'*The Billionaires Club* should be thought of as a football bestiary for our times, a brilliantly researched catalogue of the exotic, the evil and the egregious ... those who want to stop the catastrophic rise of the one per cent in the game are in James Montague's debt.'

David Goldblatt, author of *The Game of Our Lives*

'A sprawling – but fascinating – exposé of why billionaires are so keen to bankroll £200,000-a-week sportsmen ... the business-minded and the football crazy — and there are many who are both, as this book proves — will find it hard to resist.'

Sunday Times

'This is the 21st century football writer's conundrum: how to investigate this transformation and expose wrongdoings without being spat out by the system. James Montague has had the courage to tear up that tacit contract, by which silence is rewarded with access – and a job. This is not just a 'good' book (even if it is that too): it is also a brave and necessary one.'

Philippe Auclair, *France Football*

'Both surprising and insightful ... This book does a fine job of examining just why rich men choose to plough oodles of money into football.'

FourFourTwo

'An extraordinary journey across football's heartlands to try and discover the motivations and backstories behind the men who have hijacked the game.'

Irish Examiner, Sport Books of the Year

'A fascinating read for the many football fans interested in the developments off the pitch.'

Financial Times

D1079557

For Mitra and Mila

THE
BILLIONAIRES
—CLUB—

The unstoppable rise of
football's super-rich owners

JAMES MONTAGUE

BLOOMSBURY SPORT
LONDON · OXFORD · NEW YORK · NEW DELHI · SYDNEY

BLOOMSBURY SPORT
Bloomsbury Publishing Plc
50 Bedford Square, London, WC1B 3DP, UK

BLOOMSBURY, BLOOMSBURY SPORT and the Diana logo are trademarks of
Bloomsbury Publishing Plc

First published in Great Britain 2017
This paperback edition published 2018

ISBN: PB: 978-1-4729-2312-7
eBook: 978-1-4729-2313-4

2 4 6 8 10 9 7 5 3 1

Typeset in Adobe Garamond Pro by Deanta Global Publishing Services, Chennai, India
Printed and bound in Great Britain by CPI Group (UK) Ltd, Croydon CR0 4YY

To find out more about our authors and books visit www.bloomsbury.com and
sign up for our newsletters

Contents

You follow drugs, you get drug addicts and drug dealers.
But you start to follow the money, and you don't know where
the fuck it's gonna take you.

Detective Lester Freamon, *The Wire*

Introduction

Crewe, United Kingdom

The densely terraced streets surrounding Crewe Alexandra's Gresty Road stadium were eerily and uncharacteristically quiet. It was match day, a Sunday, but there was none of the pageantry that marked the usual pre-game build-up. There were no vans selling pies and sausages; no programme stands. There seemed to be no fans at all.

But at the corner of the stadium, inside a red door in a tiny, unmarked red-brick building opposite the Gresty Road Chip Shop ('Under New Management'), Harold Finch was keeping a flame alive. The 88-year-old was as busy as ever on match day, opening his programme and badge shop which he had run for over 60 years.

Inside, the tiny room was the closest thing you could find to a footballing time machine. Atop two tables were stacks of old, weathered football programmes, arranged in neat piles, dating back to the start of the twentieth century. A third, manned by Harold's son, was taken up by a glass and wood case displaying pin badges commemorating matches long forgotten. 'I'm officially the club historian and I've seen well over 3,000 games,' said Finch proudly, wearing a Crewe Alexandra training top, grey hair swept back. 'I first started watching Crewe as a supporter on 10 March 1934,' he explained. 'Crewe Alexandra 4–2 Accrington Stanley.'

There are few people alive today who can vividly recall football matches that span nine decades, but Harold is one of a shrinking club.

He has travelled to almost every football league ground past and present. There are only two missing to complete the full set: Manchester City's Etihad Stadium, 40 miles north of Gresty Road, and Arsenal's Emirates Stadium, both symbols of a game so far removed from Crewe Alexandra v Accrington Stanley in 1934 that they might as well exist in a parallel universe. The club has been in existence since 1877, making it one of the oldest in the world; the stadium has sat on this spot since 1907, squeezed in between rows of red-brick terraced housing to the west, and the West Coast main line on the other side. The railways provided the backbone of Crewe's industry and working-class fan base, bequeathing the club its nickname: 'The Railwaymen.' Harold himself had worked on the railways.

Today, the club play in League One, the third tier of English football, and have never made it to the top division. They once spent twenty straight seasons in the old fourth division. As football emerged from the dark days of the 1980s into the shiny new world of Premier League all-seater stadiums and wealthy benefactors, Crewe Alexandra retained its old identity. It was a community club with an ownership structure of old: local businessmen done good, investing in their clubs almost as an act of philanthropy rather than for profit or a short cut to fame and success. The club's chairman, John Bowler, had returned to Crewe in 1980 after making his fortune in pharmaceuticals.

By the turn of the twenty-first century, football was a new game. Millionaire local owners were not enough. Now billionaires and the super-rich were the only individuals with pockets deep enough to bankroll survival and success. The purchase of Chelsea in 2003 by Roman Abramovich, a Russian oligarch who was one of the richest men in the world after building a fortune in the anarchic capitalism of post-USSR Russia, raised the bar. The purchase of Manchester City five years later by Sheikh Mansour bin Zayed al Nahyan, a member of the royal family of Abu Dhabi in the United Arab Emirates, presented football with its richest family of billionaires.

Crewe survived under the old local-businessman-done-good model, and was a million miles away from the deals made in Abu Dhabi, Doha, Paris and Moscow. At least, it was until today. If there was one thing Harold had never seen at Gresty Road – something he thought he might never see – it was a full international match, one that brought football's old world and new into collision. Northern Ireland were about to play a friendly against the Persian Gulf state of Qatar. 'It is a most unusual one,' conceded Harold, a little guarded about the unfamiliar Arab visitors.

The Qatar national team was something of a mystery to everyone at Crewe Alexandra. No one knew when the team would turn up nor who their players were likely to be. The club hadn't heard from a single Qatari fan interested in purchasing a ticket either. Ever since the former president of FIFA Sepp Blatter announced on a stage in Zurich in December 2010 that the tiny, natural-gas-rich state would host the 2022 World Cup finals, Qatar had become something of a pariah in the British press. For the tabloids this frightening new football force from far away in the alien Middle East possessed an ability to punch above its weight almost everywhere except on the football pitch (they had started the year ranked 95th by FIFA, alongside the likes of Liberia and the Faroe Islands) – and most football fans in the West were simply incredulous. Qatar was pilloried for investing its extreme wealth in football, and for assembling a national team of mostly naturalised players from other countries – their various first XIs during 2018 World Cup qualification saw players appear who had been born in nine different countries. Beneath this lay widespread condemnation for Qatar's appalling treatment of the Asian migrant workers building the country's new infrastructure.

So, in a bid to try to show a different face to the country it regarded as its biggest critic, a mini-tour had been planned for the United Kingdom, kicking off in Crewe against Northern Ireland, before moving, a few days later, north to Scotland for a fixture in Edinburgh. The English FA had welcomed the Qataris with open arms, hosting them at the

St George's Park National Football Centre in Burton-on-Trent about 50 miles away. Somehow, that series of decisions had led to Qatar's arrival in Crewe. 'This is the first time I've seen Qatar play,' admitted Harold, as a few curious middle-aged Northern Ireland fans began filtering in to view the pages of football from a bygone age. And he wasn't happy that the game was being held in a strangely secretive manner. 'From a personal point of view I am very disappointed that the club hasn't arranged a programme for today,' he said. 'I thought they would have done.'

There might not have been a programme, but outside Harold's hut a lone scarf seller was hawking his wares: 136 split scarves, half in the green and white of Northern Ireland, half in the maroon of Qatar. 'A lot of people go on about the split-scarf thing,' said Martin, a Mancunian, 'but you've got to give people what they want, 'aven't yer?' On a normal weekend, Martin – a man switched on to the commercial possibilities football's new gilded elite have brought – would be shifting 500 split scarves outside Old Trafford, a position that affords him an informed insight into the increasing numbers of Japanese, Thai, Malaysian and Scandinavian fans that form his customer base. You might never sit next to the same person again inside Old Trafford, he reckoned, but 'Liverpool hammer United for tourists'.

Today he had shifted just 30 scarves, to Northern Irish fans. 'I've not seen a single Qatari fan. Just the team,' he said, pointing to the huge, blacked-out luxury coach parked outside the ground's front entrance, as if a UFO had just landed. Perhaps Qatar's fans had chosen to watch the game from the comforts of The Shard, the luxury, multibillion-pound skyscraper funded almost exclusively by the Qatari state (cost: roughly half a billion pounds) that was now London's, and Britain's, tallest building? 'Well,' Martin replied before leaving to try to offload 106 more green, white and maroon scarves, 'they're not likely to come up all the way to Crewe, are they?'

**

Football in the twenty-first century is unrecognisable from the working-class game that captivated and captured the world in the twentieth. Sky and BT paid over £5 billion for the 2016–19 three-year Premier League broadcasting deal. Once foreign rights sales are taken into account, that figure rises to above £8 billion. The sale of the English league's foreign rights alone are comparable to the entire TV rights deals of Spain, Germany and Italy. The 2016–19 deal will likely secure just as much. In comparison, the Premier League's first five-year contract signed with BSkyB in 1992 was for £191.5 million, less than 4 per cent of the 2016–19 deal.

Less than three decades earlier, the game was very different. The story of 15 April 1989, Hillsborough – the 96 Liverpool fans who died in a stadium crush during the FA Cup semi-final against Nottingham Forest; the Taylor Report, which painted a picture of a dilapidated game housed in decrepit, crumbling, Victorian stadiums where supporters were treated little better than cattle; and the subsequent rebranding of the game that would consign football's negative image to the past – has been well documented elsewhere.

But 1989 also saw a year of seismic political and social upheaval that would go on to play an important role in football's economic evolution. In November of that year the Berlin Wall finally fell, which marked the beginning of the end of Europe's communist partition, the disintegration of the Soviet Union and what seemed to be total victory for free-market capitalism and liberal democracy over state-dictated socialism. It was dubiously dubbed the 'end of history' by political theorists like Francis Fukuyama, and marked a fundamental shift in the global economy, the roots of which had been laid by the free-market economics of Margaret Thatcher in the UK and Ronald Reagan in the US that preached the gospel of privatisation and deregulation. The fall of the Berlin Wall brought freedom to millions but also heralded a period of plunder unseen in modern times. It handed the opportunity to a group of businessmen to take advantage of the chaos to make fortunes in an opaque fashion. It gave rise to the oligarchs – a Greek word that approximates to 'rule by the few' but which is largely now used in relation to Russian business figures connected to the country's political elite. Around the world, the post-communist economic settlement accelerated a system of privatisations and deregulations that concentrated wealth and increased inequality, whether in the United Kingdom or Russia. As the historian Niall Ferguson wrote in the *Boston Globe* after the election of US president Donald Trump: 'Back in 1989, we thought we were witnessing the triumph of capitalism and liberal democracy. Alas, we were wrong. It turns out the winners were oligarchy and the populism that legitimises it.' Millionaires became billionaires, and football, in particular the Premier League, was in the right place at the right time to benefit from the largesse of this new class of super-rich. Within years the Premier League model was being frantically copied, with minor cultural tweaks, everywhere from Australia to the US to India, attracting a new breed of club owner, one that had been largely unseen in world football until the mid-1990s: members of the super-rich with little or no local connection to the club they had bought, who, at best, possessed hazy motives and even hazier pasts.

By the end of 2016 foreign owners had bought, or held significant shares in, 15 of the Premier League's 20 teams. Dozens more, from Charlton to Blackpool, had bought clubs further down the league pyramid. But more important than nationality was wealth. Fourteen billionaires from Russia, Iran, China, Thailand, the UAE, Germany and Switzerland, the US and the UK now had a say in the fates of Arsenal, Chelsea, Crystal Palace, Everton, Leicester City, Manchester United, Manchester City, Liverpool, Sunderland, Stoke City, Southampton and Tottenham. And it wasn't just in England. In France, Paris Saint-Germain had been bought by Qatar Sports Investments, an investment vehicle funded by the Qatari state. Qatar was now one of the richest countries – when judged by GDP per capita – on earth. Other investments had spanned the globe, with money from Sheikh Mansour connecting Manchester City to New York City FC to Melbourne City FC. Clubs in the

It's not as if buying a football club has traditionally been a sure-fire way to enhance riches. Simon Jordan, a multimillionaire by the time he was 32 years old, bought the club he supported as a child – Crystal Palace – for £10.175 million in 2000. He lost his fortune and the club was later put into administration. He had found that football was a tough business to make money in. For all the huge revenues generated by bumper TV deals, profits, if they ever came, were minuscule in comparison. Lord Alan Sugar, the technology entrepreneur now worth £1.4 billion who was Tottenham Hotspur's chairman from 1991 to 2001, famously described the 'prune juice effect' in relation to football club finances. The money came in then disappeared out of the back door almost immediately in the form of players' wages. 'Despite the rhetorical hype of the new football industry, in absolute terms it remains a pygmy,' David Goldblatt wrote in *The Game of Our Lives: The Meaning and Making of English Football*. 'The average Premier League club has a turnover only slightly larger than the average Tesco supermarket.'

That, however, may be about to change. In *The Billionaires Club*, in trying to explore what the motivations of this new breed of owner might be, I've followed the trail of wealth to four different continents and have spoken to those who've benefited and those who have been crushed by the money-making machine. The story is not just about the game, but also concerns the profoundly unequal, murky economic system that supports it. Although this book has a global outlook on the connections in the world of football club ownership, it necessarily concentrates on English clubs for two reasons. Firstly, because the sheer popularity, interest and investment in the English game remain unsurpassed in world football; and secondly because the English, uniquely, opened the door to this kind of investment and control in the first place, way back in the nineteenth century. Quite simply, it is far easier to buy a football club in England than it is in any other major European league.

The passing of the Limited Liability Act into law in 1855 signalled a watershed moment in the development of Anglo-Saxon capitalism.

Up until that point, the owners of businesses were personally liable for any debts or failures. But as Professor Stefan Szymanski points out in his book *Money and Football: A Soccernomics Guide*, 'It allowed the company rather than the owners directly to borrow money, and if the business failed only the company was liable, not the owners.' In 1888 Birmingham City FC – then as Small Heath FC – became the first football club to become a Limited Liability Company (company number 27,318, according to the Companies House register).

Within a few years, virtually every club was a Limited Liability Company. With access to loans, this led to a boom in stadium building across the country, creating the vast temples of football that attracted hundreds of thousands of people every Saturday, and cementing football's place as a collective, mass movement. 'It is an odd coincidence of history,' writes Professor Szymanski, 'that organised football developed just at the time when the new type of corporation became popular.'

The English FA legislated to prevent profiteering at football clubs, clinging to the notion that football clubs were not businesses. But by the 1980s the FA's so-called Rule 34, which restricted dividend payments to shareholders, among other things, was being circumvented by club owners like Tottenham Hotspur's Irving Scholar. Many of these restrictions were dropped with little fanfare in 1998. In 2004 the Premier League, Football League and the body that represents non-league football agreed a set of criteria that owners and directors would have to pass. It became known as the 'Fit and Proper Persons Test' (now known as the 'Owners' and Directors' Test') and was introduced to weed out those with convictions for fraud or a track record of bankruptcy. The Premier League also included rules preventing clubs being bought by those who held significant investments in other clubs.

But so far Thaksin Shinawatra's human rights record, Massimo Cellino's tax affairs, four different owners of Portsmouth FC in as many seasons, and the leveraged buyouts of Manchester United and Liverpool, saddling both clubs with heavy debts, have all failed to trouble English football's new guidelines. 'The FA, Premier League and Football League have spent too long behind the curve on ownership matters,' concluded the 2011 Football Governance Report by the British House of Commons' Culture, Media and Sport select committee. 'Between them they have allowed some startlingly poor business practices to occur, and have tolerated an unacceptably low level of transparency.' Anyone who has the money, it seems, can buy an English football club, with virtually no serious questions asked.

Crewe Alexandra was registered as a limited company on 31 May 1899 (company number 62,367), exactly 116 years to the day that the Qatar team bus arrived at Gresty Road. Qatar's players headed straight into their dressing room. No one had been given any access to them or their officials. A noisy handful of Northern Irish supporters dotted the stands. Several had brought signs to protest about Qatar's treatment of migrant workers building the infrastructure to host the 2022 World Cup. 'I work with a lot of Nepalese guys who have worked in Qatar, and they are treated like slaves,' said Martin Lowry, a supporter who worked for the Royal Air Force.

The match itself was a surprisingly even affair (given that Northern Ireland were on the verge of qualifying for the 2016 European Championships while Qatar had little international pedigree) and finished 1–1, Karim Boudiaf, a naturalised midfielder born in France, equalising late on with a stunning volley. The Qataris had been born in France, Algeria, Morocco, Ghana, Egypt and Saudi Arabia, and a few were graduates of the Aspire Academy, the state-of-the-art training and player-development facility, which had caused controversy for allegedly hoovering up and naturalising talent from across Africa, Asia and central America, thus bypassing FIFA's tough rules against such schemes (toughened up in the first place only because of Qatar's previous attempts to fill its team with Uruguayans and Brazilians).

There was no post-match press conference, and the Qatar players quickly disappeared back onto their luxury coach. But José Daniel Carreño, Qatar's Uruguayan manager, dressed in a dapper blue suit, stopped outside the fire exit to smoke a quick cigarette before leaving. It had been his first game in charge. I asked him how he communicated with his team of multinational players. 'In football, there are a lot of gestures going on,' he replied, through an interpreter. 'We speak a little bit of everything: a little French, a little Arab, a little English, a little Spanish.' He stubbed his cigarette out and boarded the coach.

'After Ireland scored the first, I thought they were going to flatten them,' said Harold, Crewe Alexandra's living encyclopedia, cheerily after closing up his shop. The money and the circus that surrounded football didn't interest him. Just as when he first saw Crewe play in 1934, or even as he watched them get hammered by Spurs in the FA Cup in 1960 (13–2), it was always about the football. Those 90 minutes on the pitch were sacrosanct and worthy of respect, whomever it involved. 'Qatar showed some very, very good football,' he said, impressed. 'And their goal was a beauty.'

PART ONE, EASTERN EUROPE:

Rise of the Oligarchs

1. London, United Kingdom

The view from the apartment at the top of building number 4 Whitehall Court must be magnificent. The 5,380-square-foot, six-bedroom luxury apartment faces out over the Thames, overlooking the Ministry of Defence and Whitehall Gardens. On the opposite bank of the Thames, the London Eye dominates, across from the curved, neoclassical façade of County Hall. Further down, on the right, is Westminster Bridge, the Palace of Westminster and Big Ben. It would be hard to think of a more sought-after vista, nor a more sought-after piece of classical real estate in the world.

Vladimir Ashurkov is standing on the street outside, and pointing up to its windows. The building once housed, he says, an MI6 office. It used to be two addresses, before being bought and transformed into one glorious mega apartment. 'This is the home of Igor Shuvalov, Russia's first deputy prime minister, one of the top five officials in the government,' says Ashurkov, short and snappily dressed, with long boyish blond hair that makes him look much younger than his 43 years. A group of journalists and activists are clustered around him. Although, technically, this is the home of Igor Shuvalov's wife. Shuvalov is a rare liberal presence in Putin's inner circle, described by *Foreign Policy* magazine as having a reputation for 'the cleanest hands in the Kremlin'.

And yet Ashurkov is here to tell the story of how he had bought the two apartments through a network of offshore companies in 2003 before selling them in 2014 to another Russian shell company, ultimately controlled by his wife. 'Igor Shuvalov paid a sterling equivalent of 77 million roubles [just under £1 million] in stamp duty – eight times his official declared income for 2014. The price of this property is 114 times his annual income. So how did the humble bureaucrat make so much money?' Ashurkov wondered. It was a question that had weighed heavier on his mind ever since he fled his homeland and claimed political asylum in London. How did Russian elected officials and bureaucrats come to accumulate seemingly impossible amounts of cash in Russia before investing it in London real estate?

A few years ago Vladimir Ashurkov was a sharply dressed banker, working for Russia's Alfa Bank. He'd even once supported Putin. But after becoming disillusioned with what he believed was state-sanctioned corruption, he began working with Alexei Navalny – the most prominent critic of Putin still in Russia. Navalny headed up the Anti-Corruption Foundation and tried to encourage other leading businessmen unhappy with what they saw around them to join. He made his leap into the political arena just as Russia was rolling back the reach of civil society. Corruption was draining the country of its best minds. The state now controlled the most influential media outlets. Activists and opposition politicians had been jailed on trumped-up charges. The highest profile opposition figure had been Boris Nemtsov, a former vice prime minister once part of Boris Yeltsin's inner circle. Nemtsov was executed in February 2015, near the Kremlin. Five Chechen contract killers were convicted of his assassination, but Nemtsov's family denounced the trial for failing to examine who had contracted them in the first place.

Whether you had money or not, speaking up in Putin's Russia was a bad idea. Ashurkov was chased out of the country after being accused of embezzlement. His apartment was raided twice by the police.

A tactic, he says, to silence those who speak about the huge flow of money out of Russia and into places like building number 4, Whitehall Court. Ashurkov was granted political asylum in the UK and is now one of thousands of Russian exiles preparing for the day after Vladimir Putin is not in power. They live in a city that has also become a second home for Putin's inner circle, a place to park money. To keep such wealth, they have to keep the man at the top happy at all costs.

Much of that wealth is tied up in grand properties in central London, or other investments. Like football clubs. Vladimir Ashurkov is currently working with anti-corruption activists in the city he now calls home, helping to run the Kleptocracy Tour: a bus journey around central London that eschews Big Ben and the Tower of London, and instead points out the lavish properties bought by Bahraini kings, Egyptian dictators and Russian oligarchs. He describes many of these properties as the 'ill-gotten gains of Russian officials or of cronies of the current people in the administration . . . they bring their money to Britain, they buy property, they buy companies, and with this money comes the corrupt practices that people are used to at home.'

Few people in London would recognise Igor Shuvalov. Yet how he made vast amounts of money – enough to purchase prime British real estate – and who enabled him to make that money, is illuminating. Shuvalov was seen as a pro-business, pro-privatisation figure who foreign investors could do business with. Before rising to become one of the most powerful politicians in Russia, he was Putin's economic advisor and had represented Russia at a G8 summit. But, most importantly, he was perceived to be untainted by corruption. Before he entered government he had trained as a lawyer, becoming a senior advisor at ALM, a successful Russian corporate law firm that advised several clients in the oil industry, among others. It was here in the mid-1990s that he met a client who would change his life. Roman Abramovich was in the middle of constructing the deal of his life:

purchasing a company that had been formed, called Sibneft. According to a *Guardian* profile of Abramovich in 2004, 'in December 1995, four oil exploration, drilling, refining and distribution companies in Noyabrsk and Omsk came up for auction, in a deal that would see them combined into a holding company to be named Sibneft.' Ten years later Abramovich would sell 72 per cent of Sibneft's shares to government-owned energy giant Gazprom. It was sold for $13 billion. But, as Ashurkov explained, Shuvalov earned more than his fee. Back in 1996 he had also received a small percentage of the company in return for his legal work for Abramovich and Sibneft. 'The option supposedly covered 0.5 per cent of Sibneft shares – an unheard of payout for an outside legal counsel!' explained Ashurkov. 'While Shuvalov and Abramovich confirm the existence of the option contract, neither party could ever produce any proof of it.' A profile of Shuvalov in *Forbes Russia* describes how Shuvalov and Abramovich had become close friends. A spokesperson for Millhouse Capital, a UK-registered company that manages Abramovich's assets, justified the option due to the complex nature of the Sibneft case. Another spokesman confirmed the option, but declined to confirm its size.

Shuvalov's family was made fantastically wealthy thanks to this option from Abramovich, the owner of Chelsea FC. Then, in 2004, a Bahamas-registered trust called Sevenkey, with Shuvalov's wife as the main beneficiary, invested elsewhere, buying $18 million in Gazprom shares. Four years later they were sold after the government had, in the words of the *Financial Times*: 'prepared to liberalise share trading, a reform which greatly increased their market value.' The reforms allowed foreigners to invest in domestically traded stock and the value of Gazprom's shares soared. There was also another deal with a prominent Russian billionaire who had invested in English football: Alisher Usmanov, whose Red and White Holdings owns 30 per cent of Arsenal FC's shares. 'Shuvalov was ostensibly asked by the Russian metals tycoon Usmanov to lend him $50 million for the acquisition of a stake in [formerly British-owned steel manufacturer] Corus Steel,' says Ashurkov. Usmanov is, by some margin, one of the richest men in Russia. Ashurkov couldn't understand why Usmanov, one of Putin's key oligarchs, would need to borrow money from a Russian advisor in the Kremlin. That deal eventually netted Sevenkey a $119 million payment from Usmanov's company. Taking into account the Gazprom shares, Sevenkey would stand to make $200 million from deals signed while Shuvalov worked as Putin's economic aide. 'A top government official reaps millions in profits with the help of the nation's wealthiest businessmen. That definitely sounds illegal,' wrote Leonid Bershidsky for Bloomberg, shortly after news of the deals became public. 'In Russia, however, things are much more complicated . . . it appears that he truly has not broken any Russian laws, such as they are.' As Vladislav Inozemtsev, director of the Institute for Post-Industrial Studies in Moscow, said in a 2012 interview for Reuters: 'The current system in Russia is based not on corruption in the traditional sense, but on a complete merger of public service and private business interests.'

For Ashurkov it wasn't necessarily the money that was the best proof of Russia's slide towards kleptocracy – a Greek word that means 'rule by thieves'. Money flows could change and disappear. They were ephemeral and hard to pin down. Nor was it the now well-known potential conflict of interest between state officials who were doing business with the very same oligarchs they were involved, at least in part, in regulating. No, the best proof was the properties themselves, the London bricks and mortar that represented the physical manifestation of their dealings. Money can be hidden from view. A house? Less so. 'The story of Igor Shuvalov is quintessential for the history of modern Russia,' says Ashurkov. 'Russia is a country where 16 years of Putin's regime have succeeded in establishing an absolute rule of state-sponsored corruption. It is a perfect kleptocracy.' The Russian authorities have always denied that such corruption exists, and insist that Shuvalov and his wife have paid all taxes owed on her investments in Russia. In fact, many in Russia believe that it was Shuvalov's lack of corruption that got him into trouble. He was the first major Kremlin figure to publish his earnings to try to prove that he was indeed the lawyer with the clean hands. 'As a lawyer, I have without fail followed the rules and principles on conflicts of interests. For a lawyer, this is sacred,' he said in a statement after the deals were revealed. 'I welcome rigorous journalistic and legal scrutiny. I am confident of my record as both a private businessman and subsequently a government technocrat.'

The party of journalists and activists board the bus and inch through London's heavy midday traffic. It passes by London's most affluent streets and opulent houses; past Roman Abramovich's £125 million mansion in Kensington, which was once the Russian embassy. Past One Hyde Park, the single most expensive residential development in the world. The building is part owned by a property development company belonging to the former Qatari prime minister Sheikh Hamad bin Jassim bin Jaber al Thani, but it's not entirely clear who owns the 86 ultra-luxury apartments there, as most are registered in the names of offshore shell companies set up in tax havens like Jersey and the British Virgin Islands to hide the owners' true identities. But one proprietor is known: Rinat Akhmetov, Ukraine's richest man, who also owns Shakhtar Donetsk, Ukraine's most successful football club. He bought two apartments for close to £200 million then merged them into one.

The bus turns north, towards Hampstead, and past the £50 million mansion of Arsenal FC minority shareholder Alisher Usmanov. All three men – Abramovich, Akhmetov and Usmanov – have risen from nowhere to become fabulously wealthy, before investing in football and changing the game for ever. Where did their money come from? And how did the cash end up being poured into three of Europe's most famous football clubs?

2.

Apart from the sums of cash involved, the final game at Stamford Bridge, which brought the 2002–03 season to a close, looked much the same as it would today. The English Premier League appeared to be booming, attracting big-name foreign players. Large TV revenues were on offer. The stadiums were full. Liverpool were the visitors for what had been dubbed the '£20 million game'. Chelsea were fourth in the league table and in the final UEFA Champions League spot. Liverpool had the same points but an inferior goal difference. Whoever won the game qualified for European football's premier competition. Whoever didn't qualified for the UEFA Cup instead. The shortfall was £20 million. The two teams came out of the tunnel into a gloriously sunny May day. The packed stadium was in full voice. Stamford Bridge was one of the best stadiums in the country, completely renovated under the ownership of businessman Ken Bates, who'd bought a struggling, debt-laden club, which had spent the late 1970s and early 1980s bouncing between the first and second divisions, for £1 in 1982, and transformed it into a top ten Premier League team with the occasional foray into European football.

Bates had long been a controversial character, but when he arrived at Chelsea in the early 1980s Stamford Bridge was in terrible shape. Every few years my father brings out a VHS tape he's kept from 1986 – a recording of the TV highlights from West Ham playing Chelsea at the Bridge, with commentary by Brian Moore. With Tony Cottee and Frank McAvennie ascendant, West Ham thrashed Chelsea 4–0 on their way to a best ever third-place finish in the league. Every year the quality of the recording fades a little more, but the image remains unmistakable. The pitch is a mud bath, West Ham's all-white kit is caked in brown. The stadium itself looks as if it belongs to another century. One stand behind the goal is completely uncovered, and fans standing in the famous Shed End fare little better. A running track separates the fans far from the pitch. The gap created by the old race track is so big that it was filled with parked cars, an assortment of beige, green and orange Cortinas, Escorts and Jags. The fans are kept behind a metal fence. In fact, Bates went as far as installing an electric fence, which he threatened to turn on if the hooliganism that had blighted Stamford Bridge from the late 1960s onwards continued. It was never turned on after he was rebuked by the league.

By the early 1990s, after a long battle against developers who wanted to demolish the ground, Bates finally acquired the freehold and managed to deal with the issue of the club's debt, but in a controversial way. He set up the holding company Chelsea Village plc in 1990, and transferred the players' registrations from Chelsea Football and Athletic Club (which had existed since 1905) to the new entity in 1992. CFAC promptly went into receivership, owing over £2 million. By 2003 the stadium was all-seater, with a restaurant and health club, and Chelsea Village plc had long ago been floated on the AIM Stock Exchange. The pitch, turnstiles and the actual name of the club were owned by Chelsea Pitch Owners, a non-profit group set up by Bates to ensure that the ground could never be sold to property developers. The club pays a tiny rent and, in return, CPO allows the club to use the name.

On that day back in May 2003, Chelsea fought back from 1–0 down to beat Liverpool 2–1, Danish winger Jesper Grønkjær scoring the vital goal. Things, however, were not as rosy behind the scenes. Chelsea, like most other clubs, had invested speculatively for success and had taken on huge debts. By 2003 Leeds United had reached the semi-finals of the Champions League but had gone £100 million into debt as a result. Chelsea had a £23 million debt repayment to make in six weeks with no way of paying it. They had already mortgaged the next tranche of TV money. 'It was a massive game for Chelsea,' recalled Grønkjær in an interview a few years later with the *Independent*. Trevor Birch, the club's then CEO, had warned the players before the match that losing would have dire financial consequences for both them and the club. 'We all knew what we were playing for,' recalled Grønkjær. 'I remember the stories about our financial situation.'

And then a knight in shining armour arrived. No one had heard of Roman Abramovich before. There were a few vague pieces of public information. He was a Russian billionaire who had made a fortune in oil and gas investments. He was young and was also the governor of a far-away Russian region in the frozen northeast of the vast country. But he wanted to buy Chelsea and he wanted to buy it quickly. A meeting was arranged at Stamford Bridge to do the deal and within 15 minutes, Birch later recalled, the sale was agreed. The dark financial clouds lifted immediately. On the second day of pre-season training, Abramovich arrived with a translator. 'There were rumours about everything – new coach, new players, new training ground, new stadium. He wanted us all to calm down,' said Grønkjær. Come the new season, Abramovich also started sitting in the dressing room with the players, in silence: 'I don't know if he could understand [what was being said] but he would just sit there, like one of the boys.' The purchase of Chelsea FC was a transformational moment not just in English football but in the global game as a whole. The books no longer had to be balanced in the traditional sense. Abramovich had bought the shares and taken the club private, netting Bates at least £17 million from his initial £1 investment. Abramovich could spend an open-ended amount of money on players and wages. If anyone else wanted to compete, they had to find a comparable source of income. Clubs had to get rich or die trying.

But important questions remained unanswered. Who was Roman Abramovich? And, more importantly, why had he bought Chelsea? He was a notoriously shy man who rarely spoke to the press. The era from which he had emerged as a member of the super-rich had been dark and chaotic. The early years of Russian capitalism had created an anarchic brew of bravado, risk, organised crime and corruption. Blood had been left on the floor as fortunes had been made. 'I want to know whether this individual is a fit and proper person to be taking over a club like Chelsea,' said Tony Banks, who had been sports minister in the Labour government between 1997 and 1999 and who was also a high-profile Chelsea fan. 'Until that question is answered, then I'm afraid the jury is out.'

In those chaotic few days in the summer of 2003, Abramovich gave one interview, to the BBC, who described him as bearing an 'astonishing resemblance to Woody Allen, without the glasses'. He laughed at the idea that he was in it for the money, given that investing in football gave tiny returns. In pure business terms, trying to make money from football just wasn't worth the effort. 'No, it's not about making money. I have many much less risky ways of making money than this. I don't want to throw my money away, but it's really about having fun and that means success and trophies,' he said. 'I know what people say. But there are lots of rich, young people in Russia. We don't live that long, so we earn it and spend it. I'm realising my dream of owning a top football club. Some will doubt my motives, others will think I'm crazy.' A few days later, the crazy spending began. Within six weeks, Abramovich had spent £140 million on players.

Roman Arkadyevich Abramovich was not born into money. He was born in Saratov, on the banks of the Volga river, in 1966. His mother died of blood poisoning before he was one. His father was killed in a construction accident when he was four. The young Abramovich was taken to Ukhta, a barren and cold place in northern Russia where the winters could plummet to -49 degrees, to live with his father's brother and his wife. He had, by all accounts, a happy life there. 'To tell the truth I cannot call my childhood bad,' he said of his early years, in the last interview he ever gave, to the *Observer*, in 2006. 'In your childhood you can't compare things: one eats carrots, one eats candy, both taste good. As a child you cannot tell the difference.' When he was eight he moved to Moscow to live with his grandmother.

He was not a great student, or athlete, nor particularly gregarious. Slight, but handsome and quiet, Abramovich studied highway engineering, although it appears that he never graduated. He did his national service in the Russian army with minimal fuss, leaving it as he had entered it: as a private. When he finished his national service in 1986 he emerged into a changing world. Mikhail Gorbachev had become general secretary of the Politburo, with his reforms of perestroika and glasnost designed to open up a space for personal freedoms as well as private enterprise. Abramovich worked as a mechanic before starting his own business. By the end of the 1980s he had filled the small Moscow apartment he shared with his first wife with toy dolls and rubber ducks. According to Dominic Midgley's and Chris Hutchins's biography *Abramovich: The Billionaire from Nowhere*, he had set up a doll-making company called Uyut and was earning 3,000 to 4,000 roubles a month, a colossal sum at the time (the average wage was closer to 900). He had started and liquidated up to 20 companies during this time, 'in sectors as diverse as tyre treading and bodyguard recruitment', incrementally increasing his wealth and hoping that one business would hit the jackpot. It was more *Only Fools and Horses* than *Billions*, but it was the collapse of the Soviet Union and the rise of Boris Yeltsin that offered him the opportunity that would change his life, and football, for ever.

Christmas Day 1991 spelt the end of the communist revolution. The hammer and sickle was lowered from the Kremlin, and replaced by the Russian tricolour. Earlier that day, Gorbachev had resigned as president. He had already resigned as head of the Communist Party following a failed coup by hardliners desperately trying to cling to the Soviet Union, and hoping that the people would rally to the Soviet cause. Instead, the coup plotters were faced with the iconic image of Boris Yeltsin in a flak jacket, riding a tank. Yeltsin was now president of a newly independent Russia. The task ahead of him was immense. Russia had to build democratic institutions from scratch as well as grow a political and civil society that had been neutered by the KGB. It also had to introduce a market economy. Those who were smart, lucky or well connected – usually all three – spotted the gaps in the system where money was to be made. And the quickest way to make money was oil. Abramovich's business sense had taken him into the lower reaches of the oil industry, which by 1991 was ripe for exploitation. Oil was an abundant and easily traded commodity, as long as you could secure an export licence. Yet it remains a mystery as to exactly how Abramovich made his money so quickly. One answer to how he made the leap from serial entrepreneur to millionaire lies in an alleged 1992 warrant issued for his arrest over the alleged counterfeiting of documents to try to get his hands on 55 train wagons' worth of diesel. He's always denied the claim.

Still, Abramovich was rich enough a year later to be invited to a special meeting on a yacht in the Caribbean with the new Russian oligarchy. There he met Boris Berezovsky, a businessman closely connected to Boris Yeltsin's inner circle, aka 'the Family'. The two men became close and worked on a deal that would make them billions. 'I was . . . very impressed with Mr Abramovich on this trip,' Berezovsky would later say. 'He seemed knowledgeable about the oil business and he was a very charming person.' Berezovsky saw that Abramovich had one skill in particular that he didn't have. 'He is good at appearing to be humble. He is happy to spend days socialising with important or powerful people if that is what is needed so that he can get closer to them.'

In 1995 the Russian economy was in bad shape and Yeltsin was trailing badly in the polls. Russia's second ever presidential election was due to take place the following year and it looked like the incumbent might lose. His main challenger was former communist hardliner Gennady Zyuganov. A win for Zyuganov would unravel Yeltsin's free-market reforms. Yeltsin had to win at all costs, so his advisors made a deal with the country's richest men. Get our man back into the Kremlin, and you'll be rewarded. Berezovsky collected an election war chest of

$120 million, as well as guaranteeing positive coverage for Yeltsin on TV and in the newspapers. That wasn't hard – Berezovsky owned 49 per cent of the state broadcaster ORT. Thanks largely to the positive media coverage, Yeltsin won the 1996 election, but the price was high: the now-infamous 'Loans for Shares' programme – a fire-sale privatisation of state assets, including Russia's marquee oil, nickel and aluminium operations. Almost overnight it made billions for the handful of men who had kept Yeltsin in power.

Through the scheme, Berezovsky and Abramovich managed to buy Sibneft, one of Russia's largest oil companies, for $100 million – $50 million each – a fraction of what it was really worth (it is thought the true value was closer to $3 billion). Yukos Oil was bought by Mikhail Khodorkovsky, who went on to become Russia's richest man. With his new-found wealth, Abramovich moved into the aluminium business, which had become something of a disputed battle ground, with oligarchs, foreign businesses and the Russian mafia all vying for control of Siberia's smelters. As many as a hundred people were murdered in what became known as 'the Aluminum Wars'. 'Every three days, someone was being murdered,' Abramovich would later recall. Abramovich was a central figure in trying to unify the fractious industry. For his pains, he emerged even wealthier.

Boris Yeltsin wouldn't serve out his full six-year term. Soon after his re-election he had a quadruple heart bypass. During his term, corruption worsened. The 1998 financial crisis saw the rouble devalued again and the Russian government default on its debt. With his health fading and his approval ratings hovering just above zero, Yeltsin's thoughts turned to a successor, and in 1999 – at the urging of his inner circle of oligarchs – he appointed a largely unknown insider to prime minister. Vladimir Vladimirovich Putin was a former KGB officer stationed in East Germany during the end of the Cold War, who had risen to power thanks to a loyal clique he had maintained from his power base in

St Petersburg. When Yeltsin resigned in an emotional speech live on television, Putin stepped in as acting president and won the subsequent 2000 election.

If the oligarchs thought they had found a malleable, easily influenced character, they were soon proved wrong. Famously, in July of that year, Putin hosted a meeting of the country's richest men in a dacha outside Moscow, telling them in no uncertain terms that they would only be able to keep their fortunes if they showed absolute loyalty to him. Berezovsky and Khodorkovsky were already supporting opposition movements: the former using his ORT to criticise Putin; the latter by funding opposition parties and media. Abramovich, though, had already made his move. Unbeknown to his former mentor Berezovsky, Abramovich had thrown himself fully behind Putin, interviewing prospective cabinet members for the former KGB man's first government. 'I respect him a lot,' Abramovich said of Putin in a rare 1999 interview with the media arm of Russia's state-owned oil and gas company Gazprom. 'Putin is an independent figure. He knows in which direction to lead the country . . . In my opinion, everything that Putin does, he does almost without making any mistakes.' It had long been alleged by Berezovsky and others that Abramovich had chipped in alongside a group of other oligarchs to buy Putin a £25 million yacht, the 57-foot-long *Olympia*, as a birthday gift shortly before he became president. Berezovsky had refused to contribute. When those allegations were aired on the BBC's *Panorama* programme in 2016, Abramovich's lawyers dismissed them as 'a rehash of speculation and rumours'.

There were other alleged acts of generosity. After the famous meeting of the oligarchs in July 2000, where Putin laid down the law, Boris Nemtsov said, 'The era of the oligarch is over.' He was only partly right. As long as they showed absolute loyalty to Putin, and kept their own political ambitions in check, they could, as promised, keep their fortunes. Part of the 'loyalty' deal allegedly involved finding cash for projects Putin thought were important. 'Donations' of hundreds of millions of dollars were sought. One Russian whistleblower detailed how one such famous scheme worked. Sergey Kolesnikov once ran a medical supplies company and was, in 2000, part of Putin's inner circle. When his medical supplies company was approached to procure state-of-the-art equipment from Siemens, he was told that 35 per cent of the contracts would be put into foreign accounts and that oligarchs would honour these contracts. The first oligarch to contribute was Roman Abramovich.

Instead of all the money going towards much-needed medical equipment, Kolesnikov saw the state funds diverted to two huge multibillion-dollar construction projects on the Black Sea coast. Kolesnikov, seeing what was going on, eventually quit and wrote an open letter to Dmitry Medvedev, who was now Russian president (although he would later step down for Putin to stand again in 2012). 'We were told that these contracts would be funded by oligarchs willing to make charitable donations to help the new president,' wrote Kolesnikov. 'The first contribution came in 2001 from Roman Abramovich who donated $203 million.' One project was a wellness centre on the Black Sea. The other was a villa being built named 'Project South', which he believed was being designed for Putin's personal use and has subsequently become known as 'Putin's Palace'. When the financial crisis hit in 2008, all other projects were stopped, except Project South. Kolesnikov wrote of the 'ten billion roubles [that have] been diverted – out of funds desperately needed to protect so many jobs and industrial projects important to Russia – [to] an enormous Italian palazzo-style palace with a casino, winter theatre, summer amphitheatre, church, swimming pools, sports grounds, heliports, landscaped parks, tea houses, staff apartments, technological buildings – a modern day version of Peterhof, the tsar's palace near St Petersburg . . . I am appealing to you publicly because not only Russians but the entire world is waiting for you to take clear and resolute action; action that would demonstrate that Russia has ceased to be a corrupt haven.'

Medvedev did nothing, and construction continued. Abramovich denied he funded the palace, stating that the money was for medical equipment. Shortly after the letter to Medvedev, Kolesnikov fled Russia and now lives in exile. Vladimir Putin, through his spokesman, has always denied that 'Putin's Palace' was built for him. According to Reuters, the Kremlin 'dismissed Kolesnikov as an aggrieved man, saying he left Russia because of business disputes'. Its ownership structure is complex – reportedly, it is owned by a Cyprus-based firm, which in turn is owned by a company in the Caribbean tax haven of the British Virgin Islands. Ultimately, Kolesnikov said in an interview with Radio Free Europe: 'No one really knows who the ultimate beneficiary of that palace is.'

The breaking point with Yeltsin's oligarchs came with the *Kursk* submarine disaster in August 2000. The pride of Russia's nuclear fleet had malfunctioned and sunk to the bottom of the sea. All 118 sailors on board died. Putin reacted slowly to the tragedy, not immediately returning to Moscow from his holiday in Sochi. Berezovsky's ORT television station showed pictures of Putin in the sun jet skiing while devastated relatives of the sailors wept. Putin furiously summoned Berezovsky to the Kremlin. Berezovsky later recounted he informed Putin that the negative coverage was a positive, as it would look like Russia had a free media:

'Putin listened to what I had to say. After I had finished, he produced a file. He then read from it. I do not recall his exact words, but the gist of what was said was that both ORT and I were corrupt. He also accused me of hiring prostitutes to pose as widows and sisters of the sailors killed aboard the *Kursk* to attack him verbally. These allegations were completely untrue and I told President Putin this.'

Berezovsky claimed that in the meeting, Putin demanded he sold his shares of ORT to the state. Berezovsky refused. A few months later

Putin announced in an interview with French newspaper *Le Figaro* that he wouldn't tolerate media criticism from outlets owned by oligarchs and that a 'cudgel' was waiting for anyone who opposed him. A criminal case was launched into Berezovsky's stake in state airline Aeroflot. By the time the tycoon was called in for questioning he had already left for France, then the UK, where he remained and claimed political asylum.

Abramovich was now making a break from his former mentor Berezovsky. He travelled to Le Bourget airport, on the outskirts of Paris, to meet with Berezovsky and persuade him to sell up his remaining Russian interests, including the TV station that continued to air stories critical of Putin. The details of their conversation became public record thanks to the largest civil litigation in British history, the 2011 Berezovsky vs Abramovich High Court trial.

During the trial, the transcript of their Paris meeting – secretly recorded by Berezovsky's Georgian business partner Badri Patarkatsishvili – appeared to show Abramovich eager to please Putin.

When discussing ORT's sale, Abramovich said, 'Should we sign then so I could take it to Vladimir Vladimirovich [Putin], show it to him and say, "Here you are, the deal is done"?'

Later that month the sale was agreed for $150 million. 'Abramovich said from the very beginning that he was acting as a messenger in agreeing the terms for the state getting control of ORT,' Berezovsky said in his witness statement to the court. 'He did not even try to pretend that there was any other agenda.' In court, Berezovsky described how this was the end of his friendship with Abramovich. 'I told him: "It's the last time that I will meet you, Roma, I never want to see you again."'

When Abramovich was later asked by a barrister whether he wanted to buy Berezovsky's TV channel ORT on Putin's behest, and that Putin was assisting him in doing that, Abramovich replied, 'President Putin didn't want the shares. It was not the shares he wanted. He wanted Mr Berezovsky and [his businesses partner Badri] Patarkatsishvili to leave

[the] management of the company and relinquish control [and] stop influencing the content of the programmes.'

The case shone a spotlight on several of Abramovich's opaque dealings for the first time, not least that, 'It was Abramovich who was sent to Berezovsky to inform him of the new rules of the game,' wrote Karen Dawisha in her book *Putin's Kleptocracy: Who Owns Russia?* The 1992 arrest warrant for forging official documents over the alleged attempt to steal the consignment of fuel that was travelling from Ukhta to Kaliningrad also came up. Abramovich had always vehemently denied it had happened. In Midgley's and Hutchins's biography, an anonymous figure high up in Abramovich's inner circle said that they were told personally: 'It never happened.' The *Financial Times*, on the other hand, reported that Berezovsky's barrister had done his homework. 'Mr Rabinowitz produced a 1992 order by Moscow prosecutors to detain Mr Abramovich, who was an oil products trader at the time, after 55 train wagons of diesel fuel went missing from the Ukhta oil refinery in northern Russia. Investigators accused Mr Abramovich of forging documents with officials at the refinery. The missing diesel was recovered and Mr Abramovich said no further action was taken. "I was released and there were no problems," he said.'

Berezovsky had claimed Abramovich owed him billions for stakes in various businesses, Sibneft in particular. Abramovich claimed the only money he paid Berezovsky was for *krysha*, otherwise known as protection money, as well as access to Yeltsin's inner circle. The court ruled in Abramovich's favour and found that Berezovsky was an unreliable witness. The judge had believed Abramovich's well prepared version of events, rather than Berezovksy's freewheeling and flawed testimony, especially when it came to ORT. The Chelsea owner claimed he was buying the shares simply to avoid problems with Putin in the future and was actually doing Berezovsky – who was clearly going to end up in jail eventually – a favour. When the ruling was read out, stating that the evidence didn't prove that Putin had ordered ORT's forced sale, the Russian journalists covering the trial burst into laughter. Yet even in victory, the judgement proved something important. 'In defending himself, Abramovich had made an important admission,' wrote Masha Gessen while covering the trial for *Vanity Fair*. 'Being in opposition to Putin was dangerous to businesses and the people who ran them, and had been from the earliest days of Putin's rule.' A year later, Berezovsky was found dead on his bathroom floor with a scarf around his neck. The British police suspected suicide. The coroner's court left an open verdict.

Jail or death follows Yeltsin's oligarchs. Badri Patarkatsishvili died in 2008 of a heart attack, in his early fifties. Stephen Curtis, a British lawyer who claimed to have witnessed many of Berezovsky's versions of events, died in a helicopter crash in 2004. Mikhail Khodorkovsky, once Russia's richest man, who had used his wealth to challenge Putin's power, was jailed in 2003 and had his assets taken by the state. He now lives as an exile in London. Each one had their lives destroyed.

But not Abramovich. He was canny enough to know where the true power lay. In that context, buying Chelsea – just at the time Putin was consolidating his power, destroying any opposition in the media and removing any wealthy threats to his power – made sense. Chelsea offered something that Berezovsky and Khodorkovsky never had: international visibility. On what had become a short timeline, every Russian oligarch's life expectancy was reduced to near zero. Chelsea FC was Abramovich's insurance policy.

In 2005 Gazprom, the Russian state-owned gas giant, bought Sibneft for $13.1 billion, making Abramovich even richer. He'd now turned most of his assets liquid. While more troublesome oligarchs had their companies taken from them, or were offered a fraction of their market rate, Abramovich walked away with the true worth of his assets intact. The deal meant that Gazprom was now one of the largest companies in the world. Oil and gas prices were booming, with Western Europe and neighbouring countries heavily dependent on gas exports, which gave Russia and Putin important political and economic leverage. 'The group of individuals who control the country's energy resources will be the real political and economic power brokers in Russia,' analyst Peter Lavelle wrote for the Russian news agency RIA Novosti.

Abramovich had survived, making his 1999 interview with the media arm of Gazprom all the more prescient. He was asked two final questions. What do you think your success is based on? 'On good luck.' In the right place at the right time? 'You could say that.'

3.

It seems strange for him to admit it now but the exiled anti-corruption activist Vladimir Ashurkov once believed that Vladimir Putin was the man to take Russia into the twenty-first century. 'In the beginning of the last decade I was quite in favour of Putin. I voted for him in the 2000 elections,' he confessed. 'Life was different. The transition from Soviet era to capitalism was not straightforward. I always recognised there were people who were forces of the future and people who wanted to keep the country in the past. Russian politics was a battle between those.'

Still, Ashurkov had become a success in the new Russia. He'd made good money working as a banker for Alfa Bank, Russia's largest bank, owned by one of the original oligarchs present on the Caribbean yacht in 1993 where Berezovsky and Abramovich first became acquainted: Mikhail Fridman. But by the end of 2010, Ashurkov believed Putin wasn't the force for the future any more. 'It became clear that corruption was on the rise and that political and civil freedoms were being repressed,' he says.

Ashurkov had never delved in politics before, knowing that money and power had often led to trouble in post-Soviet Russia. But he had started reading the blog of Alexei Navalny, a dedicated anti-corruption campaigner and a trained lawyer with knowledge of finance and investment, who had started his activist career buying shares in large Russian companies like Yukos in a bid to change the climate of corruption from the inside. Navalny's attempts at shareholder activism won him publicity but the companies he targeted saw him as little more than an annoyance. He was not seen as a serious threat . . . at least not until the large street protests that broke out across Russia in 2011 and 2012, shortly before Vladimir Putin's inauguration after winning the presidential election. Navalny had been angered by the alleged electoral fraud of Putin's party United Russia, which he had famously called the 'party of crooks and thieves'. He was subsequently arrested on embezzlement charges relating to the purchase of some timber while working as an advisor for a governor. The charges were a stretch at best. Ashurkov felt that his own knowledge of the corporate world might help. 'I wrote to him and said, "Here's some things you are doing wrong,"' he recalls. 'I had experience in corporate governance. He was dealing with graft in large state-owned companies. We met and I started to help him.'

The task ahead of them was vast, but Ashurkov joined Navalny's campaign to highlight how sharp business practices were undermining the fundamental foundations of Russian civil society. One of Navalny's most high-profile cases occurred in 2012 when he exposed the deal between Roman Abramovich, Alisher Usmanov and the first deputy prime minister Igor Shuvalov, a deal that saw Shuvalov bizarrely lend Usmanov $50 million to buy Corus Steel. 'This is not a case of somebody in Siberia stealing pipes,' Navalny told the *New York Times*. 'It occurred within the oligarchy that lives abroad and with a Western-oriented official. It will be remembered. Now, every time the fight against corruption comes up, so will Shuvalov's name.'

'Abramovich was one of the key people making decisions to put Putin in power and he was a major beneficiary of it in terms of business favours and privatisations,' explains Ashurkov, on how Chelsea FC's owner remains today at the heart of the political and economic system.

'All big business in Russia is subject to the influence of government. People can influence government in decisions that affect their businesses. This is in many cases the source of wealth for the richest people in Russia. In many cases business people are front men for government officials. They hold stakes on behalf of their patrons in the government.'

Neither Ashurkov nor Navalny were making friends with the rich and powerful. But Navalny was sufficiently emboldened to run for mayor of Moscow in 2013, with Ashurkov arranging the fundraising and financing. Navalny lost but managed to get close to 30 per cent of the vote and come second, a huge achievement given that most TV channels and newspapers were pro-Putin. He claimed that the percentage would have been even higher if it hadn't been for voter fraud. Shortly afterwards, Ashurkov's apartment was raided, live on television. Navalny's campaign had fallen foul of Russia's restrictive campaign finance laws, and Ashurkov was being punished. 'I had two apartment raids. You are sitting there and early in the morning there's a ring at the door and the police come and use some pretext to search and go through your things,' he recalls. 'In the first instance they took all my computers and phones and electronic equipment. You don't know if you will spend the night at home or [they'll] take you with them on some politically motivated charge. You [already] notice that you are followed . . .'

After the second raid Ashurkov decided to flee the country with his heavily pregnant wife. He had seen for himself what the alternative was. Navalny had already been in and out of prison on tenuous financial charges. And then there was the case of Boris Nemtsov, the politician who had been a key figure in the Yeltsin government of the mid-1990s, one of its young reformers, and had once held the position of deputy prime minister. He'd become a staunch critic of Putin since his first election victory in 2000 and, in particular, of the corruption that Nemtsov saw was endemic in the president's inner circle. His report on alleged widespread embezzlement caused particular embarrassment for the Russian government. The Sochi 2014 Winter Olympics were supposed to be a show of financial and sporting power by Russia but Nemtsov's report exposed how friends and allies of Putin had enriched themselves, pushing the cost of the project through the roof. (Putin had always understood the importance of sport in building a political narrative. When waving off the athletes for the 2000 Sydney Olympics, shortly after being elected to his first term, he said: 'Victories in sport do more to cement the nation than one hundred political slogans.' He was a keen judoka and ice hockey player. Although he had little time for football, the prestige of hosting big tournaments like the 2018 World Cup finals was seen as of paramount importance.) In the original bid document, it was estimated that Sochi Olympics would cost just over $14 billion. It ended up costing $51 billion, by far the most expensive Olympics ever held. Two men in particular enriched themselves: the Rotenberg brothers, Arkady and Boris, who were part of Putin's St Petersburg clique – old school friends and judo sparring partners who had grown rich as Putin had grown powerful. According to Nemtsov, the brothers received 21 non-bid contracts, which amounted to 15 per cent of the entire budget, around $7 billion according to the US treasury department.

'Everybody who is participating in Russian opposition politics understands this is a dangerous game. People are thrown into jail for false cases or driven out of the country like myself,' says Ashurkov. 'After Litvinenko no one can be sure they feel safe,' he adds, referring to the murder of Alexander Litvinenko, the former officer of the FSB – the successor to the KGB – and ally of Berezovsky who had also fled to the UK. He was recruited by MI5 and had been highly critical of Putin, accusing the Russian president of ordering the assassination of Anna Politkovskaya, the journalist and human rights activist. A few weeks after making the claim, Litvinenko died after his tea was poisoned with the radioactive element polonium. A British murder investigation concluded that it had been an FSB hit, and that Vladimir Putin most likely ordered his murder. 'I feel safer than in Moscow,' Ashurkov says

power and support. Born in Uzbekistan in 1953, Usmanov alternates between Russia's richest and third richest man, depending on the fluctuations in iron ore prices. He started out making money by filling a gap that hadn't existed before the fall of communism: plastic bags for a new generation of consumers. He later moved to Gazprom, where he was credited with restructuring the company into the formidable political and economic entity it is today. He made his fortune in mining and steel but has now diversified his wealth, investing in mobile phone operators, publishing and internet businesses, like Facebook and its Russian equivalent VKontakte (VK). Today, he's worth an estimated $14.5 billion. Unlike Abramovich, who grew up poor and was orphaned before he was five, Usmanov's upbringing was decidedly Soviet *nomenklatura*. His father was the chief prosecutor in the Uzbek capital Tashkent, which afforded Usmanov the chance to attend the prestigious Moscow State Institute for International Relations, where many of the then Soviet and now Russian political and diplomatic elite study. Usmanov's fledgling diplomatic career was derailed by a six-year spell in jail between 1980 and 1986. What is disputed is what landed him there.

Lurid accusations as to the reason for his imprisonment were raised by Craig Murray, the former British ambassador to Uzbekistan who returned home with tales of massive corruption under the president Islam Karimov, obscene human rights abuses and an untouchable political and economic elite. One of the many things Murray highlighted about Usmanov was his ambition of succeeding Karimov, who had been the only president Uzbekistan had known since independence. In a diplomatic cable from as far back as 2009, released by Wikileaks, Usmanov was mentioned as a potential successor. ('Moscow-based Uzbek oligarch Alisher Usmanov appeared to be trying to curry favor with President Karimov's eldest daughter Gulnara, noting, for example, that Usmanov was a main benefactor of Gulnara's cultural organization Fund Forum,' read one cable from the US embassy in Tashkent, worried about who would succeed an ageing Karimov.) It took another seven years for Karimov to die, and there were no immediate signs of an Usmanov power grab.

But Usmanov did do the time, for fraud and extortion. When he first bought Arsenal's shares in 2007, the story of his incarceration resurfaced. In an email interview with the *Guardian*, he claimed that he had been arrested alongside a man called Bakhodir Nasimov, whose father was the deputy head of the Uzbek KGB, in a bribery sting that went wrong. In 1986 he was released after repenting for his crime. The Uzbek courts later quashed his conviction. 'He's certainly not an open book,' Arsenal's then chairman, Peter Hill-Wood, said at the time. 'Business is murky in Uzbekistan, and that in itself is an argument against him being involved in Arsenal. I wouldn't want him to be the owner of the club.' The club made moves to lock down Arsenal's remaining shares to prevent Red and White Holdings – ownership of which was shared between Usmanov and British Iranian businessman Farhad Moshiri – from ever taking a controlling stake in Arsenal. Not to be deterred, Usmanov engaged in a boardroom battle with US billionaire Stan Kroenke, whose KSE UK Inc. also owns a stake in the club. Kroenke won, securing a 67 per cent stake by 2016. Usmanov has to this day been denied a seat on the board.

While questions were asked about Usmanov's past, his status as one of Putin's most loyal oligarchs was never in doubt. When Putin called on Russia's rich to bring their wealth back to the country to prove their patriotism, Usmanov was one of the first to answer his calls. He repatriated a majority share of his two most valuable assets – his mining company Metalloinvest and Russia's second biggest mobile phone operator MegaFon – to Russian entities. 'I am proud that I know Putin, and the fact that everybody does not like him is not Putin's problem,' Usmanov said in a 2010 interview with *Forbes* magazine. 'I don't think the world loved Truman after Nagasaki.' So when leading liberal business newspaper *Kommersant*, which he had bought in 2006 from Badri Patarkatsishvili (who in turn had bought it from Berezovsky), ran critical coverage of the 2011 state Duma election, Usmanov sprang into action. Putin's United

Russia party had won 49 per cent of the vote but lost 77 seats. It was again the biggest party, despite widespread unhappiness in Russia.

Kommersant ran a whole issue dedicated to alleged vote fraud benefiting Putin. The front cover had a remark – a quote one activist had given – that the Kremlin considered to have demeaned Putin. Usmanov was swift, and sacked the editor and the holding company's CEO. 'These materials border on petty hooliganism,' he told the Russian press after the firings. As far back as 2008 there had been fears that the newspaper had begun toeing the Kremlin line. '*Kommersant*, while one of the few publications to criticize the Kremlin and Medvedev, was also suspected of toning down its language because of owner Alisher Usmanov's ties to Gazprom,' read one diplomatic cable sent from the US embassy, and released by Wikileaks. Ever since, *Kommersant* has indeed largely toed the line, although its editor in chief was fired in 2014 when it overstepped the mark in reporting a story about Russian state oil company Rosneft – whose president Igor Sechin is a feared former deputy prime minister and perhaps one of Putin's staunchest allies. 'It has been a gradual decline,' Leonid Bershidsky, a publisher who founded the Russian edition *Forbes* magazine, told the *Moscow Times* of *Kommersant* post-Usmanov's purchase. 'Right now, there is no reason to read it.'

The Arsenal shareholder's investments in social media have had a similar effect. Usmanov owns a stake in Russia's biggest internet company Mail.Ru Group and in 2014 he purchased Russia's version of Facebook, to add to the lucrative 2 per cent stake he briefly held in the actual Facebook. VK had been a rare online space for free expression in Russia. There were six times as many VK users in Russia than Facebook users, taking advantage of its freedoms to post controversial political opinions as well as illegally share films and music with little fear of ever being punished for doing so. But the website had become an important tool for activists during the protests that rocked Putin's re-election campaign in 2012. Supporters of Alexei Navalny used the network to send messages and arrange protests. When the FSB asked for certain activists' pages to be taken down, the young founder of the company, Pavel Durov, refused to do so. Durov has often been described as the Mark Zuckerberg of Russia, but with a more libertarian streak. He is a fan of the *Matrix* trilogy and leads a monastic life, not drinking alcohol and not smoking. His brand of anarchic freedom doesn't fit well with the Kremlin's careful control of traditional media. After refusing the FSB's request, Durov's company's offices in St Petersburg were raided and the computers taken away. A heavily armed SWAT team turned up at Durov's house. He was aggressively pursued over an alleged incident where a police officer accused him of running over his foot in a company car. Durov denied it ever happened. When he was summoned for questioning, Durov fled the country. He had fallen out with his partners, too, which allowed Kremlin-friendly investors to move in. Usmanov had, in effect, taken over the company by 2014. Durov has been in exile ever since.

Control of the internet has been vitally important for the Kremlin. Putin himself once called the internet a 'CIA plot', yet in the years following his re-election in 2012 it was clearly becoming an ever more important way of influencing people. While state-owned Channel One – formally ORT – recorded an average of 19 million viewers, almost 50 million messages were being sent on VK every day. Putin needed his trusted oligarchs to help him control the message and the medium more now than ever before. In 2014 Ukraine was in the throes of a revolution. With his popularity falling, Putin embarked on a foreign adventure that would bring the Russian economy close to ruin, and his popularity back to life.

4. *Kiev, Ukraine, August 2014*

The dark wooden desk in Anatoliy Konkov's office is surrounded by three portraits. The first is an awkward-looking picture of the 64-year-old president of the Football Federation of Ukraine shaking hands with a smiling Sepp Blatter. The picture looks as if it has been taken very recently. Konkov, a solid man with grey hair, smiles proudly when he points to it. The second is a photo of Kiev's beautifully renovated Olympic Stadium, the jewel in the crown of Ukraine's 2012 European Championships, which the country co-hosted with Poland. Ukraine kicked off their campaign there with a 2–1 victory against Sweden. England beat Sweden there too, before losing to Italy on penalties. On 1 July 2012, 67,000 supporters sat in the stadium and watched Spain destroy Italy 4–0. It was history. No team had ever won back-to-back European Championships before, nor – when you considered the 2010 World Cup – three major titles in a row. Up in the stands during that game, Ukraine's then president Viktor Yanukovych stood next to Blatter. Michel Platini, Blatter's expected successor, was nearby, as was Gianni Infantino, then UEFA general secretary but ultimately Blatter's successor. Konkov was there too.

Soon, of course, Viktor Yanukovych's Ukraine changed beyond all recognition. Not that you would guess from outside Konkov's office. It is a beautiful sunny day, the Olympic Stadium just a few minutes' walk away. But the picture is an illusion, a snapshot of a past so brief as to make you wonder if it had really happened at all – a bit like looking at old sepia-tinted photos of Afghan girls on their way to school in miniskirts in Kabul in the 1970s; or watching Torvill and Dean win figure skating gold at the Winter Olympics in Sarajevo in 1984. A time before the time after.

The third picture is the closest to hand. It is the picture that Konkov – himself a former international player who represented the Soviet Union in the 1970s – has been most drawn to in recent weeks. 'This is the faith that helps us to survive,' he says wearily, pointing to a gold and wood icon of the Virgin Mary. 'It is a difficult situation we find ourselves in.' A 'difficult situation' is quite an understatement. Ukraine is at war. What kind of war is still hard to say. It is not quite a civil war, nor a traditional war between clearly defined adversaries. But the result is the same. Less than two years since Iker Casillas lifted the trophy for Spain, marking the end of the most high-profile event ever staged in Ukraine, the Russian-speaking east of the country is on fire. Donetsk, the industrial city that also hosted Euro 2012 matches, is a war zone. The Sergey Prokofiev International Airport, which was renovated for the tournament, lies in ruins. The Donbass Arena – named after the region of which Donetsk is the cultural and business capital, and home to Ukraine's biggest and most successful club Shakhtar – has been shelled.

Barely 18 months after the final, Yanukovych had an important decision to make. Since independence in 1991, Ukraine had tried to reconcile two identities: on the one hand West Ukraine, which had been part of the Austro-Hungarian Empire until the twentieth century, and then briefly part of Poland, with its European-leaning populace; and on the other the largely Russian-speaking peoples in the east and south, formerly part of the Russian empire. Russia's cultural, linguistic and economic influence remained strong in the south and east, and Ukraine as a whole remained an important ally for the Russian government. The main gas pipeline to Europe travels through Ukraine; Russia's Black Sea fleet is moored in Crimea. But in November 2013 Yanukovych was due to sign a European Union Association Agreement, putting the country on a path to EU membership. The possible expansion of the EU to Russia's border infuriated Putin, and Yanukovych declined to sign the agreement. Massive protests broke out in Kiev's Independence Square. The young people in Kiev, at least, wanted closer ties with Europe; some in the east pulled the other way, towards Russia. The Euromaidan revolution saw hundreds of thousands of Ukrainians take to the streets, already fuelled by a groundswell of anger at the endemic corruption in the police and judiciary and the power of Ukraine's oligarchs who had – as in Russia – got rich thanks to an opaque post-Soviet fire sale of state assets. Viktor Yanukovych was seen as Moscow's man. He was deposed and fled to Russia, leaving behind a trail of opulence hidden from public view – from his own personal zoo to a loaf of bread and golf clubs made of gold. When he became prime minister in 2002, Yanukovych claimed he didn't own a car or any property and earned just $11,000 a year. He'd even applied for a hardship grant from the government. As Ukraine's pro-Russian president fled, Vladimir Putin looked to secure Russia's assets. Russian forces invaded Crimea to secure its Black Sea fleet, before a creeping war fuelled by pro-Russian separatists engulfed the east.

Konkov thinks a lot about Crimea today, and in particular the three Ukrainian football teams from the region. When Russia finally annexed Crimea after a disputed referendum in March 2014, it took with it the peninsula's football infrastructure too. A few days before I saw Konkov in Kiev, Ukraine's football federation heard the news it had been dreading. TSK Simferopol, who finished second bottom in the previous season's Ukrainian Premier League, SKChF Sevastopol, who finished ninth, and Zhemchuzhina Yalta all played in a qualifying round of the Russian Cup. Only a few weeks earlier, the Russian Football Union (FUR) had met and approved their incorporation into the Russian football pyramid. The clubs were to begin the new season in the third tier of Russian football. 'The first time I heard about it was on Tuesday when everything began,' Konkov explains as he sat down. 'We cannot understand how our Ukrainian clubs on the territory of Ukraine can play in Russia.' A letter of complaint demanding Russia be punished for 'illegally and arbitrarily' taking Ukraine's clubs was written and sent to UEFA president Michel Platini as well as Sepp Blatter. The law seemed to be clear. UEFA's statutes outlaw 'combinations and alliances' of clubs from different associations while FIFA would only accept such a move if both associations agreed. Which, of course, hadn't happened. 'Of course we didn't allow this to happen,' Konkov says. 'Our strong position is that Ukrainian teams have to be in Ukrainian competition, and there is no right for them to take part in Russia.'

**

Football appeared to be an unimportant luxury when compared to the death and privation taking place in the east of the country. And yet some of the richest men in Russia and Ukraine had invested in the game and were now involved – directly and indirectly – in the direction their two countries travelled in, orbiting around Vladimir Putin's presidency. Since coming to power in 2000, Putin had undergone a transformation. It had been a long time since Vladimir Ashurkov believed him to be a 'force of the future'. For many Russians, Putin had been an overwhelmingly good thing after the chaos and humiliation of the Yeltsin years. He had brought the most disobedient oligarchs to heel, Russian living standards had dramatically improved, there was economic stability, even a boom. But, as ever, there was a trade-off. Like Abramovich and Usmanov and the other oligarchs who had facilitated Putin's rise to power but kept quiet and out of political life to keep their fortunes, many Russians accepted Putin's growing authoritarianism as long as life continued to improve. In 2012 Putin was re-elected president for another six-year term. But as economic growth began to lag, so did his popularity. And then the revolution on Independence Square, painted in the now overwhelmingly pro-Putin Russian media as a fascist overthrow of a democratically elected leader, took place.

Putin exploited it to its fullest. With TV stations, newspapers and (following the takeover of VK) most of Russia's internet in the hands of pro-Kremlin businessmen, a propaganda war ran parallel with the very real war raging in Ukraine's east. Russia maintains that a home-grown separatist movement emerged on its own two feet. But few believe this, especially since the shooting down of Malaysian Airlines MH17 on 17 July 2014, a tragedy that took 283 lives. The Joint Investigation Team set up to investigate the tragedy concluded that a BUK missile fired from a rebel-held area was responsible, and that the BUK missile was moved into Ukraine from Russia. It was moved back over the border the same day. The Kremlin derided the report as anti-Russian propaganda.

Russia's actions in Crimea led to retaliatory sanctions, pushing the country's economy into recession. The rouble was devalued by almost 50 per cent, reviving memories of the bad old days in the 1990s. The war also put in doubt one of the biggest showpiece events ever to be staged in Russia: the 2018 World Cup. Figures high up in Russian football, and close to President Putin, expressed concern that incorporating Crimean clubs into the Russian leagues could lead to the country's suspension from the global game, a ban from the lucrative UEFA Champions League and the loss of the finals themselves. An extraordinary transcript of a leaked recording from the vote that approved the entry of Crimea's three clubs into the Russian system was published by Russian investigative magazine *Novaya Gazeta*. It appeared to show, among others, Evgeny Giner, the president of CSKA Moscow, complaining about the vote's potential consequences. 'I have a club to support,' he is alleged to have said. 'And tomorrow they'll pull us from 2018.'

Back in Ukraine, the fate of Crimea's clubs was just one aspect of how the war impacted on the league. The bigger issue was how to deal with Ukraine's football clubs in the east of the country. Some of the country's biggest clubs, including Shakhtar Donetsk, champions the past five seasons, are based in the east. Konkov had once played for Shakhtar, as well as appearing in the Soviet Union side that made it to the final of Euro '72. He scored the only goal of the semi-final win against Hungary. (They lost to the great West Germany team of Beckenbauer, Netzer and Breitner, Gerd Müller scoring twice in a 3–0 victory.) 'It is difficult to compare those times with the Soviet Union and right now with Ukraine in Europe and Russia,' he says, evidently conflicted. Konkov grew up in the east and speaks Russian. 'During Soviet times there was no division between people from Belarus or Moldova. We were all actually the same. I had an experience playing for Shakhtar. I didn't feel any different being a Ukrainian there. In both teams I enjoyed playing. We were all the same. We had the equality between players from the Soviet Union.'

regime, and the Western businessmen who made their commission doing business with them. But since the start of the 2014–15 season, a very different crowd has lived here. In the main lobby a mix of Ukrainian and Brazilian international footballers pad along the marble floor in slippers. They play for Shakhtar Donetsk, Ukraine's richest and most successful club.

Shakhtar had enjoyed modest success before Rinat Akhmetov took over. Akhmetov is Ukraine's richest man, the Donbass' largest employer, and a former ally – some say kingmaker – of the deposed president Viktor Yanukovych. He took control of the club after his predecessor had been killed in a bomb attack at Shakhtar's stadium in 1995. According to *Forbes*, Akhmetov, the son of a coal miner, was worth $12.5 billion in 2014. He made his money in steel, iron ore and in the region's famous coal mines, all of which form part of the club's identity – the club's crest includes two crossed coal hammers. Akhmetov's fortune allowed Shakhtar to pay wages and transfer fees comparable to Europe's biggest teams, attracting players who might not have otherwise contemplated a move to eastern Ukraine. The club became adept at scouring South America and especially Brazil for young talented players, offering them a route into Europe and a shop window in the Champions League. Players like Manchester City's Fernandinho and Chelsea's Willian both gained European experience playing for Shakhtar.

But padding along the marble floors of the Opera, the players are now a long way from Donetsk. Since the civil war broke out in the east, it has been impossible to play any games there. The Donbass Arena has been shelled twice in recent months. Akhmetov's SCM group owns the Opera. The staff and players are living here temporarily, eating breakfast at the buffet among the guests, training in the hotel's small but plush gym, on treadmills alongside well-to-do middle-aged Ukrainian women doing their weekly exercise. It isn't ideal, but it is paradise compared to life for those left behind: as Donetsk prepared for the derby, back home in the nearby city of Luhansk the residents were enduring a fifth week with no water and no electricity. The bodies of dozens of civilians killed in the fighting were decomposing in the streets.

Shakhtar Donetsk's captain, Darijo Srna, has lived through one war already. The Croatian international was a young boy when the Yugoslav war tore his country apart. He was born in the small Croatian city of Metković, on the Croatia–Bosnia border near the Adriatic coast. His father was a Bosniak Muslim, his mother a Croatian Catholic. 'It is a strange situation and strange for us,' he explains as he sits in the lobby of the Opera, waiting for his teammates. 'I had the war in Croatia too and, as we say in Croatia, "What doesn't kill you makes you stronger."' Srna has spent more than a decade in Donetsk. He has been the driving force on the pitch for much of Shakhtar's recent success and fallen in love with the city and the country. 'It is not easy when every day we wake up, open the newspaper and open the television and see,' he explains. The match against Olimpik Donetsk, a small, relatively new team that had just been promoted to Ukraine's top tier, was only a few hours away (Olimpik had also moved to a temporary home, in Kiev, but in far less salubrious surroundings). The Shakhtar players walk through the lobby and onto the luxury orange and black team coach waiting outside. 'The day that will be the end of the war we will return to Donetsk and kiss the street,' says Srna, as he gets up and follows the last of the squad onto the bus.

There was no sign of Akhmetov at the Opera. He rarely gives interviews to the press these days. But his position had, in recent months, become increasingly unsure, largely down to his close ties to Yanukovych – famous in the West for losing the 2004 presidential election following the Orange Revolution (a popular uprising that followed massive voter fraud) and the near death of Viktor Yushchenko, Yanukovych's opponent, after he was poisoned before the vote and subsequently left with his face disfigured. According to the *New York*

Times back then, even the secret service, the SBU, had reservations about Yanukovych. 'Several SBU officers said the premier, who was once convicted of robbery and assault and has close links to the corrupt eastern businessmen who have acquired much of Ukraine's material wealth, was a man they preferred not to serve, especially if he were to take office by fraud.'

Akhmetov had acquired his mineral wealth much like Russian businessmen had in the anarchy of post-Soviet capitalism: juggling the competing forces of the state, the military and organised crime. Wealth had given him political influence. Akhmetov had bankrolled Yanukovych's rise (as well as his Party of the Regions), and also secured a seat in parliament which, handily, brought with it immunity from prosecution. A 2006 cable from the US embassy in Kiev, released by Wikileaks, revealed remarks from the then prime minister Yulia Tymoshenko, who had been the face of the Orange Revolution, witnessing Akhmetov making his first speech after entering parliament: 'While Akhmetov was popular in Donetsk due to "local boy patriotism" the rest of the country perceived him as a criminal; this was even true in Luhansk and Crimea, two strongly pro-Regions provinces. Thus, most people watching Akhmetov would not have concluded "good speaker" but, in contrast, would have thought, "A major criminal is poised to enter the Rada [parliament]." Tymoshenko opined that any effort by government authorities to go after Yanukovych for his misdeeds would boomerang, boosting Yanukovych's political standing, but that the authorities should pursue Akhmetov for his crimes.'

Tymoshenko would perhaps rue that decision. Yanukovych would go on to make a stunning political comeback after hiring American political consultant Paul Manafort, who gave him a US-style political makeover. Yanukovych won the 2010 presidential election as a result. Manafort went on to take charge of Donald Trump's 2016 US presidential campaign, before questions about his work in Ukraine and connections to Russia forced him to resign. Tymoshenko would later be jailed on widely condemned charges of signing a gas deal with Russia that was seen as particularly disadvantageous to Ukraine. But few saw her imprisonment as anything but score settling.

Yanukovych's decision to jail Tymoshenko was criticised around the world, especially as she had also fallen into ill health. Yanukovych's refusal to release her led to almost all Western heads of state boycotting the 2012 European Championships, a tournament already mired in a series of corruption scandals after hundreds of millions of pounds evaporated from state coffers and into a shadowy network of companies in the Donbass and then into a network of opaque offshore companies.

As Yanukovych inched back into popular favour, Akhmetov continued to be a key figure behind the scenes. He has always denied any involvement in criminal activity or being part of the so-called 'Donetsk clan', a network of businessmen, politicians and gangsters that effectively ran the city. 'Akhmetov was Yanukovych's financial backer before he came to power and he benefited a lot financially by being close to the president,' explained Orysia Lutsevych, a research fellow on Russia and Ukraine for the Chatham House policy institute. 'He was never a political animal. He was a politician for a while. He preferred to be in the shadows, controlling from behind.'

When the rebellion in the east broke out, Akhmetov initially stayed silent, before coming out in favour of the Kiev government. Several rebel commanders had made suggestions that some of the money used to fund the rebellion had initially come from Akhmetov. 'It turned out that two-thirds of the activists are already dependent on oligarch Rinat Akhmetov,' said Pavel Gubarev, the self-styled governor of the People's Republic of Donetsk. He was later arrested by forces loyal to Kiev before being released in a prisoner swap with the Ukrainian secret service. Akhmetov strenuously denied the accusation, pointing to how he raised his workers to successfully defend the port city of Mariupol that came under attack by pro-Russian forces associated with the

People's Republic of Donetsk. He remains Ukraine's biggest employer, keeping the mines and factories running during the conflict, although some of his factories have been commandeered and forcibly nationalised by rebel groups.

According to Lutsevych, Akhmetov's fence-sitting during the early part of the war led many in Kiev to question his allegiances. He has since tried to win hearts and minds in the Donbass region by giving large pay rises to the quarter of a million staff in his coal mining and energy businesses. When Russia controversially sent a humanitarian convoy to the war-ravaged east, Akhmetov sent his own convoy with over 2,000 tonnes of aid. But many in Ukraine don't believe that is enough, and that the oligarch class should now 'pay back' large sums of what they see as plundered cash. 'In Kiev the thinking is that he should pay a price and it should be high,' said Lutsevych. 'There are demands he provides direct assistance to the army. The question is how high should the price be for creating Yanukovych as a political animal?'

And yet, Akhmetov maintains a semblance of popular support, largely through the success of Shakhtar. The club has received hundreds of millions of pounds from European football clubs for its players, bought for a fraction of the cost in South America.

Abramovich, Usmanov and Akhmetov – the three oligarchs who featured on Vladimir Ashurkov's Kleptocracy Tour – may come from different countries, from very different backgrounds, and have made their money in different industries. But they are from the same club, making their fortunes in hazy circumstances before investing heavily in football, giving a sliver of legitimacy to business careers with dark episodes.

'In a way, he really loves football, and has a genuine interest in the game,' Lutsevych says of Akhmetov, although she could have been talking about any of the three. 'It [the bankrolling of Shakhtar] was done to project soft power in the region. To show how much he cares about the community. It was the place he could meet other oligarchs for business. It was quasi-political. Russian oligarchs are a good model for Ukrainian ones. They operate in the same political system.'

<h1 style="text-align:center">5.</h1>

Plumes of thick black smoke and the rapid-fire echo of explosions rise into the afternoon sky. Several hundred people from the east of Ukraine, almost all of them men in black t-shirts and balaclavas, are singing nationalistic songs in one stand at Kiev's Bannikov Stadium as they throw smoke bombs and flash grenades onto the pitch in front of them. At the centre is a young man with a shaven head and sunglasses, dressed in black. His t-shirt bears the name of his home city, Severodonetsk, near Luhansk, the letters coloured the yellow and blue of the Ukrainian flag.

Vladyslav is a member of the Shakhtar Ultras, a group of hardcore fans that support Shakhtar Donetsk anywhere they play, even if that involves a ten-hour journey west to Kiev through a raging war zone. The Donetsk derby has just begun in front of a small crowd. The stadium is next to the offices of the Football Federation of Ukraine, where I had earlier met the FFU president Anatoliy Konkov, and just a stone's throw from the Olympic Stadium. The Bannikov is only half full, filled mostly with Shakhtar's fans who live in Kiev. But the ultras have all travelled from the beleaguered east to be there. In the previous round of the Premier League, Shakhtar had played in the majestic Arena Lviv in the west of the country, but the team had been booed by some sections of the crowd – Ukrainian nationalism is at its strongest in the west and Shakhtar, its fans and its owner were perceived to be supporters of the pro-Russian uprising. But for most fans it's not so simple. 'Some part of the people want to be part of Russia,' explains Vladyslav, who is a 21-year-old finance student. 'Normal people want to stay. I am a patriot. I love my country. I love Ukraine.'

Ukraine's football ultras played a significant role in the country's revolution. As the protests grew, and Yanukovych attempted to crush them – firstly with a new 'dictatorship law' to ban any gatherings and then by brute force – Ukraine's ultras vowed to bury their traditional enmities towards each other and protect the protesters in the square. When the restart after the winter break of the 2013–14 season was postponed because of the growing conflict, the ultras of Shakhtar Donetsk and Dynamo Kiev met in the capital anyway to show solidarity. 'Let us applaud the heroic soccer fans of Dnipro Cherkasy, Karpaty Lviv, and Vorskla Poltava! This is where solidarity starts. This is where patriotism starts!' said Oleh Tyahnybok, the head of the nationalist, far-right Svoboda party, praising the nation's ultras.

Even the ultra groups of the two main clubs from the overwhelmingly ethnically Russian Crimea expressed their solidarity with the protests. Where once Ukraine's ultras had been derided as nihilistic hooligans, now they were fêted as protectors of the revolution. 'We all speak Russian,' says Vladyslav the ultra from Severodonetsk of his gang. 'Since a kid, Russian is my mother tongue. Our problem is corruption, not Russian speakers.' On the pitch, the Donetsk derby was going to form. Shakhtar had close to 100 million Euros worth of talent on the pitch; Olimpik Donetsk, on the other hand, could only bring on a 41-year-old striker from the bench, a huge, barrel-chested bear of a man who is also the club's owner. 'When I play I feel the fans and players on the bench stare at me, that's why I have the bigger responsibility than other players,' says Vladyslav Helzin, scorer of five goals over the past five seasons. 'Every time I go on the pitch I have to prove that it's not for nothing. I'm trying to do my best.'

Helzin isn't just the club owner and striker. He was also a leading regional figure in the Party of the Regions, Yanukovych's old party. He set up Olimpik in 2001 as a way of nurturing young talent in the city, and won successive promotions until making it to the Premier League for the first time in 2014. Like Akhmetov, he too has had to bankroll the club's temporary move to Kiev. The match is nominally a 'home' game for Olimpik. 'We don't leave the players alone with their problems,' says Helzin of how the war is affecting his squad. 'Each employee of the club is provided financial assistance in order to help rent apartments in Kiev and protect their families. Our team is a family. We share joy and sorrow together.' The match ends in a rout and Helzin doesn't get on the scoresheet. Shakhtar thrash Olimpik 5–0. After the full-time whistle is blown, Darijo Srna and a handful of players run towards the Shakhtar fans. The players are mobbed as the ultras shake hands, hug them and have photos taken together. 'This was the best day of the season,' says Vladyslav, beaming as he leaves the stadium. 'I don't know how I'll get home. Maybe I'll hitch a ride on a tank.'

**

In the weeks after the Donetsk derby, the Donbass Arena was hit by shelling again. The club's offices were also, briefly, overrun by unidentified armed men. The Shakhtar ultras, meanwhile, continued to travel hundreds of miles every week to see their club, even if their numbers had been reduced somewhat. The day after the Shakhtar–Olimpik game in Kiev, the Shakhtar ultras' Twitter account announced that a number of its members had stayed in Kiev and joined the Azov Battalion, a 500-strong right-wing volunteer militia fighting in the east of the country that has been accused by some of harbouring a neo-Nazi ethos. 'Some boys who were at the match today took the military oath and will go to Donbass,' Vladyslav later told me. He said that as many as 75 ultras had taken the Azov Battalion oath. Vladyslav was eager to join the fighting too. 'I wanted to go to the military unit,' he said. 'But my parents wouldn't let me.'

After winning the league five seasons in a row, Shakhtar initially struggled in exile. But as war became normality, the club adapted and won the 2016/17 league and cup double. Ukraine's Crimean clubs were told by UEFA they could not compete in the Russian league. UEFA's compromise was to set up its own Crimean league. Anatoliy Konkov, the former Soviet Union player in charge of the Ukraine FA, was not happy. But bigger issues – namely making sure that Ukraine qualifies for the next World Cup in Russia – are on his plate. Qualification, he says, would send a message to Russia and the rest of the world. Meanwhile, the war in the east continues. It has taken 10,000 lives so far.

6.

The war in Ukraine has cast a long shadow. Outside of the destruction wrought in Donetsk and Luhansk, the hundreds of other towns and villages destroyed barely get even a passing mention. The Russian economy is in recession as EU sanctions bite. An asymmetrical propaganda war is ongoing, with newspapers, TV stations and websites churning out a one-sided, often false reading of events and history. But the leaders and politicians – not to mention the wealthy oligarchs who have been instrumental to their rise – are largely immune. Their wealth and their power continue. What happens in Russia and Ukraine seems a world away. And perhaps it is. The question is, at what point do we accept some culpability for humanising those that have played a role in dismantling the freedoms we hold dear, or even dismantling whole countries? Should we ignore the Gazprom adverts that wrap around the Champions League, when Russian gas supply is used as a tool of war? Or the transfer goings-on at Chelsea when they are funded by one of Putin's closest oligarchs? Or ignore the role that some of the world's richest football club owners have had in neutering Russian newspapers, eviscerating investigative reporting or strangling a country's embryonic civil society?

'You can draw up a blacklist of about a thousand people who will no longer be allowed entry into Western countries, and you can do it quietly, without any big announcement, but you have to hit the propagandists of war, the ones who finance the war, the real party of war,' Alexei Navalny told the *Financial Times* in 2015. He was speaking just after he had been released from his latest stretch in prison. For Navalny, Western sanctions against Putin's inner circle have not had the desired effect. 'Usmanov, Abramovich, and their families – if they can't get to their residences in London or in Switzerland, that will make a difference.'

Ukraine didn't qualify for Russia 2018 but the usual accusations of large-scale graft around the tournament's building projects proliferated. 'I can promise you will never regret it,' said Russian deputy prime minister Igor Shuvalov – the same Shuvalov with the fancy apartment in Whitehall – as he accepted the winning bid in Zurich back in 2010. Shuvalov played a key role in delivering the tournament. It was alleged that several deals had taken place behind the scenes too. A 2014 British parliamentary report outlined how an ex-MI6 agent, later named as Christopher Steele, had been spying on the Russian delegation on behalf of the failed England bid. 'Roman [Abramovich] was absolutely integral to the Russian bid,' an anonymous source, thought to be Steele, told the *Sunday Times*. It was also claimed a huge natural gas deal struck between Qatar and Russia was connected to the bids. 'I remember seeing him [Abramovich] attending private meetings with Sepp Blatter in South Africa and thinking to myself, "We don't do that, so we are fucked . . ." Roman was very visible. Any suggestion that he paid money, I don't know. The way he operates, you'd never find out.' Steele later went into hiding after being outed as the author of a salacious dossier detailing the connections between Russia and the US president Donald Trump.

When the murky world of the 2010 FIFA votes began to be investigated, FIFA's ethics committee asked to see the Russian federation's computers. They refused, saying that they had only borrowed the computers and they had all now been destroyed. As a reward for his efforts in securing the finals, Abramovich was handed a large bill to pay. 'I don't rule out that Mr Abramovich may take part in one of these projects,' Putin said when discussing who would contribute to the cost of building the stadiums for 2018, shortly after the announcement on Russian TV. 'Let him open his wallet a little. It's no big deal – he won't feel the pinch. He has plenty of money.' And, sure enough, Abramovich and Usmanov have 'opened their wallets'. After all, no one wants to become the next Berezovsky. 'There seems to be something of an emerging understanding that the government will help the titans of the economy to maintain the liquidity they need to stay in business,' Sam Greene, the director of the Russia Institute at King's College London, told the *Independent*. 'In return for that, they remain quiet, they remain loyal, but they also maintain employment and they keep moving money through the economy.'

There are other ways to maintain influence. The annexation of the Crimean peninsula, the London court cases, the business deals and the ongoing war in Ukraine are revealing of how football has become inseparably intertwined with how oligarchs maintain their power, interests and influence: football and the Russian state-owned gas supplier Gazprom are both different but important tools of power. For a long time Gazprom, which presides over the largest natural gas reserves in the world, had the power to turn off the gas and – more importantly – the heating in Ukraine and the other parts of Europe. With 80 per cent of Russia's gas supply to Europe coming through Ukraine – Germany gets 46 per cent of its gas from Russia; Poland, 88 per cent – Russia had political and economic leverage, setting prices that furthered political ends. The head of Gazprom, Alexey Miller, is an ally of Putin's from his days in St Petersburg. 'In fact, Putin is the acting CEO of Gazprom,'

Vladimir Ashurkov is not much of a football fan but he understands the game's attraction to oligarchs. 'Soccer is really popular in Russia, and the Premier league is one of the most watched sports,' he says. 'The other thing, of course, is that the UK is convenient for doing business for Russians. It is a safe place to keep money and invest in property and has a favourable tax regime. Investing in a soccer club in Britain is a good way to become acquainted with the British establishment. It works well for Abramovich at Chelsea,' who has spent as much as £2 billion on Chelsea so far without an end in sight. There are other benefits, of course. 'Primarily in Britain, if you think you might have some issues with your money or money-laundering investigations, you would have an easier time if you had some public profile in England. Owning a soccer club does that.'

Roman Abramovich changed the way money was invested in football forever. While Chelsea fans could bask in a new and scarcely believable dominance on the field, off it rival clubs were scrabbling around to find ways to compete, to find a sugar daddy of their own. Football had always been a global game, but global capital was now crossing borders and into clubs, even when the provenance of that investment could not entirely be accounted for. There were rumours that other wealthy Russians would join the fray, buying European clubs to compete with the Abramovichs of the world. But that investment never materialised. Instead, billionaires on the other side of the Atlantic Ocean would provide the next wave of investment. It would be American investors who would try to compete with the Abramovichs.

Ashurkov, meanwhile, continues to see London as his home. His young daughter was born here and he has the freedom to continue campaigning against the complex network of corruption between the state and oligarchs that he believes is destroying his own country and beyond. '[London] is the best city in the world,' he says. 'After Moscow, of course.' He won't be here for ever, though. He believes Putin's regime is doomed. As with all regimes that eat their young, there is no one to

PART TWO, AMERICA:

The Money Men

1. St Louis, Missouri, United States

Soulard is starting to turn dark. The historic neighbourhood in St Louis is the city's oldest, famed for its tightly packed terraced housing that once housed workers from the Anheuser-Busch brewery – home of Budweiser – and long lines of blues and jazz bars. It is also home to St Louis' Mardi Gras, considered the second biggest after the more famous parade in New Orleans. But both share a common French heritage despite being 700 miles apart down the Mississippi river.

St Louis was founded by two French fur traders and named after Louis IX, who ruled France in the thirteenth century. The settlement changed hands between the French and Spanish before being sold to the Americans as part of the 1803 Louisiana Purchase. Napoleon offered to sell a huge swathe of what is now central USA to Thomas Jefferson for a combined price (including debt relief) of 68 million francs. It was, by any standard, a bargain, not to mention one of the biggest land sales ever. At current land prices it would be worth upwards of $1.2 trillion.

Many European customs and communities remain in St Louis. For one, it is arguably the crucible of soccer in America, where immigrant communities from the end of the nineteenth century onwards have played and organised the game, setting up the country's first professional league in 1907. Six of the players who travelled to the 1950 World Cup with the US national team played in St Louis, including the captain, Harry Keough. Today, the city is home to the biggest Bosnian community outside of the Balkans.

The party on the litter-strewn streets of Soulard is coming to an end. Huge speakers outside each bar pump out a disorienting mishmash of EDM. Fights are breaking out. It is Super Bowl weekend – Super Bowl 50, no less – between the Carolina Panthers and the Denver Broncos. But no one seems to be in a particularly happy mood, and not just because the city's team, the St Louis Rams, failed to make the playoffs. No one seems happy with football, the National Football League (NFL) and – most tellingly of all – everyone is unhappy with one man in particular: Stan Kroenke, the Missouri-born billionaire who is one of the country's richest men, owns a majority stake in Arsenal FC and is the sole owner of the Rams. Although it isn't to remain the city's franchise for much longer. A month earlier Stan Kroenke had announced that, after 20 years in St Louis, down the road from the tiny town where Kroenke grew up, the Rams franchise would move back to glitzier and wealthier Los Angeles.

As the Super Bowl party winds down and drunken partygoers, covered in garish plastic beads and necklaces thrown from floats at the earlier carnival parade, stumble back to waiting buses laid on by the city, five college-age bros are venting spleen. 'Fuck Stan Kroenke, dude. He moved the Rams to LA. I hate him. Fuck him,' says Sean, who seems the most angry of the group.

But isn't Kroenke from Missouri? I ask.

'He's not from Missouri! He don't give a fuck about anything! Just himself and making paper!' he says angrily, chugging back the plastic cup holding the last of his beer. 'THAT'S WHAT I'M TALKING ABOUT!' he shouts as he throws it behind him. 'He don't care, he just wants to get out of St Louis. He's always wanted out of St Louis. We are all pissed. St Louis people are pissed that the Rams are leaving.'

It isn't the first time a city has been faced with losing a beloved sports team. Since the 1920s teams have gone on the road, usually due to dire financial situations that could only be remedied by upping sticks and moving to the big city. But American football is a different game these days. The NFL is now the most valuable league in the world: of the names on Forbes.com's list of the 50 most valuable sports teams in 2016, 27 hail from the NFL. At the time of writing, the number one team, overtaking Real Madrid and Manchester United, is the Dallas Cowboys, bought by oil and gas magnate Jerry Jones in 1989 for $150 million, and now worth over $4 billion. The average worth across all 32 NFL teams is $2 billion. Roger Goodell, the NFL commissioner, earned $32 million in 2015. By comparison Richard Scudamore, the man who has overseen the TV rights bonanza that has made the English Premier League the world's richest soccer league, earns upwards of £3 million a year including bonuses.

American football is the biggest of big-money sports, but profit isn't necessarily based on success on the field of play. The Dallas Cowboys have not made the Super Bowl in nearly 20 years. Instead, they have increased their wealth thanks to booming TV contracts, clever sponsorship deals and an unusual form of protectionism. Essentially, the NFL is a cartel of 32 teams untroubled by failure unless it is a failure to make money. There is no promotion or relegation, nor any fixed geographical identity. Any history is connected to the brand, not necessarily the city that hosts them, allowing owners to shop around from host to host and state to state to get the best deal for its franchise, largely in the shape of tax breaks for building their stadium. Kroenke had simply done what others had done before him: found a place that would offer the best deal for the greatest profit. That place was Los Angeles. Kroenke had bought a 40 per cent stake in the LA Rams and had been an integral part of the same consortium that took them to St Louis in 1995, and into the then brand new Trans World Dome, a 70,000-seater state-of-the-art, covered stadium built at a cost of $301 million, paid for by St Louis' taxpayers. As was a $30 million renovation 15 years later. 'I'm born and raised in Missouri,' Kroenke told the *St Louis Post-Dispatch* when he was seeking approval to purchase the remaining 60 per cent of the team in 2010. 'I've been a Missourian for 60 years. People in our state know me. People know I can be trusted. People know I am an honourable guy.'

But then suddenly, for Kroenke at least, the stadium wasn't good enough any more. Negotiations with the city for a new publicly funded stadium failed. So, in January 2016, the NFL voted 30 to 2 to allow the Rams to up sticks and move back west. 'This has been the most difficult process of my professional career,' Kroenke said in a statement after the decision was taken. 'This is bitter sweet. St Louis is a city known for its incredibly hard-working, passionate and proud people. Being part of the group that brought the NFL back to St Louis in 1995 is one of the proudest moments of my professional career.'

The reaction was furious, not least from the city's Democrat mayor Francis Slay, who had convened a task force to recommend a $1 billion waterfront stadium in downtown St Louis in order to keep the Rams in the city. 'Let me do something Stan Kroenke did not – thank the St Louis fans of the Rams. St Louisans stood by their team, supporting them through far more losing seasons than winning seasons. The NFL ignored the facts. They ignored the loyalty of St Louis fans. They ignored a viable plan for a new stadium,' he said after the decision. 'The NFL sent a loud and clear message: their home cities and hometown fans are commodities to be abandoned once they no longer suit the league's purposes,' before adding, 'I have no real interest in the NFL.'

Others were less polite, like the editorial in the caustic *Riverfront Times* entitled 'Fuck You, Stan Kroenke, and the Toupee You Rode in Under', whose diatribe went viral: 'You're worth an estimated $7.7 billion. You're so rich you bought a goddamn professional lacrosse team, which is dumber than leasing a sports car. But consider this, Stanley: maybe St Louis is suffering economically because of you. The city (and the county) both pay $12 million a year in upkeep on the team's current home, and both governments will continue to pay it for years to come.' More pressing, that figure would rise if no tenant was found to actually use the stadium and share the costs. The piece signed off by pointing out Kroenke's way of doing business would not be restricted to the NFL: 'Have fun counting your pennies. It's clearly your main joy in life, other than buying winning sports teams like the [ice hockey team Colorado] Avalanche and Arsenal and running them into the fucking ground . . . You're hated on two continents. At least it pays well.' The sign off was at least verifiable. While he is public enemy number one in St Louis, Kroenke isn't much liked in North London either.

Kroenke's heavy investment in sport extends to not only buying NHL's Colorado Avalanches but also the NBA's Colorado Nuggets (both of which he spun off to his son to comply with conditions set by the NFL allowing him to take full ownership of the Rams in 2010) and the Colorado Rapids in Major League Soccer. But his most surprising move wasn't his left-field swerve into American lacrosse ownership with the Colorado Mammoth – it was his investment in English soccer with Arsenal. Kroenke Sports Enterprises (now Kroenke Sports and Entertainment) started acquiring shares in Arsenal Holdings plc (Arsenal FC's parent company) in 2007, sparking a battle for control over the club's shares with controversial Uzbek oligarch Alisher Usmanov. By 2011 Kroenke had won that battle and now owns 67.05 per cent of Arsenal Holdings. Usmanov meanwhile solidified his position when British Iranian banker Farhad Moshiri – Usmanov's long-time business partner – sold his stake so that he could then launch a successful £200 million bid for just under 50 per cent of Everton FC's shares. Kroenke's interest in English soccer was piqued on a business trip to Hong Kong. 'I walk up to a newsstand on the waterfront, pick up a magazine, and it's all about the English Premier League,' he said in a 2011 interview with *Sports Illustrated*. 'Maybe we have something here.'

In 2007 the English Premier League was enjoying booming revenues but shrinking margins. According to Deloitte's 2007 *Annual Review of Football Finance*: 'Premier League clubs' revenues increased by 3 per cent to set another European record at £1,379 million, an average of £69 million per club.' But operating profits had fallen for the first time in seven years, by 15 per cent. The number of clubs recording a profit fell from 14 to nine. The arrival of Roman Abramovich in 2003 had altered the game, and the fans' expectations. He had spent hundreds of millions of pounds at Chelsea, which had delivered two league titles and the FA Cup in four seasons. The report thought it a particularly positive sign that Chelsea's finances had improved, cutting their pre-tax losses from £140 million to a mere £80 million. But the report also predicted a boom that would explain Kroenke's interest. A huge new TV rights deal had been signed with Sky Sports and Setanta that would kick in in 2007. The three-year deal was for £1.7 billion, and represented a two-thirds increase on the previous arrangement. It was the deal that, for the first time, meant that match-day revenue would not be the main source of income for most clubs. By the end of the deal almost every club in the Premier League, including Manchester United, would earn more from broadcasting money than gate receipts. Every club bar one, that was. Arsenal had invested heavily in the new 60,000 Emirates Stadium, built without public subsidy and financed largely through debt, from selling off the old ground, naming rights and, most controversially and counter-intuitively in a league where sums spent on the playing squad and silverware are directly proportionate, player sales. Broadcasting would overtake match day revenue only in 2014.

Despite being awash with cash – with reserves of £226.5 million in 2016 – Arsenal have only won three FA Cups since Kroenke's investment in the club, while rivals Chelsea, Manchester United, Manchester City and Leicester City have all won the Premier League. Kroenke is not popular with Arsenal's fans for his perceived thriftiness and aloofness – a matter not helped when the BBC revealed Kroenke had bought a mammoth 520,000-acre, $725-million ranch in Texas, making him the ninth biggest landowner in the US. Nor were they happy when Kroenke was quoted saying that he didn't buy Arsenal to win things. 'If you want to win championships, then you would never get involved,' he told a sports analytics conference in Boston, in 2016. 'I think the best owners are the guys that sort of watch both sides a bit.'

The exponential growth of Premier League TV deals has now attracted a different kind of investor: a raft of American businessmen who have learned how to extract profit in the NFL, MLB and NBA, Kroenke being one of the canniest. They have learned an important lesson. Sports teams, franchises, aren't tethered: they are entertainment products; a studio from which a never-ending series every bit as engrossing as *The Wire* or *The Sopranos* plays out season after season after season. And the best bit? The network will never cancel it. But characters are bumped off or moved on, as St Louis Rams' fans learned the hard way. Perhaps there are lessons here for what European soccer, especially English soccer and in particular Arsenal, can learn from what had happened to the Los Angeles né St Louis Rams.

'Soccer? I don't know, bro, they should WATCH OUT,' shouts Sean. The college bros agree, but then begin arguing about the Rams' lack of a quarterback. 'You heard it here first, if the Rams had stayed [in St Louis] we'd have got Peyton Manning and won the Super Bowl, so fuck Stan Kroenke. Everyone hates him, dude,' says Sean. Sean's polite friend offers an alternative: 'Come on,' he says quietly. 'No one gave a shit about the Rams until they left. All we needed was a quarterback.' Sean doesn't take it well. 'Fuck Stan Kroenke!' he shouts. 'And that's all I got to say on the matter.'

2.

Enos Stanley Kroenke was born in the tiny village of Mora in the heart of Missouri, roughly equidistant from Kansas City, Springfield and Columbia (where he studied for an MBA and became interested in international trade at Missouri University). St Louis is 200 miles and a three-hour drive away. As Jeré Longman explained in his 2010 *New York Times* profile of Kroenke shortly before he would take control of Arsenal, his father owned a lumber yard, where Kroenke would work sweeping up wood chip while doing the books on the side. He played basketball in college but grew up following his grandfather's beloved St Louis Cardinals baseball team – in fact he is named after two Cardinals Hall of Famers, Enos Slaughter and Stan Musial. His upbringing was modest. 'I know this will sound corny,' he said in a 2012 *Sports Illustrated* interview, 'but I really walked to a one-room schoolhouse, two and a half miles each way.'

His life would change after a ski trip to Aspen. There he met Ann Walton, the niece and heir to the fortune of Stan Walton, the founder of the world's largest retailer, Wal-Mart. The Waltons are the richest family in America. The seven heirs – including Ann – are worth a staggering $130 billion. Still, Kroenke and his surrogates have always stressed he is a self-made man, who was already wealthy from his dealings in real estate before he joined the family, although many of his strip mall developments took place around existing Wal-Mart properties, with Wal-Mart as the anchor tenant. Both Ann and Stan are listed separately on *Forbes'* rich list.

Even after owning numerous sports teams – although, interestingly given the story behind his name, not a baseball team – Kroenke still sees himself as a real-estate man first and foremost. His company THF Realty (an acronym of To Have Fun) developed parcels of land into retail spaces around St Louis and the rest of Missouri, at least half of which were connected to Wal-Mart developments. The business also taught him another important lesson. Profits could be bolstered by government dollars. The Waltons have been long-time supporters of the Republican Party, donating millions of dollars to the party as well as outside groups – PACS and Super PACS – that campaign on conservative issues, like fighting any rises in the minimum wage or abolishing estate taxes. According to a 2014 report by US think tank Demos, Wal-Mart spent $80 million on campaign contributions and lobbying between 2000 and 2014, heavily skewed towards a Republican Party that believes in small government and small government spending.

Kroenke, for his part, has personally donated close to $300,000, overwhelmingly to Republican campaigns between 2000 and 2013. (Yet according to filings at the Federal Election Commission he also donated $105,400 to Hillary Clinton's failed campaign against Donald Trump for the US presidency.) Despite the Walton family's apparent championing of small government policies, Wal-Mart has famously become a huge recipient of government subsidies, dubbed by critics as 'Corporate Welfare': by paying rock-bottom wages to its 1.4 million staff, the state effectively has to subsidise them with food stamps, housing and other benefits. A 2014 report by the political advocacy group Americans for Tax Fairness placed that figure at a staggering $6.2 billion. Wal-Mart's employment practices became a campaign issue during the 2016 American presidential election primaries, and that perhaps explains why Kroenke backed Clinton. 'Wal-Mart is the major beneficiary of welfare in America,' Senator Bernie Sanders said during a January 2016 campaign speech in Des Moines, Iowa. 'Isn't it weird that many of the people who work at Wal-Mart are on Medicaid, which you [the taxpayer] pay for. On food stamps, which you pay for. They are in government-subsidised housing, which you pay for. Because the Walton family refuses to pay the wages and benefits their workers deserve.' This has, according to the Demos report, helped redistribute wealth from the poorest in America to the richest. 'This outcome exacerbates inequities because companies like Wal-Mart rely on a business model that depends on taxpayers to support their low-wage workforce, while simultaneously aiming their political spending to reduce their own tax burdens.'

Kroenke spent five years on the Wal-Mart board between 1995 and 2000, when he had to disclose that he held close to 2 per cent of the company's stock. In a 2011 *Denver Post* profile it was revealed that Kroenke had enjoyed massive tax breaks during his real-estate career. 'THF Realty . . . received $117 million in tax breaks from local governments on ten shopping-center developments from 1994 to 2006,' investigative journalists Robert Sanchez and Greg Griffin discovered. 'Of that, $54 million went toward Wal-Mart stores.' US sports-franchise owners had worked out that corporate welfare worked for them too.

**

Even as late as 1980, the news that an NFL team was moving to another city was rare. A move hadn't been approved by the football league for the best part of two decades. The last time had been in 1960 when the Chicago Cardinals moved to St Louis. Owner Violet Bidwill and her late husband Walter Wolfner hadn't wanted to move. But the league wanted it, as did CBS Television. There were no protests and no denunciations of the owner. On the contrary, 'No impartial observer can shed any tears over the Cards' departure,' wrote legendary true crime and sports writer Jack Olsen in a 1960 *Sports Illustrated* feature on the prospective move to St Louis. 'The Cardinals bored Chicago and the Bears did not.'

But in the early 1980s, America was changing. Ronald Reagan had come to power promising a diet of supply side economics and financial deregulation. The NFL was growing in power and wealth thanks to cable TV. Cheap air travel had made America a smaller place. People were moving south and west in large numbers to warmer climes, opening up new markets and new opportunities for sports team owners and TV networks. In 1979 the notorious Oakland Raiders owner Al Davis (who tried his hand as first-team coach too) decided that his publicly owned home stadium – the Oakland Coliseum in the San Francisco Bay Area – needed an upgrade: a new press box, new locker rooms, a state-of-the-art PA system and, most importantly, luxury boxes for high net worth individuals. It would cost up to $10 million, which Davis wanted the public purse to fund, or he'd move the team to LA. The Coliseum Commission – run by the state of California plus the city and county of Los Angeles – understandably refused. So did the NFL, who voted 22–0 against the move. But Davis launched an anti-trust lawsuit against the NFL and won. The Oakland Raiders became the LA Raiders, a traumatic split that Oakland fans still remember to this day. 'Sure, I expected the Oakland fans to get angry at me,' Davis said after the successful verdict. 'But I don't remember any of them parading on the Oakland Coliseum, saying, "Give him what he wants [in terms of funding]." In their mind, it's their team. In my mind, it's not.'

That, and the subsequent 1984 move by the Baltimore Colts to Indianapolis – done in the dead of night as the state scrambled, but failed, to effectively nationalise the team to prevent the move – can be seen as the original sin: the moment when billionaire owners began leveraging a franchise's popularity for large state subsidies to stay in town. According to Neil deMause, co-author of *Field of Schemes: How the Great Stadium Swindle Turns Public Money into Private Profit*, this is little more than blackmail. Today, he estimates that taxpayers are ponying up more than $2 billion a year to sports teams, most of it going to the richest 1 per cent of the 1 per cent. 'They say: "Sports subsidies are good for economic development, the old place is obsolete, you'll lose your team if you don't build one,"' says deMause. Almost always, he adds, that is at best unproven, at worst untrue. 'Who can put a number on how many people can come downtown to see a game? Economists have tried to look at it and put a value on it, and it is very small. Zero by some estimates, maybe ten million dollars [by others]. But certainly not the hundreds of millions owners say.'

Stan Kroenke was just one of a club of owners who took full advantage, arguing that their teams brought huge economic benefits and that it was only right the state enticed them to stay, much as they would with any large corporation thinking of relocating or leaving the city. There were the intangible benefits too: the prestige of having a team from your city in the NFL. And who can put a dollar amount on that? The original deal offered by St Louis in 1995 and negotiated by the LA Rams was, for deMause, one of the 'worst examples of stadium deals in the history of stadium deals'. It saw the city of St Louis pick up the tab for the entire TWA Dome, a 70,000-seater multipurpose stadium costing $301 million to build; but the total costs would actually set back St Louis $1.07 billion. According to deMause, the rent paid by the team was set at just $250,000 a year, the Rams got 100 per cent of luxury box and concession revenue, 75 per cent of naming right and sponsorship deals, plus a $46 million 'relocation fee'. A 'state of the art' clause was also inserted into the contract, stating that the city had to ensure that the stadium remained one of the 25 best stadiums in the league – or the team could break the lease and leave without censure or fine. In 2008 it became clear that, given the number of top of the range publicly subsidised stadiums being built, to ensure that clause wasn't invoked St Louis would have to build another stadium rather than renovate its old one, merely to keep up.

The stadium had been a boon for the franchise owners, especially Kroenke who took full ownership of the Rams in 2010. With highly profitable luxury boxes, revenues rose by $10 million in the first year. 'The lovely thing about the advocates of small government is that they almost always mean smaller government for everyone apart from them,' says deMause. 'You see this time after time. People who are making lots of money on public spending in one way are saying that we have to cut down public spending in another. Scott Walker, governor of Wisconsin, is a perfect example of that. He's been cutting public spending on everything from employees to public education, but when it came to buying an arena for the Milwaukee Bucks [basketball team], well, oh, this is different. It is an investment.' Walker, a failed 2016 Republican presidential candidate, signed a deal handing $250 million to the Bucks to stay in Milwaukee.

Still, one saving grace for Rams fans was that things could have been even worse. When it was clear that the majority owner of the St Louis Rams – the family of the late Georgia Frontiere who had inherited the club after her death in 2008 – wanted to sell a year after taking control, a consortium headed by the owner of the St Louis Blues ice hockey team, Dave Checketts, announced that it wanted to buy a 60 per cent stake in the Rams. There was one problem. One of the minority investors was Rush Limbaugh, the ultra-conservative radio shock jock who had made a slew of controversial and highly offensive comments, not just about the black community but also black NFL players as well as US president Barack Obama. In 2007 he said watching an NFL game was like watching '. . . a game between the Bloods and the Crips without any weapons. There, I said it.' He later resigned from his ESPN gig covering the NFL after suggesting that a black quarterback was only getting good coverage because of the colour of his skin. In 2009, 78 per cent of NFL players were black.

In the build-up to the 2008 presidential election, Limbaugh had trained his aim on Barack Obama. 'Barack Obama is not real,' he said on his show. 'He's just there to assuage white guilt. In other words the only reason Obama is anywhere is because whites are willing to support him because they feel so guilty about slavery.' Using that reasoning, plus a phrase he had seen in an *LA Times* piece, he repeated the phrase 'magic negro' 27 times and ended one section of his show by singing 'Barack, the magic negro' to the tune of 'Puff the Magic Dragon'. Unsurprisingly, there was uproar. Several prominent players vowed never to set foot in St Louis if Limbaugh was part of the ownership structure. NFL commissioner Roger Goodell spoke out against Limbaugh, and the shock jock was dropped from the consortium. Limbaugh took to the airwaves and attacked those who had criticised his involvement. It was, he said, 'Obama's America on full display.' He railed against what he called the racist left-wing media and 'race hustlers' in the civil rights movement, who he believed were ultimately responsible for him being dropped. But it didn't change anyone's mind. He was out, for breaking the one law that the NFL holds dear. 'Rush's existence among this exclusive fraternity of billionaires would violate the number one rule of ownership,' wrote Dave Zirin, who described the Rams–Limbaugh saga in his book *Bad Sports: How Owners are Ruining the Games We Love*. 'He was simply too toxic for their billion-dollar brand.'

Even without Rush Limbaugh, the bid failed. Kroenke's closest rival was Shahid Khan, a Pakistani American billionaire based in Illinois who had made an attractive offer for the Rams. But under the terms of the deal he made when investing in the Rams back in 1995, Kroenke was allowed to match any offer, which he did, buying the rest of the shares for $750 million. Khan got his NFL franchise in the end, buying Florida's Jacksonville Jaguars. He also dipped his toe into English soccer, buying English Premier League team Fulham FC, although they were relegated to the second tier shortly afterwards.

A decade after the Rams moved to St Louis, revenues stood at $179 million a year. In 1995, that figure had been $76 million. The franchise's value had risen from $193 million to $757 million. But it still wasn't enough. 'Fifteen years down the road, they [the St Louis Rams] say, "Oh, we don't have the newest stadium in the league any more, you either have to upgrade it for hundreds of millions of dollars or we are going to break the lease,"' explains deMause. After a five-year will-they-won't-they saga, Kroenke finally put the St Louis Rams out of their misery. 'So they upped and left. St Louis are still paying off the old stadium and won't have a team. But you could argue that was cheaper than paying to keep them.'

Ironically, the NFL announced in January 2016 that the Rams would move to the Los Angeles Memorial Coliseum – where the LA Rams had played before leaving in 1979 – for three years before moving into a specially made and privately owned stadium in Inglewood, south of Los Angeles. It is set to be the most expensively built sports stadium in history. But back in St Louis the city, and the fans, had lost a team they had invested their heart, soul and cash in. This kind of leverage – inter-city or even inter-country rivalry to host a team – is anathema to most European soccer clubs. In England, the only comparable example is that of Wimbledon FC, a team from southwest London that operated on a shoestring budget yet, for a decade, were one of European soccer's greatest underdogs. With the shaven-headed bulldog Vinnie Jones in midfield, the Dons beat Liverpool – then arguably the best side in the world – in the 1988 FA Cup final. But by the early nineties they were homeless, living at Crystal Palace's Selhurst Park, and badly mismanaged. Eventually, the English Football Association agreed that the club could move to Milton Keynes, a post-Second World War new town 80 miles north of Wimbledon. They were renamed MK Dons and re-entered the league, although they were forever considered with distaste. Meanwhile, a consortium – disgusted that their team could effectively be taken away from them and their club's ancestral home – founded AFC Wimbledon, beginning life again at the very bottom of the football pyramid. Their first squad was chosen after an open trial on Clapham Common. After successive promotions, AFC Wimbledon – controlled by a supporter's trust – made it to the league in 2011. In 2016 they were promoted to League One, English football's third tier, while MK Dons were relegated from the Championship, meaning the two teams were now in the same division for the first time.

Such movement is impossible in American sport today. 'You have promotion and relegation in European soccer but in the NFL and all the sports leagues you have a situation where the team owners have the monopolies,' says deMause.

Things might not stay that way forever in Europe. Recent moves to protect the position of so-called 'legacy' clubs in European soccer, and the often-raised spectre of a European super league, are proof that the American model could start to become a reality. In 20 years' time, why couldn't Arsenal move to another city, or even another country to play its games? 'Kroenke would love to be able to take advantage of European cities and threaten to move somewhere else,' believes deMause. 'The huge advantage in England is that you do not have the tradition of cities bidding against each other. If you go up to a mayor in the US and say, "We want to talk about you giving us a load of money to move our team here," they will say, "Sure, that is our business. Our job as mayors is to lure business here and win elections."'

3.

While Stan Kroenke was hustling for the LA Rams to switch to St Louis, another wealthy American family were negotiating an NFL deal that would, eventually, see them become the first to invest in English soccer. At the time, the Glazer family's $192 million purchase of the Tampa Bay Buccaneers in 1995 seemed like throwing money down the drain. The Bucs founder and owner, Hugh Culverhouse, had recently died, and the Glazers offered a then record price for what was seen as a fraying franchise. 'It was a team with a string of losing seasons and a real doubt in people's minds, including my own, where the club would end up,' former general manager Rich McKay told the *Tampa Bay Tribune*. 'Some people were saying Tampa was a college town, not big enough or strong enough to support an NFL franchise.'

The family patriarch was Malcolm Glazer, a sharp-minded businessman who built a fortune with myriad businesses, from healthcare to broadcasting to oil, buying what was left of one exploration business set up by George H. W. Bush, the 41st president of the United States of America. The bedrock of Glazer's fortune was real estate – primarily shopping malls – but what he always wanted to get his hands on was a sports franchise: he had tried, and failed, on three separate occasions to buy an NFL team despite not knowing a thing about the game. He struck gold on his fourth attempt with the Bucs. Glazer hired his sons – Joel, Bryan and Edward – onto the board and straightaway made a case for how the Bucs would be a success. The franchise, the Glazers explained, needed a new stadium to make the team financially viable. Glazer would pay half, but the city would have to cough up for the rest. Otherwise, they'd have to move the Bucs somewhere else.

A variety of methods was suggested for how to raise the money. Seat licences, bond issues and taxes on cigarettes and alcohol were all considered. When nothing worked, a city politico came up with an ingenious solution to find the hundreds of millions of dollars needed to build the stadium. The Community Investment Tax would be a 30-year, half-cent sales tax that would be used to pay for public infrastructure projects as well as education and law enforcement. It was projected to raise $2.7 billion over three decades, with the construction costs of the new stadium piggybacking on whatever was raised. Six per cent would go towards building the Bucs' stadium.

Local politicians and activists were outraged, arguing that – as a sales tax – the burden disproportionately fell on the poor. Worse, the money would then go into the pockets of a private business. It was a reverse Robin Hood situation, opponents argued. So the tax was put to a public vote in 1996. It passed: 53 per cent for, 47 against. The main opponent of the scheme was the former mayor of Tampa, Bill Poe, who sued using $750,000 of his own money, taking the case all the way to Florida's Supreme Court – the same court that famously heard Gore versus Bush over the recount of the 2000 presidential election and, effectively and controversially, handed the 43rd presidency of the United States of America to George W. Bush.

In court, the figures offered by the city for the financial rewards from building the stadium were rubbished. Local politicians vowed never to set foot in the new stadium. But the court approved the tax and in 1998 the Raymond James Stadium opened, complete with a

103-foot, 43-tonne pirate ship which has a cannon that fires every time a point is scored. 'The stadium was a terrible deal for the taxpayers,' Poe told Jeff Testerman of the *St Petersburg Times* in 2001. 'The public paid for the whole thing. It's ridiculous.'

Malcolm Glazer didn't pay a cent towards the building of the stadium. He didn't need to. His deal with the Tampa Sports Authority was especially lucrative. Under the terms of the lease, the Bucs paid a combined $4.9 million in rent and ticket surcharges, less than what it costs the authority to actually run the stadium. The Glazers would receive anything they got from naming rights and the vast majority of money made on everything else from hot dogs to parking. '[People on] low-income[s] get hit the worst, and they can't even afford to get in,' said Poe, who died in 2014. But the tax lives on, and today the Bucs are worth $1.8 billion, with revenues of $341 million. When the Bucs needed $100 million for renovations to improve luxury boxes, build a Hall of Fame and install two 9,600-square-foot video screens (the third largest in the NFL), the Tampa Sports Authority agreed to cough up $29 million more. 'And the Glazers are still trying to get money out of Florida for a new stadium,' Neil deMause points out. 'They've already got money out of Tampa. And now the state of Florida for renovations, saying they are eligible for additional subsidies.'

Ten years after finally buying into an NFL franchise, Malcolm Glazer turned his attention to English soccer. He knew as much about the game as he knew about the NFL when he purchased the Buccaneers. A third son, Avram, however, was a keen fan of the game, and the family knew how to make money out of a sports team; and this time Glazer wasn't taking over an undervalued, high-risk, down-on-their-luck franchise as he had with the Bucs. There was no better club in world football that could be wholly owned and commercially exploited than Manchester United.

The Red Devils had thrived in the new era of Premier League football after a long two decades in the wilderness. The club had, like many English teams formed at the turn of the twentieth century, become a limited company in 1907. Things changed with the death in 1980 of Louis Edwards – the Manchester butcher who had accumulated Manchester United shares by literally knocking on the doors of shareholders and offering to buy them. His son, Martin Edwards, became chairman.

Manchester United had seen a renaissance on the pitch after hiring – and almost firing – Scottish coach Alex Ferguson. In 1991 Edwards floated the club on the stock exchange, opening the club up to anyone who had the money and the skill to take it. The 1990s also saw the boom in TV rights money; in an era when United dominated matters on the pitch, they became an integral part of Rupert Murdoch's new pay-per-view Sky brand. United's success had mirrored Murdoch's. So it wasn't a huge surprise when Murdoch launched a bid in 1998 to buy the club for £623.4 million, a huge sum at the time. Silvio Berlusconi, the Italian billionaire media tycoon who would go on to become Italian prime minister, had already pioneered a similar move when a tangled web of holding companies secured control of AC Milan in 1986. The club, almost bankrupt at the time, was one of a host of entities owned by his holding company Fininvest, which included Mediaset, Italy's biggest private media company. The move had been especially lucrative for Milan and Berlusconi. Milan dominated Italian football for a decade, winning five *Scudettos*, two European Cups and the newly rebranded Champions League in its second year. Paris Saint-Germain had also enjoyed a windfall in 1991 when it was bought by TV channel Canal Plus, becoming the richest club in France.

But there was deep distrust at the move in England. Fans were outraged at the clash between the game's working-class culture and its rapid commercialisation – from rising ticket prices to all-seater stadiums to being asked to pay large amounts of money every month for TV subscriptions. Aside from a perceived conflict of interest, there was also unease in the Labour government. Newly elected Labour prime minister Tony Blair had courted Murdoch's right-wing tabloids to secure their endorsement ahead of the 1997 general election. It was duly granted and Labour won with a landslide, ending 18 years of Conservative Party rule. But Labour MPs remained deeply suspicious of the power Murdoch wielded in British life, and the bid was referred to the Monopolies and Mergers Commission. 'Under almost all scenarios considered by the MMC, the merger would increase the market power which BSkyB already has as a provider of sports premium channels,' said Stephen Byers, Labour's trade and industry secretary, when the deal was rejected. United fans rejoiced, as did Labour Party MPs. But Murdoch's newspapers were less happy. 'This is a bad ruling for British football clubs who will have to compete in Europe against clubs who are backed by successful media companies,' said Mark Booth, then BSkyB's chief executive, referring to the likes of AC Milan who enjoyed just such an advantage.

It took a very human set of circumstances for the Glazers to arrive at United in 2005: a legal battle steeped in greed, mistrust and revenge – concerning the ownership of a horse. By the mid-2000s coach Sir Alex Ferguson was virtually untouchable at Manchester United. He had won eight Premier League titles, five FA Cups, a League Cup, a UEFA Cup Winners' Cup and, most famously, the 1999 Champions League final after dramatically beating Bayern Munich with two goals in the final minutes. It was the first time an English club had won Europe's top competition for 15 years. But at the turn of the century Ferguson, a horse-racing enthusiast, was involved in an unseemly feud with the club's majority shareholder over the ownership rights of a horse. Rock of Gibraltar had won a world-record seven Group 1 races in a row. Ferguson part-owned the horse with the wife of racing magnate John Magnier, who alongside fellow racing investor J. P. McManus owned close to 29 per cent of Manchester United.

Ferguson believed that he had not received his dues over Rock of Gibraltar's success and sued the Magniers, souring his relationship with an important ally at the club. Magnier and McManus even allegedly hired private detectives to look into Ferguson's transfer dealings. Eventually Ferguson agreed to a £2.5 million settlement. Bad blood remained but the fans wholeheartedly backed Ferguson. Magnier and MacManus had to go. Two men were waiting in the wings to buy their shares. One was Malcolm Glazer. The other? Libyan dictator Colonel Muammar Gaddaffi. 'The deal was a whisker away from going to Libya,' Mehmet Dalman, the chairman of Cardiff FC, told the *Sunday Times*. Dalman helped broker the sale of MacManus and Magnier's stake. 'That's how close it got – literally you're talking about a few hours.' But Gaddaffi couldn't agree a price and Glazer could. Six years later Gaddaffi was executed in the street.

Within a month of acquiring the stake owned by Magnier and his partner J. P. McManus, Malcolm Glazer's Red Football Ltd had acquired 98 per cent of the club's shares, forcing the rest to be sold. It gave him complete control of the club and allowed him to take the company off the stock exchange and into private hands. The move was categorised as a leveraged buyout, or LBO. Essentially, the club had been bought not with the Glazers' money but with debt they had raised against the club they wanted to buy. After 75 years of being debt free, Manchester United was suddenly hundreds of millions of pounds in the red and the Glazer's Red Football Ltd holding company owned the club without having put much capital in themselves.

LBOs were particularly controversial. Although they were devised in the 1950s, and considered an obscure financial instrument, LBOs boomed in the 1980s in the deregulated financial world that made credit cheap and easily accessible. They were seen by many, including the US Treasury, as a predatory financial instrument, used by investors to turn the financial success of a company against itself, force a hostile takeover, take it private, break it up and then asset strip. In financial terms, it was a clever piece of business, where the acquired asset continues to make revenue, services the interest payments on the debt and leaves a handsome profit at the end of it. In the case of the Glazers' leveraged buyout the asset, Manchester United FC, effectively paid for its own takeover, as well as its continued upkeep.

In football terms it was seen by the fans as a disaster waiting to happen. Not only had debt been laid onto the club like never before, its revenues were not being ploughed back into the team but into servicing the interest payments of the debt used to buy the club in the first place. Sensing trouble ahead, some fans set up a group that ended up buying 17 per cent of the club's shares to try to prevent the takeover. But that failed. 'He's not turning up with a suitcase full of his own cash and he is, in effect, asking Manchester United fans to pay for his takeover, to pay for increased ticket prices and increased merchandising,' Oliver Houston, a spokesperson for Shareholders United, told the BBC at the time. Glazer, he said, 'was no Roman Abramovich'.

The Glazers set about importing the business model from the US. 'Being involved in sports, being an owner in sports . . . nothing can prepare you for that. I think we've seen that. It's something you learn as you go along,' said Joel Glazer in the family's only ever interview about the club, with the in-house channel MUTV. 'Judge us over the long haul, don't judge us on a day or the last several months . . . I can't make time move forward, but like we experienced with Tampa, there was scepticism at the beginning but time changed that.' Ticket prices rose and commercial deals were exploited to their fullest, with the club taking advantage of its global prominence to strike the kind of global endorsement deals an NFL franchise could never make. Debt continued to rise, at one point hitting £800 million, but Alex Ferguson's success on the pitch held it all together. After the takeover Ferguson's Manchester United won five more Premier League titles, alongside three League Cups, the FIFA Club World Cup and a second Champions League trophy. By the time Ferguson stepped down in 2013, and the hunt for his successor led to the unsuccessful reign of David Moyes, Manchester United's finances were in far better shape. By 2015 the club's debt was refinanced to much lower, more manageable levels.

With the rise in TV revenues seemingly unstoppable, the club could even see a debt-free future.

But the fans had agitated throughout. There were protests outside Old Trafford when the takeover was announced. A breakaway, supporter-owned, phoenix club was founded: FC United of Manchester. The club was against the commercialisation of football, and vowed never to have a shirt sponsor. It was entered into the North West Counties League Division Two, the tenth tier of English football. They have achieved four promotions since, and are now two good seasons away from reaching the Football League.

Rival takeovers have come and gone. A fan protest, where supporters at the game would wear green and gold scarves – the colours worn by Newton Heath, who changed their name to Manchester United in 1902 – attracted the attentions of former player David Beckham, who wore the scarf after United played his AC Milan in the Champions League. He later claimed he wasn't aware of the significance of the colours. But it was a potent symbol. Despite the success and the improving situation, the supporters refused to give the Glazers credit. 'Not investing a single penny might be considered an "ownership crime" by fans at most clubs but far worse than that they've actually extracted colossal sums from Manchester United,' the Manchester United Supporters' Trust said in a statement released to mark the ten-year anniversary of the Glazers' takeover, in 2015. 'When all interest and charges on their leveraged buyout is added up, plus money they've paid themselves, plus related debt still on the club, they've taken more than £1 BILLION and it's still rising. No owner in the history of football in any country, ever, has taken so much money from a club.'

Malcolm Glazer died in 2014, having been struck down by a series of strokes since 2006. His sons had largely steered the ship for the last eight years of his life; Joel and Avram Glazer remain as co-chairmen today. Malcolm Glazer's other four children are directors. *Forbes* consider the club the fifth richest sports team in the world, worth $3.32 billion, and with the ability to secure huge commercial deals like its ten-year $1.1 billion kit deal with Adidas. Although *Forbes* did concede that 'United has the highest debt load of any of the top 25 most valuable teams'. For those watching in the US, the Glazers' acquisition and increased commercialisation of Manchester United wasn't just a masterstroke, it was proof that their way, steeped in the cut-throat world of twenty-first century American capitalism, worked at what it does best: generating profit. Manchester United had been bought with very little of the Glazers' own money. They had nevertheless sustained success and improved revenues hugely. In 2016 the club announced that it had become the first English club to earn more than half a billion pounds in revenue in a single financial year, with a record profit of £68 million. They have doubled the revenue over the course of their tenure, massively expanding commercial contracts (Japanese firm Kansai Paint is Manchester United's official paint partner, for example) and taking advantage of rising broadcast revenue. According to *Forbes,* Manchester United's revenue from the 2015–16 season ($774 million) made it the most valuable sports team in the world, overtaking even the Dallas Cowboys. 'Their expertise in running very successful teams in two different sports, on two different continents, is a testament to their sports business knowledge,' Jerry Jones, the owner of the Dallas Cowboys, said of the Glazers in an interview with the *Tampa Bay Times.* 'That knowledge and experience have made the Glazer family a very valuable asset to the NFL on many levels.'

4.

Debt-laden buyouts didn't always go to plan, even when an expert in the field was conducting the deal. While supporters were revolting in Manchester, another of English football's grand dames – Liverpool

FC – had also attracted the attentions of American businessmen who had got rich through predatory takeovers and sports franchises. Liverpool had dominated English football in the era before the Premier League and the explosion in TV money, winning a record five European Cups and 18 league titles. But the club has not won a league championship since 1990. It maintains fervent support despite not reaching the heights of the 1970s and 1980s, when they were the most feared team in world football, with strong links to its working-class fan base, even as ticket prices have risen. But to challenge the dominance of Manchester United and compete with the advent of super-rich owners like Roman Abramovich – those willing to lose huge amounts of money to buy success – a billionaire would need to be found. And in 2007 Liverpool found two: Tom Hicks and George Gillett. The two had fended off a bid to buy the club by an investment vehicle owned by Sheikh Mohammed bin Rashid al Maktoum, the ruler of Dubai, one of the seven emirates that make up the United Arab Emirates. Both were viewed suspiciously, but it was the Americans' bid that won in the end.

Grand promises were made, including a vow to have a 'spade in the ground' within 60 days, to build the club's long-planned new stadium in Stanley Park, next door to their current home at Anfield. Few knew of the businessmen, but in the US there was a long trail of evidence to suggest that things might not go to plan. George Gillett was a former McKinsey-trained management consultant who once owned a small percentage of the Miami Dolphins in the 1960s, which he bought for $1 million and sold for $3 million a few years later. He used that money to buy a failing Harlem Globetrotters, transforming them back into an internationally successful brand. He got involved in the leverage buyout craze in the 1980s when trying to expand his broadcast holdings. He eventually applied for bankruptcy protection when the interest rates on his junk bonds went through the roof in 1991. Most of his TV channels ended up affiliated with the Murdoch-owned Fox News. With a few million dollars left to rebuild, he started a successful food processing business before getting back into sports ownership. Stan Kroenke beat him to the Denver Nuggets and Colorado Avalanche so he bought ice hockey franchise the Montreal Canadiens, as well as a NASCAR team.

Tom Hicks, meanwhile, had made his fortune in leveraged buyouts. Born into a Texas family that made money owning radio stations, Hicks had a flare for complex financial deals, forming his own company in the mid-1980s to specialise in leveraged buyouts. By 2004 he'd been involved in over $50 billion worth of leveraged acquisitions. He too had invested in sports franchises and bought an ice hockey team, the Dallas Stars. But he was most famous for buying the Texas Rangers baseball franchise – a deal that enriched the man he was buying from: George W. Bush.

Bush had enjoyed a wayward youth and had little to show for his time other than a string of failed businesses and a 1976 ticket for drink driving. But when his father was elected president, he started thinking of his own potential political career. He had one big problem: the lost years. 'My biggest liability in Texas is the question, "What's the boy ever done?" He could be riding on Daddy's name,' he told *Time* magazine in 1989 when asked about a future run for elected office. Karl Rove, the Republican Party strategist who would go on to mastermind Bush's two presidential victories (with the nickname 'Bush's Brain'), urged him to buy the Rangers when they came up for sale, especially if he wanted to be voted governor of Texas one day. 'It gives him . . . exposure and gives him something that will be easily recalled by people,' Rove said.

According to a report by the Pulitzer-Prize-winning Center for Public Integrity, Bush's ownership of the team was defined by rampant nepotism and the excessive patronage of men who perhaps knew that humouring the son of the current president and scion of one of Texas' most influential families might not do them any harm in the long run. Bush scraped together his $500,000 stake through bank loans. He was part of a consortium that lavishly rewarded him for his time. 'He had a well-known name, and that created interest in the franchise,' Tom

Schieffer, the Rangers' former president, told the *New York Times* in 1999. 'It gave us a little celebrity.'

The Texas Rangers were not a success on the field but they at least had a new stadium, persuading the city of Arlington to heavily subsidise one. The move went to a public vote, for a half per cent sales tax to pay for it all. The measure was passed by two to one. Worse, the Rangers were able to exercise eminent domain over the surrounding land of the new stadium and simply took land to make the franchise more profitable. (The former owners of the land sued the public body responsible for OKing the move and won a settlement of $11 million.)

With the Rangers ensconced in their new stadium, Bush won back-to-back governorships. Hicks had donated hundreds of thousands of dollars to Bush's election campaigns before then, buying the Rangers in 1998 for $250 million. George W. Bush made $14.9 million on the deal, after only investing $600,000 in total. The Center for Public Integrity estimates that taxpayers subsidised the franchise to the tune of $200 million. Hicks agreed to pay the $11 million settlement over the Rangers' eminent domain land grab. By 2007, and with the Glazers' experiment in leveraging an English soccer club attracting interest in the US, Hicks and Gillett joined forces to buy Liverpool for a bargain £219 million. Initially they claimed that there would be no debt at the club. They would not 'do a Glazer', whose name had itself become a synonym for risky debt-loading that threatened the long-term future of a club, even if Manchester United had, instead, enjoyed continued success. But the model of ownership was predicated on being able to make your interest payments. In Europe, success on the field has translated into financial success off it. In the NFL, that relationship is different, hence why the Dallas Cowboys were the most valuable franchise in the sport without winning a Super Bowl in years. It was a strange fit. For one, Liverpool had not won the league for years, and the club had always worn its working-class identity firmly on its sleeve: a port city that had grown rich during the Industrial Revolution, only to then suffer under Margaret Thatcher's de-industrialisation of the north in the 1980s, Liverpool engendered a strong collectivist ethos that supported socialism, the Labour Party and the union movement. Where in most of the rest of England solidarity had been transformed into a dog-eat-dog individualism, fraternity still meant something in Liverpool. When the *Sun* newspaper falsely accused Liverpool's fans of responsibility for the 96 deaths at Hillsborough in 1989, the city never forgot. The *Sun*, to this day, continues to be boycotted.

Soon, the new owners' promises came to nothing. The new stadium didn't materialise and, a year later, Hicks and Gillett took out a £350 million loan, in the process doing what they had promised they'd never do: put the club into debt. Little did Liverpool's fans know, but the 2008 financial crisis had taken a heavy toll on the owners. Gillett offloaded his stake in the Montreal Canadiens for $500 million while Hicks tried to offload the Texas Rangers. They tried to hang on to Liverpool for dear life, even as it looked like the club could go into administration, something unthinkable a few years before.

In Liverpool, Hicks and Gillett became hate figures. They had made moves to undermine the hugely popular coach Rafa Benítez, who'd only recently won Liverpool the 2005 Champions League. The pair seemed to have fallen out, too, with both giving interviews stating that their relationship had deteriorated and how they'd like to buy each other out. Billboards went up around the city, paid for by fan advocacy group Spirit of Shankly:

Tom & George

DEBT
LIES
COWBOYS

Not Welcome Here

Both men, and their families, claimed that they had been inundated with death threats. When Hicks's son visited the Sandon pub, considered the birthplace of Liverpool FC, he was soon heckled, abused and showered with beer. 'At worst, it was yet another failure to understand English football culture and proof of the failure of Liverpool's owners to grasp just how unpopular they have become,' wrote Tony Barrett, then of the *Liverpool Echo*, who had witnessed the incident. 'One thing is for sure – Tom Hicks Jr is unlikely to be going for another pint at the Sandon any time soon.' From across the Atlantic the bravado looked familiar. 'It happened because of the exporting of American style ownership into the field of European sports,' wrote Dave Zirin in his book *Bad Sports*. 'In US sports, the owner is the man on the throne. Looking out from the owners' box like a modern Caesar . . . US owners expect to be treated like they are life's great winners and they are allowing the fans to join the party.' Later, Hicks Jr would clash with Liverpool fans again, this time online. When Stephen Horner, a member of Spirit of Shankly, wrote to Hicks Jr complaining about the transfer funds made available for the coach, he got a terse reply. 'Blow me, fuck face. Go to hell. I'm sick of you.' Hicks Senior removed his son from the Liverpool board immediately.

In the end, the club had to be taken away from them. They owed so much money that they didn't have the skin in the game that they thought they had and, as a result, zero bargaining position. A potential sale went to the High Court in London, and the club was sold to the holding company of another American baseball franchise owner. Hicks and Gillett could not stop it. They were furious but the club was bought by the Fenway Sports Group [FSG], controlled by J. W. Henry. Henry was the breakout star of US sports franchise owners, and a rarity among this small, unpopular club. He wasn't universally hated. He had come to the Boston Red Sox promising to preserve the iconic Fenway Park rather than level it and move, as had been suggested in the past. He took over in 2002 and vowed to break the Curse of Bambino, the

86-year-old superstition that had hung over the Red Sox since their last World Series win, and which the Red Sox finally overcame in 2004. But he'd also become something of a celebrity. *Moneyball* is the famous book written by Michael Lewis about the general manager of the Oakland A's, Billy Beane, and a pioneering baseball statistician called Bill James. Stats gave the A's an incredible advantage, salvaging gold from a squad of players largely discarded and unwanted from other teams. As in soccer, Lewis wrote that the amount spent on wages in baseball directly correlated with success. Yet the A's spent a fraction of the sums of their rivals, and over-performed season after season. Henry was a fan of James and hired him. He was a numbers man and made his billions in commodity trading. After all, he too made a living spotting where the market had undervalued something. He believed baseball could learn some of those lessons. Perhaps soccer could too.

Brad Pitt plays Beane in the film, and Arliss Howard plays Henry. When you take the stadium tour at Fenway Park, one of the official highlights is going to sit in the press-box seat where Brad Pitt sat. Fenway Park is one of the last great ballparks. Henry saved it, and had a plan to do the same with Anfield. After Hicks and Gillett, the plan was the best the fans could hope for. 'John Henry has been as beneficial an owner as you can think of,' says Neil deMause. 'He didn't ask [for a] subsidy to tear down Fenway Park, he put a lot of money into the team and made a lot of money on the team, too.' Henry had still been involved in his fair share of controversy, though. 'He went into this owning the Florida Marlins and manipulated this three-way purchase,' says deMause. 'He got the Red Sox. He's got blood on his hands as much as anyone. But for now, he's seen as a more benign owner.'

Things almost came unstuck when FSG tried raising ticket prices. Henry's group had forwarded Liverpool £120 million to renovate and extend the Main Stand. When the club released the prospective ticket prices for the 2016–17 season, some would be as high as £77. There was uproar. Season ticket holders arranged a protest, where the fans would walk out of the stadium on 77 minutes when Liverpool played Sunderland in a home league game in February 2016. Liverpool were leading 2–0 when the walk-out happened. They ended up drawing 2–2, conceding twice after the stadium emptied. 'I'm blunt with my answer to this: if the walk-out cost us two points today but it comes at the benefit of future generations of fans who don't get ripped off then so be it,' wrote Chris Williams for *This Is Anfield*.

At Fenway Park they have a different view. During the tour, you'll be taken to the Green Monster, a high green wall that towers over left field, and given a hagiographic run-through of the Fenway Sports Group's achievements. 'We introduced dynamic ticketing,' the guide tells a group of twenty tourists, as if it were a gift to humanity, explaining a process whereby the purchase of a ballpark ticket seems suspiciously to resemble buying an aeroplane ticket. 'Now, tickets are available to everyone! Dynamic ticketing! You can have any seat you want.' If you can afford it, of course. At Anfield, FSG and Henry backed down. Tickets were capped at £59, matches would no longer be categorised, so all games were priced the same. Season ticket prices were also frozen.

Other American investors have had a mixed experience in England. Ellis Short made his fortune in bank takeovers before investing it in Sunderland. He had no sports background, but has ploughed close to £200 million into the Wearside club over a six-year period, during which time Sunderland have been involved in a relegation battle every season. One US businessman who missed out on the newly negotiated TV windfall of 2016 was Randy Lerner. The former Cleveland Browns owner had a disastrous spell in charge of Aston Villa after buying it in 2006. The club had a long and occasionally successful history. The golden years were in the early 1980s, when Villa came from nowhere to win the European Cup, an achievement almost unthinkable today. Lerner had made his money in the financial sector but had been bequeathed the Cleveland Browns when his father died in 2002. The Browns had been one of the oldest teams in the NFL but were moved to Baltimore and became the Ravens. The Browns were, in fact, an expansion franchise which Lerner had to sit on for three years before it came into existence. When they came back to life, they were a shadow of their former team. Lerner sold the Browns in 2012 for a reported $1 billion. By then Lerner had already been in charge of Villa for six years, after buying a majority stake in the club for £62.6 million.

He had supported the team ever since studying in the UK for a year during his twenties. Like any fan would, he went on a spending spree that nonetheless resulted in very little return on the pitch. The club ended up making a loss for nine financial years in a row, costing Lerner an incredible quarter of a billion pounds. Finally, after struggling every season, Villa were relegated in 2016, just in time to miss out on English football's next TV rights bonanza. Relegation has cost them £61 million from lost TV income alone. 'Much of the blame for Villa's woes has been laid at the feet of owner Randy Lerner,' wrote football finance blog The Swiss Ramble. 'Fundamentally, the American appears to be a good man, pumping vast sums of money into the club, but he seemingly has little idea how to run a football club . . . Lerner's reputation has not been helped by his lack of visibility at the club. He has effectively acted like an absentee landlord, letting his house fall into disrepair. Worse, he has chosen appallingly when hiring people to run the club for him.' In the end, Lerner sold Villa to a Chinese businessman, Tony Xia, for £60 million, a little less than what he had originally paid for it. But taking into account what had been spent, Forbes estimated that Lerner had lost as much as $400 million overall. 'It really is some kind of a special "achievement" for Villa to lose so much money in today's Premier League,' concluded The Swiss Ramble.

The rollercoaster experiences of American owners in European football haven't scared new investors from arriving. At the end of the 2015–16 season, Swansea City were in negotiations with Stephen

Kaplan and Jason Levien – the former involved with the NBA's Memphis Grizzlies, the latter a general manager at MLS club DC United – to buy a 68 per cent stake in the Premier League club from Wales for £100 million. Others have seen opportunity in smaller stakes, with private equity groups lining up purchases of significant shares of clubs. A 25 per cent stake in Bournemouth was sold to PEAK6 Investments, a Chicago-based private equity firm whose founder Matt Hulsizer had an interest in the NHL's Minnesota Wild. Crystal Palace sold a 36 per cent stake in the club to Apollo Global Management, co-founded by Josh Harris, who also controls the New Jersey Devils and Philadelphia 76ers. The deal effectively gave Apollo a controlling stake in the club. When the two sales were announced, it was heralded as a significant step: the sight of two hard-headed private equity funds investing not in a dream but in profit was an important milestone for football becoming a profit-making business. 'A corner has been turned,' Dan Jones, the head of sport at Deloitte, told the *Financial Times*. 'After two decades of being very successful at generating revenue, football clubs are now finally able to retain some of that revenue. It's quite hard now not to make money in the Premier League.'

5. St Louis, Missouri, United States

Jeanette Mott Oxford refuses any help as she eases out of her car and, with a stick, gingerly walks towards the only coffee shop on the block open this early on a Sunday morning in St Louis. 'I've only recently had a hip operation,' she explains as we sit down in the empty café, although her recovery hasn't slowed her down. 'I'm always up this early, but I have some time before church. I'm taking some older people who wouldn't otherwise make it.' She'll be attending alongside her wife, a hospital chaplain, whom she married in 2014.

Mott Oxford is not the kind of woman to let a recently installed hip stop her. For the past few years she has been a thorn in the side of Francis Slay, the city's Democrat mayor. She ran a non-profit advocacy group, Empower Missouri, which campaigned for greater funding of hospitals and schools, better treatment of immigrants and public-health issues. But the issue that has infuriated her most is sports stadiums, and in particular taxpayer subsidies. 'My involvement on whether we spend tax dollars on professional sports teams began not with the Rams but the St Louis Cardinals,' she said of the city's famed baseball team. 'In 2001 they asked for $431 million to build a stadium. I was outraged. There were so many things that we needed our tax dollars for.' Even at 7 o'clock on a Sunday morning, fifteen years on, it still angers her. She tells the story as if for the first time: 'The elevators weren't working in our public-health departments. I just thought this was ridiculous. We couldn't fix an elevator in the public-health building but we could build a ballpark for seventeen white millionaires, some billionaires, who owned the St Louis Cardinals.'

She has been campaigning against public subsidies for stadiums ever since, which brought a clash with the mayor and, by extension, Stan Kroenke. In 2002 Mott Oxford had successfully petitioned the city to include a provision that the public had a right to vote on whether any new stadium be built at public expense. It was seen as a victory for democracy by Mott Oxford, but the city was later aghast when it realised it needed to win a pubic vote as well as persuading Kroenke to keep the Rams in St Louis with its sweetener of a new stadium. City Hall believed that the Rams' 'state of the art' clause meant the only chance to keep the Rams in the city was to build a new riverfront development.

With the clock ticking, the city wriggled out of a public vote but a public hearing was held in November 2015 to make the cases for and against the new stadium plan. Instead of holding the meeting in a hall, the city's politicians in favour of the city deal hosted the hearing outside, in the depressed, derelict part of town where the stadium would be built, by the riverside, just to stress how badly development was needed. A large group of Rams fans turned up. 'It was 10 a.m. and a lot of Rams fans in jerseys had turned up to cheer on their team,' Mott Oxford recalls. 'They were drinking beer. It got louder and rowdier after each testimony. I actually thought it might turn into a riot.' When she stood up to give her speech, she was heckled. 'When I spoke about how it was a waste of tax dollars there was a really loud round of boos,' she adds, before making a loud 'booing' sound in the middle of the empty café to emphasise the point. 'It was quite the scene. The rubble on the ground; train tracks – a train went past – Rams fans drinking. It was the strangest hearing I've ever been at.'

Mott Oxford didn't see it as a partisan issue either. 'This is an issue that me and far-right conservative Republicans agree on,' she says. There are more pressing problems in St Louis. Infant mortality is high, Mott Oxford notes, 'Worse than in many third-world countries.' The city's transit system is desperately in need of expanding and upgrading. 'That is where it is more appropriate to spend our tax dollars,' she says. 'Rather than a private sports team socialising the risk of building the stadium, and privatising the profits.'

She was right. St Louis does have some pressing problems. The city has been down on its luck in recent years: businesses have left and population growth has stagnated, as have relative incomes. Half of the Fortune 500 companies headquartered in St Louis have left. When Kroenke made his application to the NFL for a potential switch to LA, he cited St Louis' faltering economy as a reason to leave. 'One recent study reports that St Louisans ranks 490 out of 515 US cities and 61st among the 64 largest US cities in economic growth in recent years,' his submission read. St Louisans pointed out that there were worse performing economies hosting NFL teams, and they weren't leaving town.

Judging by the city's billboards, some of the only people making a decent living were accident and injury lawyers. Hundreds crowded along the highways that could have featured on *Better Call Saul*. One in particular stood out due to the fact it appeared to be on every single corner:

Brown & Crouppen

(314) 222–2222

WINNINGEST

The face of Terry Crouppen – with grey beard and round glasses – was next to the phone number. I took a picture.

This part of Missouri had recently experienced a traumatic national incident. In 2014 in the city of Ferguson, only a few miles away, mass protests – some of them violent – were held following the shooting of an unarmed black teenager, 18-year-old Michael Brown, by a white police officer. Brown's death ignited a huge sense of resentment at the behaviour of the police and authorities that had been building both in the state and beyond. The ensuing violence was such that the National Guard were called in and a curfew imposed. Mott Oxford saw this as proof that money spent on stadiums was better spent elsewhere. Worse, the people who paid for the stadium would be the ones least likely to actually see a game. When the St Louis Cardinals successfully petitioned the city for a new stadium, the cheap seats were sacrificed for luxury boxes. 'St Louisans couldn't go. But lots of companies would buy them. "Monsanto Night at the Ballpark", that kind of thing,' she says before she leaves. 'You have our ruling class – the oligarch class, if you will – demanding public subsidies to build a stadium that the public can then not afford to attend! There is something just wrong about that.'

**

A few miles away from the café, St Louis' best-known soccer pub is opening its doors for early drinkers and the city's dwindling number of Arsenal fans. The Amsterdam Tavern has only recently started opening early on a Sunday to cater for the English Premier League lunchtime kick-offs, which start around 7 a.m. Central Time. St Louis has always been a soccer town, from back in the days when America's first pro soccer league was formed there. But only in recent years, with the explosion of global interest in the game, have people filled the dark-wood interior of the Amsterdam for English, Spanish and Italian matches. Inside the tavern, walls are covered in soccer jerseys from around the world. A Celtic top hangs over the bar. On most nights and afternoons the place is filled with drinkers and supporters. Arsenal had kicked off their mid-afternoon/early-morning match against Bournemouth. It was a crucial game. Leicester were still, surprisingly, at the top of the table. But the fans of the traditional giants of English football, Arsenal among them, still couldn't believe the underdog story would continue. Arsenal had to win, and keep the pressure up.

That morning, two men, both called Mike, are the only Arsenal fans present. One is wearing a retro yellow Arsenal away jersey with 'SEGA' plastered across the front; the other is sporting a traditional red 'Emirates' Arsenal top. 'I detest how Stan Kroenke is affecting my life – not only Arsenal but with the Rams in so many ways,' says Sega Mike. 'I hate the lack of control we have over things in the face of this billionaire. There's loads of Tottenham fans now. Sure, there were a lot of Americans who played for Spurs. That is one reason. But the other is that if you are a St Louisan . . . well, you're not going to pick the one with Kroenke. You'll pick his mortal enemy.' Sega Mike has been an Arsenal fan for almost 20 years. 'That's as real as an American fan can get, pretty much,' he says, of a period of time that almost exclusively covers the modern era, with TV money and all-seater stadiums. But even fans like Mike, detached from any geographical connection to north London, have felt the destructive pull of the new breed of soccer club owner – a strangely familiar feeling. 'It is something a lot of Britons are not familiar with. When the Glazers took over [Manchester United],' he says, 'there was a lot of shock that private stock owners were getting enriched. And that is just America. That is

since then the Rams had declined markedly. Over the past ten years, no NFL team had ever acquired as bad a record as the St Louis Rams. 'Me and my dad, we are not going to watch the Super Bowl. We are done with football,' Dave says. 'St Louis will be the only city in America not watching the Super Bowl. The Rams were a 20-year thing. It was the worst team ever for ten years. And we still turned up! Twenty years that just ended in an instant. It's heartbreaking.'

Arsenal ran out 2–0 winners at Bournemouth. As soon as the match finished, the bar filled to bursting. There was talk that the soon-to-be abandoned stadium in the centre of the city might now be put to good use. There had been talk of an MLS expansion team in St Louis, who might be able to take up the lease. But, of course, whether a team could compete in the league wasn't dependent on merit, on rising up through the leagues and earning your place. You had to prove your wealth and your worth, and join the same kind of financial club of rich owners that had, in the end, destroyed the St Louis Rams. 'We deserve an MLS soccer team,' Sega Mike says. 'Just don't let Kroenke anywhere near it.'

6.

It was hard to find anyone with a good word to say about Stan Kroenke – Rams fans, Arsenal fans, businessmen, barmen, mayors, activists, journalists alike. Even the Uber driver who picked me up from the Amsterdam at 11 a.m. and who stunk of weed was dismissive. Kroenke was referred to as 'Silent Stanley' in the US media for his low profile and few conversations with the press. The handful of interviews he has given painted him as an unassuming, down-to-earth guy. The title of the 2011 *Sports Illustrated* profile hinted as much: 'The Most Powerful Man in Sports . . . You Had No Idea, Did You? Stan Kroenke.' While many in the city were planning to boycott the Super Bowl, one accident and injury lawyer from St Louis had decided to make a more visible protest, paying for and starring in his own advert to be shown at half time. Super Bowl is famous for its adverts, which can cost as much as $5 million a minute. I clicked on the CBS.com story. The picture at the top looked familiar. It was Terry Crouppen, the lawyer of the 'Winningest' billboard all over town. I checked the picture on my phone and called the number, but it went straight to answerphone. I left a message. He called back within five minutes. Ten minutes later he is sitting next to me in a bar. 'We were voted the "winningest" law firm in the state and we are very proud,' he says, ordering an orange juice. 'It didn't cost $5 million, but it was a lot, the most I've ever paid for an advert,' he says when he sits down. 'If I had five million dollars spare I'd probably hire a hit man.' There's a moment of silence. 'That's a joke, by the way.'

Crouppen supported the Rams from the start, when they arrived in 1995. He'd seen the Kroenke takeover in 2010 and suspected this day may come. He wasn't prepared for how it would be done. 'You come in, ruin a city's reputation and status, put hundreds of people out of work, break the heart of millions of fans who supported the team – and the team has been terrible for years, three good years – and what for?' Crouppen was genuinely bereft and angry. So much so he decided to make an advert after watching the playoffs. 'I'm sure somewhere he has a little gold dial that clicks how many billions of dollars he has, and it is all to click that dial from $8 billion to $9 billion.' Crouppen took a breath and a sip of orange juice. 'How much money does this guy need? What does he not have that he wants? These people want everything everybody has. It is a sickness. People enjoy a glass of wine; there are people who drink eight bottles of it. These are people [who] don't want to make money to be comfortable, and for their family. They just want everything for themselves. It is greed, greed to a level that is unimaginable by normal people. These are not normal people. I think these are sick people.'

What was the feeling towards the team and Kroenke when he first came to the city? I ask.

'We were thrilled. In America, football is like European soccer. When I was a kid everyone played the sport, it's our sport. Our heart and soul. We had lost a team before in similar circumstances . . . a greedy owner. Thought he could make more money someplace else. In fairness we took the team from Los Angeles. And in fairness they took the team from Cleveland. That is what the NFL does. That is what it breeds. People will compromise decent moral principles. They will steal from each other. Cities steal from each other. It is not right. It is not a good thing.'

Why does it happen?

'Because we are foolish people and pathetic in some ways. We'll do anything and it is sad. We will do anything to get these teams and make them [the owners] happy. And these people know that and they work it to such an extent that normal people would feel some shame. [Normal people] would say that is enough. I'll leave something to you people. But [these owners] they would take everything if they could.'

Because Kroenke is from Missouri, did you feel he would be more loyal?

'That is what he told us. He was from Columbia, Missouri. He went to the university there. So, of course, you know he is one of us. But he is not one of us. I think the world is in danger. Whether you are Republican or a Democrat, we have developed a system where a few greedy people have accumulated obscene amounts of wealth and they do whatever they want. Buy votes. Get things they want with no regard of what is good for everyone. Just themselves. And their greed knows no bounds.'

Why did you need an advert that criticises Kroenke for taking the Rams away?

'I was watching a playoff game leading up to the Super Bowl and I thought about it. I thought they might leave for a while, but they strung us along. And we spent a lot of money, this town, to keep them. It was clear from the get-go that Kroenke had the ability to make another billion elsewhere.'

Did you go to the games?

'Yes! We had to buy a PSL – a Personal Seat Licence. Just for the privilege to buy season tickets: $4,500 each. We bought four because we were so excited. So that's $18,000. Season tickets, $1,000 every season. So that's $22,000. Then you have to buy new season tickets. I'm embarrassed. I guess any sort of outrageous passion when held up to the light might look foolish to an outsider because you are seeing it realistically, and I am seeing it emotionally. But we did it. The jerseys we wore. One of the things that bothers me: some people believe that just because something is legal and you have the money to do something, anything you do is OK and right, and I think that is just a terrible message. You know, I am a capitalist. We have a law firm. We have a good living. We help people and we earn a good living. But there's got to be some bounds, some limits – even on capitalism. How many people can you hurt? How many people's lives do you have to diminish the quality of? Is there a point where it is too much? Even if it is technically legal?'

What do you hope to achieve with the advert?

'I hope Stan is sitting there watching it and has an epiphany that . . . can you say the word "dick"?'

You can say 'dick'.

'. . . What a bad thing he's done. The result will be the people of this community – who have gone through a bad few years, and losing the team is [the latest in] a long run of bad things happened around here – [well,] I hope it gives people a feeling like it gives me. Fighting back a little. To show we are strong and resilient and we understand what they did, [that] we don't like it and we want the world to know about it.'

A few hours later, in an empty downtown bar near St Louis' famous Gateway Arch, Crouppen appears on the TV during the half-time Super Bowl break, under the Twitter hashtag #slamstan. The centre of town was dead. A year ago, the city's bars would have been heaving with parties watching the big game. But not this year. A handful of people had arrived in the one place showing the game. Next to me, a drinker had his head on the bar, asleep. Crouppen's voice blasted out of the TV: 'I'm Terry Crouppen. You know my hometown, St Louis. We were loyal to our football team. We bought their tickets, wore their jerseys, drank their overpriced beer. We cheered them year after losing year, and in return they trashed us then left us. Stan, you're worth eight billion dollars. That's not enough? Well, here's some free advice. Just because it's legal and you're rich enough to do it – that doesn't make it right.'

Someone shouted, 'Yeah!' at the back of the bar, before the second half began and the quiet, almost funereal atmosphere returned. The Denver Broncos beat the Carolina Panthers 24–10. Peyton Manning, the Broncos' 40-year-old star quarterback, retired after the game. He wouldn't be coming to St Louis or the Rams or anywhere else.

**

In September 2016 the new-look LA Rams walked out onto the turf at Levi's Stadium, the home of the San Francisco 49ers, for the first game of the regular season. It did not go to plan. They were annihilated 27–0. 'Los Angeles,' wrote ESPN's Alden Gonzalez, 'was subjected to one of the ugliest, most uninspiring season-opening performances imaginable.'

Things got better for the Rams at their first home game in the LA Coliseum. The Red Hot Chili Peppers, dressed in full yellow and blue Rams kit (without shoulder pads and helmets) performed a pre-match show as Stan Kroenke hobnobbed with LeBron James on the touchline. CeeLo Green sang the national anthem and the Rams won their first game at their new home 9–3, against the Seattle Seahawks. It was estimated by *Forbes* that the value of the Rams doubled in the few months between moving from St Louis to Los Angeles, to $2.9 billion. Still, the LA Rams finished the season in even worse shape than their final season in St Louis. They finished with a 4–12 record after losing all but one of their final 12 games. Coach Jeff Fisher was fired and they missed the playoffs for the 13th consecutive year. Only two teams now had a worse record than the Rams. And yet there was one surprising figure to emerge from the chaos. The Rams still enjoyed a large viewership in St Louis. When the Rams played the Seahawks again a few months later, the ratings tracking company Nielsen discovered that 10.6 per cent of viewers from St Louis watched the Rams get hammered 24–3, beating the 10.2 per cent of viewers in LA. It appeared that St Louisans were tuning in, not for the team, but to enjoy the meltdown.

Meanwhile, wealthy investors in the city of St Louis were up to their old tricks again. Jeanette Mott Oxford had continued with her legal fight against the city, even after the Rams had left. For her it was a matter of principle that taxpayers should have a vote to approve any public funding of stadiums. The Missouri State Supreme Court agreed to look at whether taxpayers should indeed be given a vote before any stadium is built with state subsidies. It was, for Mott Oxford and her lawyers, important for another reason. A consortium of local businessmen – including executives from the Blues, the Cardinals and the NFL, and others involved in the failed $1 billion riverside project – had formed MLS2STL, which later morphed into SC STL, a body that hoped to finally bring an MLS franchise to the city. The city proposed an $80 million subsidy but the new governor-elect for Missouri had poured cold water on the project.

'This project is nothing more than welfare for millionaires,' said Eric Greitens – a former Navy SEAL and registered Democrat voter who nevertheless was elected on a Republican ticket – at a press conference shortly after winning election. 'Right now, because of reckless spending by career politicians, we can't even afford the core functions of government, let alone spend millions on soccer stadiums.'

While the consortium would have to think again about how to fund an MLS expansion team in St Louis, Mott Oxford was right.

The issue of the state subsidising stadiums for private businessmen wasn't a partisan political issue. It was something that people both on the left and the right of the political spectrum were in agreement on. Still, a vote was finally planned. The issue would be put to St Louisans.

The day after watching the Denver Broncos beat the Carolina Panthers in the one American city that had wanted nothing to do with American football, the Lambert St. Louis International Airport is quiet. I pass a shop with a table of St Louis Rams merchandise. 'Thanks for the Memories,' reads a blue sign propped up next to a pile of hoodies, t-shirts, baseball caps and beer coolers. '50 per cent off Apparel! 75 per cent off Souvenirs!' I buy a jumper, figuring that one day it might be a curiosity, something unashamedly retro; like an LA Rangers hat, or a Chicago Cardinals t-shirt – a piece of history from a time when the city once had the Greatest Show on Turf.

How many of these have you sold? I ask the cashier.

The teenage boy behind the counter laughs. 'Yours is the first I've sold,' he says, handing me the bag. 'I couldn't sell them if they were free.'

7. *Sarasota, Florida, United States*

It is often said that learning a language is harder the older you get, but at the grand old age of 34 David Villa had surprised even himself. 'Last year I didn't speak nothing, and right now I take a lot of classes,' he says, in surprisingly good English. Villa didn't have much cause to learn English before, but now, sitting in a quiet backroom of the Ritz–Carlton in Sarasota, an upmarket city on Florida's west coast, south of Tampa, it had become something of an imperative. He is now captain of his new team, New York City FC, one of the newest franchises in Major League Soccer. Communicating via the medium of goals, as he had largely done in his first season with NYCFC when he scored 18 in their debut season, wouldn't cut it any more.

Villa has won virtually everything in the game: two league titles with Barcelona as well as the Champions League, where he scored in the final against Manchester United, plus another La Liga title with Atlético Madrid. He was part of the all-conquering Spain team that won back-to-back World Cups and European Championships. When he retired from international football after the 2014 World Cup, he did so as Spain's all-time top scorer.

The first time I saw Villa play wasn't in America, even though it had been announced that he had signed for NYCFC. It was in Australia. Shortly after announcing the move, Villa instead travelled down under to join Melbourne City FC. Far from simply signing for NYCFC, Villa became part of something much bigger: City Football Group, a holding company that owns several teams across the world in emerging soccer markets. The group is owned by Sheikh Mansour bin Zayed al Nahyan, a member of the royal family of Abu Dhabi, the biggest and most powerful emirate in the United Arab Emirates. The UAE, an oil-rich country and key Western ally on the Persian Gulf, has virtually zero democracy, a deteriorating record on human rights, and is a country that has been lambasted by rights groups for its use of *kafala*, a form of employer–employee sponsorship that has been categorised by human rights groups as a form of modern-day slavery. The vast majority of the UAE's population are low-paid construction workers and domestic servants from Bangladesh, India, Pakistan, the Philippines and elsewhere in Asia. They live as third-class citizens, unequal in front of the law and separated from the rest of the country in labour camps, often kept in appalling conditions. Their wages, even by standards in their home countries, are derisory.

Sheikh Mansour is one of the richest men in the world, but he also holds political sway. He is a vice prime minister and also the minister for presidential affairs in the UAE government. He had come to prominence in 2008 when, at the age of 38, he purchased Manchester City, spending hundreds of millions of pounds, securing the club's first Premier League title, as well as Champions League football. But Mansour and City had larger ambitions and in 2014 City Football Group was founded as a holding group for its sports properties. As well as owning 100 per cent of Manchester City and Melbourne City FC, the group owns 20 per cent of Japanese club Yokohama F. Marinos, has interests in China and Singapore, and owns 80 per cent of NYCFC – the other 20 per cent being held by Yankee Global Enterprises, the American owners of the iconic New York Yankees baseball team, controlled by the family of George Steinbrenner, the legendary franchise owner who virtually wrote the book on extracting state subsidies by leveraging the fear of moving elsewhere. Until NYCFC can find the space to build a stadium – a huge problem in overcrowded New York City – the club continue to play their home games at Yankee Stadium.

Historically, it hasn't been unusual for players like Villa to move abroad to play in less developed leagues in exchange for one last pay day at the end of their careers. That practice had been going on for 60 years before Major League Soccer – in Colombia, England, Qatar and, most recently, China, countries who had all spent big in the past to attract big names to raise the standard and profile of local leagues as quickly as possible. MLS famously did the same with David Beckham's move to LA Galaxy. But David Villa was in an unusual position. Rather than playing for one team, he was playing, potentially, for a group of teams. The A-League and MLS seasons don't overlap, so Villa could switch between the two without the paperwork needed for an official transfer. 'I had the opportunity of signing for the City Group. It is not only about one club: Manchester United—' he stopped to quickly correct himself. 'I mean City, Melbourne, Japan, maybe more. It was very nice, it was only one month.'

Villa scored a handful of goals in Australia as he built his fitness up and was called back to New York after four games, rather than the planned ten. Back in the US, he quickly realised how popular soccer had become in the States: 'Our season tickets are 20,000 people, the club feels like it is ten years old. Three times [so far], 45,000 people have been in the stadium. This is [in] one year. In Europe, the best leagues in the world, they had one hundred years.' Villa wasn't the only foreign star to join the project. Patrick Vieira became the team's coach, after playing at City and later having a string of backroom roles at the club. Also headed to New York City was Frank Lampard, but his acquisition would prove far more controversial than Villa's. When it was announced he was to leave Chelsea, where he had become the club's all-time top scorer, it was initially thought he was heading straight for New York. Not so. Instead, he went on loan to Manchester City. City Football Group later said the NYCFC announcement had been a mistake, but one that had far-reaching consequences – not least for Lampard, who managed to alienate both Chelsea fans who'd believed him when he said he wouldn't play for another Premier League team and American soccer fans who saw it as a snub to their league and their country. 'I was asked from the top to stay in Manchester,' Lampard said when he arrived in America. But the damage had been done. NYCFC fans booed him from the outset. The whole affair had shone a light on a way of doing business: City Football Group were creating a network of clubs where players and staff might be interchangeable, and which could theoretically circumvent existing transfer rules. There had long been worries about owners taking control of multiple clubs – UEFA instigated rules now prohibiting an owner from holding more than 50.1 per cent of controlling shares in another club – but this complex, multi-continental ownership structure was unprecedented.

The investment by Mansour and others has proved that the super-rich's money doesn't flow one way. The domestic game in the US, and soccer in general, were, and still are, huge potential growth areas, and helps explain why there has been such crossover between owners of established franchise sports and MLS clubs. Robert Kraft, one of

America's richest men and the owner of the second most valuable NFL franchise, the New England Patriots, is an enthusiastic backer of the New England Revolution. Paul Allen, the co-founder of Microsoft (worth $18.6 billion), owns MLS side Seattle Sounders as well as the Seattle Seahawks. Philip Anschutz owns the LA Galaxy via his Anschutz Entertainment Group, which also has stakes in the LA Lakers and LA Kings. According to its website, AEG is the largest owner of sports teams and events in the world.

Villa and NYCFC sporting director, former US international Claudio Reyna, sitting next to us, didn't talk too much about a team, but a group. Pep Guardiola was 'a perfect coach for Manchester City and our group', Villa says. But the passion in New York was real. And Sheikh Mansour's City Football Group was in a position to clean up. Supporters' groups had been set up. One group, The Third Rail, would publish lyrics for songs on their website, to be sung from the Yankee Stadium bleachers on match day, including 'We're Blue, We're White':

> We're Blue! We're White!
> We're freaking dynamite!
> NYC!! NYC!!!
> (Repeat)

There was even a song for Villa called 'Chant for David Villa':

> Illa, Illa, Illa!
> Villa Maravilla!
> (Repeat)

For Claudio Reyna it was strange building everything from scratch. 'You actually don't know, when you first are told, "We will build a club," where to begin,' he says. 'There's everything to do: hiring staff, training facility, our logo, supporters. So just to see how far we've come is amazing.' Reyna isn't precious about the recent history. When he was growing up, there were few opportunities to play. 'When I left the US back in 1994 to go to Europe there was no league,' he says. He went on to play in Germany, Scotland and then in the English Premier League for Sunderland and Manchester City. He captained his country and played in three World Cups. 'When I was growing up, you either went to Europe and started playing or you got another job.' Now that the US interest in soccer is huge he isn't surprised that some of the world's wealthiest men are interested in investing in it. 'Soccer is on all the major news and sport channels. Kids love following it domestically and internationally. It's a sport that has the biggest upside in growth. It is incredible to see. I never imagined it. Soccer-specific stadiums! We used to play in American football stadiums. There's a lot of commitment from owners, who believed in the sport when not too many did.'

The biggest issue with Reyna's new club, though, isn't passion, or money, or attracting crowds. It is building a stadium. Everywhere they've tried – whether it was the Bronx, the banks of the Hudson River or near the famous tennis stadium in Flushing Meadow – no one has wanted the stadium in their backyard. Locals had successfully fought off the plans for a mixture of reasons, ranging from the UAE's blemished human rights record to the fact that some plans would take away existing soccer pitches. 'It has to be somewhere accessible by mass transportation, in one of the boroughs,' says Reyna, as the hunt continues. It also has to be wanted. 'We have to make sure we find a home not just for a stadium. A neighbourhood and boroughs where we find a stadium that wants us too.' The future, though, is already set. Too much money has already been invested for it to fail. 'This league could be one of the best leagues in the world in ten years,' he believes. 'We have big cities; big markets have embraced MLS. We have more teams coming in. We've only scratched the surface. I don't think there is another country in the world [where football] has evolved as quickly as the US.'

The look and sound of European soccer has been recreated in MLS – aside from the heated debate that ensues about the merits of promotion and relegation, something that franchise owners have traditionally opposed on the grounds of endangering investment, but fans want, as the trapdoor makes the sport more exciting and meritocratic. But European football is having second thoughts about that too. While NYCFC were losing to the New York Red Bulls 7–0 in the sweltering heat of a New York summer, Qatar-owned Paris Saint-Germain, American-owned Liverpool, Russian-owned Chelsea and Thai-owned Leicester City (alongside Barcelona and Real Madrid, Inter and AC Milan) were all in town for the 2016 International Champions Cup. The tournament was being organised by a company run by Charlie Stillitano, a well-known voice on American soccer radio. 'Forming a European Super League is being discussed by leading clubs across the Continent,' he said, before meeting with the representatives of said top European clubs. They'd had enough of the Champions League as it was, he remarked, and discussions of a revamped Champions League were back on the agenda – with 'legacy places' available for the biggest teams, regardless of results. The alternative was a breakaway European Super League, for which Stillitano believed his competition provided the basis. 'They're talking about it all over Europe. At least a change in format,' Stillitano announced on his radio show. 'When they came up with the Champions League, the idea wasn't to have PSV and Genk playing in the knockout stage . . . there are several different groups among Europe's top clubs that want a fairer share from the Champions League. When you see the teams we have in the ICC, you're going to want to go see us.'

There was predictable outrage at his comments in Europe, and the clubs scrambled to deny they were plotting a breakaway. I thought of Stan Kroenke, standing on the touchline of the LA Coliseum with LeBron James as he watched the Red Hot Chili Peppers playing 'Under the Bridge' wearing the LA Rams' yellow and blue kit. I thought of the drunken bros at Mardi Gras, and the anger that bubbled up every time the lawyer Terry Crouppen mentioned Kroenke's name. I thought of

NYCFC and the lyrics for chants printed out before a home game. It's true, soccer had finally found a home in America, and more pertinently, the American way of doing business had finally found a home in football. But even as American owners were sizing up European football's profitability, a new player had arrived. In the space of a few months, a new superpower emerged with deeper pockets and even bigger ambitions. China wanted some of the action too.

PART THREE, ASIA:

Dawn of the East

1. The Hague, The Netherlands

A storm had blown into the Dutch coastal city of The Hague. Night had long fallen and a vertical hail of rain stung the skin of anyone foolish enough to expose themselves to a North Sea squall at this time of year. Yet the Kyocera Stadium on the outskirts of the city is floodlit and busy as supporters of ADO Den Haag, the city's Eredivisie football club, hurry towards their seats and the relative shelter of the stadium.

Many are carrying large plastic bags bursting at the edges. Instead of seeking respite from the howling December wind, they head for a green and gold coloured bus – the colours of the city's 111-year-old club – parked by the kerbside. Inside, Jacco van Leeuwen greets each visitor by their first name, enquires about their work or family and empties the bags out onto a table in front of him. He sorts the contents into the piles of pasta, cookies, soup, sugar, marshmallows and powdered milk; the bags have grown in such numbers that they now gather up around his feet and almost completely cover the floor.

Jacco looks like a punk who's never accepted its demise. Tall, in his mid-forties, with a shaved head down to the skin and a bomber jacket on top of dark jeans and heavy boots, in a certain light he might come across as intimidating. But he also carries a boyish excitement. 'Every year ADO is doing a lot for the poor and sick people,' Jacco explains in blunt English, as he gathers more bags of provisions from passing supporters on their way to the match against Willem II, the club's last before the league's winter break.

Christmas is approaching and the club's supporters are collecting for a food bank to distribute the packets to the local poor. As head of ADO Den Haag's supporters' association, Jacco had organised the bus and the collection. After a few moments of mental arithmetic, he announces that 451 separate packages now cover the floor of the bus, his best haul yet. 'In this rich country, that so many people need to use the food bank, it's not right,' he says, aghast that he lives in a world where this kind of action is still necessary.

Many people, he adds, have volunteered to help the huge numbers of refugees arriving in Europe from Syria and elsewhere since the start of the year, making it harder to attract donations for those already in the Netherlands who are struggling too. 'Whether they were born in Turkey or Suriname or Holland, it doesn't matter,' he says hastily, so as not to appear that he is favouring one group of the needy over another. 'There are people that need help here too and you want to do something. Football is a way of life. Not just a match.'

The Hague is a city with an international, urbane reputation. It is the Netherlands' seat of government and home to the International Criminal Court, where the most egregious violators of the rules of war are tried. Outside of its pretty city centre full of multinational bureaucrats, The Hague is a different city. To the northwest, towards the sea, you'll find the *Hagenaren*, the city's well-to-do middle-class residents. But to the southeast, below the Laan van Meerdervoort, the avenue that splits the city, you'll find the *Hagenezen*, the city's vast working-class community from which ADO's support is mostly drawn. The division, it is said, is down to the earth. Below the Laan the ground is made of clay and was cheaper to build on. To the north, the ground is made of sand, making it more attractive for expensive houses. 'In Den Haag the character of the people is that when you don't like [something], you say it directly. You don't hide. So we have a rough reputation,' Jacco happily explains. Nowhere is that identity and directness more proudly worn than at ADO, an acronym in Dutch of *Alles Door Oefening*, which translates as 'Everything Through Practice'.

The club gained a fearsome reputation in world football for its tough fans, possibly only eclipsed by Millwall FC when it comes to an international notoriety for skulduggery. 'That was before my time,' Jacco says. 'The club made it to the *New York Times* though!' he adds with pride. And indeed it had. In 1982, back when they were known as FC Den Haag, the *New York Times* reported that the club's famous Zuiderpark stadium had burned down. Except, this appeared to be no accident. The supporters had allegedly burned their own stadium to the ground in an act of self-harm that took hooliganism to a whole new nadir. 'According to team and police spokesmen, the fire was set after a 4–0 loss to Haarlem,' read the *New York Times* report. 'Earlier Saturday evening, most of the windows of the stadium's executive wing were smashed. Damage was estimated at $500,000. Club officials and sponsors will meet Monday night to decide whether the club should continue in professional soccer.'

But continue in professional soccer they did, playing in a shabby and patched-up Zuiderpark that remained famous for its small size and horrifically intimidating atmosphere. 'I wasn't there that night – I was too young – but the atmosphere in the old place . . .' Jacco trails off. 'But now we are here.' He points outside to the Kyocera Stadium, a gleaming silver 15,000 all-seater venue whose naming rights were sold to a multinational with interests in everything from telecommunications to ceramics. When the new stadium was opened in 2007, the city's then mayor announced that it was the safest in the world. The violence and hooliganism that had made the city's fans the planet's most feared would now be a thing of the past. CCTV cameras covered every inch of walkway outside and every seat inside. The Orwellian-sounding 'Happy Crowd Control' (HCC) system, which uses facial recognition to prevent *persona non grata* from entering the stadium while also identifying troublemakers inside, had also been introduced. 'And there's more!' boasts the HCC website. 'Access to the stadium is via a unique entrance system: a sluice.' The accompanying picture shows a line of miserable fans standing in a metal corridor waiting for the HCC facial recognition software to decide whether they should indeed be granted access to watch their team. 'I miss the old stadium,' Jacco says wistfully, before greeting another famous old fan. 'He was always there, in the old days,' Jacco says, pointing to the old man, now in his seventies, bald, but short and powerfully built, walking slowly past sporting a black bomber jacket with an ADO Den Haag badge on the back with the words '*OPA HOOLIGAN*' – 'Grandfather hooligan' in Dutch. It was all a long way from the dark days of the 1980s, when Den Haag reached the 1987 Dutch Cup final against Ajax but had no venue to play it in after every municipality refused to host the match. In the end they had to play the match in The Hague. Marco van Basten scored twice in extra time to hand Ajax the cup. I wondered where *Opa Hooligan* might have been then.

The violence departed and modern football arrived at ADO. But just as the supporters were begrudgingly getting used to the new rules of the game, the club received the most unexpected of phone calls. ADO had become the target of a big-money investor who wanted to transform them into one of the best in Europe. ADO had never really enjoyed much success. They had won the KNVB Cup twice, and the league a couple of times before the start of the professional era in the 1950s. But they had also spent long stretches over the past 30 years in the second tier of Dutch football. Plus there was the reputation of the supporters. Only Ajax, PSV Eindhoven and perhaps Feyenoord had any kind of international success to warrant a reputation outside of Holland. Yet a wealthy but unknown Chinese businessman had decided that it was ADO that had the untapped potential. His name was Wang Hui, a 53-year-old patent lawyer from Beijing who had moved into sports marketing. His United Vansen International Sports Co. Ltd had, among other things, helped to organise the closing ceremony for the 2008 Beijing Olympics, as well as several high-profile football matches including the Italian Super Cup, which had been moved to China in an effort to tap into the country's vast 1.4 billion-strong market.

So, in 2014, Wang Hui bought a 98 per cent stake in ADO for £6.8 million. The move puzzled many within the city. What exactly was Wang's connection to The Hague? And, with a huge array of clubs for sale across Europe, why did he want to invest in ADO? 'It was always a mid-table club,' explains Dick Advocaat when I call him. The former Dutch national team coach grew up in The Hague and started his playing career there. 'But it is a good club, with good young players coming from the city.' For Advocaat, the city, the club and its supporters all shared the same forthright attitude. 'In The Hague, black is black, and white is white,' he says.

No one at ADO had heard of Wang but they had certainly heard of the Chinese money – billions of dollars – being invested in the game by Chinese businessmen (for they were all men) buying up clubs across the Continent. Little was known about many of these buyers, but it was common knowledge that China's new premier Xi Jinping was a huge football fan with big ambitions to host a World Cup and become central to the world's sports business industry. The Chinese business elite responded to the leader's call with huge investments. There was Spanish La Liga side Atlético Madrid: at the start of 2015 the Dalian Wanda property group purchased a 20 per cent stake in the club for $52 million – a snip for the company's owner Wang Jianlin, China's richest man who, according to *Forbes*, is worth $13.2 billion. Spanish club Espanyol, Barcelona's second team, also saw investment by the Rastar Group, a toy manufacturer that specialises in model cars and video games. This time €50 million bought a 54 per cent stake in a club that was deep in financial crisis. A few months earlier French club FC Sochaux was bought by Ledus, an LED-lighting specialist based in

Hong Kong, for €7 million. Sochaux were in the second tier of French football but were still one of the country's most historic clubs, having spent a record 66 seasons in a row in France's top flight. The club is famous for being founded by car manufacturer Peugeot, who built the side for its workers. To this day the stadium is next to the Peugeot plant, where 1,000 people still work.

In the Czech Republic CEFC China Energy, a vast conglomerate whose main business lies in oil, gas and financial services, bought a 59.97 per cent stake in Slavia Prague. In Portugal too, Chinese investment has been flowing in for years, largely to the lower reaches of the league. Although that investment backfired somewhat when Ledman, another Chinese lighting manufacturer, signed a sponsorship deal with Portugal's second division that compelled the league's top ten clubs to have at least one Chinese player. There was uproar, not least because it appeared to be against UEFA and FIFA rules on third-party influence. 'We don't understand why the league is allowing a company to force players onto clubs and their managers,' Joaquim Evangelista, president of Portugal's players' union, told AFP. In the end the Chinese backed down, citing a misunderstanding. A few months later Ledman expanded its football business by purchasing the Newcastle Jets in Australia's A-League.

But a much bigger, and more significant, deal had just been made. When China's president Xi Jinping arrived in the UK for a state visit in the autumn of 2015, he headed for Manchester City where he visited the Etihad Stadium and had a selfie taken with the British prime minister, David Cameron, and Argentina striker Sergio Agüero. Xi was also present – alongside Manchester City's Emirati chairman Khaldoon al Mubarak – when former China international and Manchester City midfielder Sun Jihai, the first Chinese player to ever score in the English Premier League, was inducted into the National Football Museum's Hall of Fame alongside some of the game's greatest players.

Sun was a cult hero at City, and the step up from Asian to elite European football is a steep one that deserves some recognition. But he was considered a journeyman footballer at best, and the decision was widely ridiculed. The Hall of Fame was an elite club of only 36 names, and Sun was only the seventh foreigner to make the grade. Almost no one except Xi, Cameron and Manchester City believed he deserved a place alongside the likes of George Best, Eric Cantona or Bobby Moore. British tabloid the *Mirror* said the PM was 'kowtowing' to the Chinese.

But six weeks later, Sun's induction at least had an explanation. It was announced that Sheikh Mansour's City Football Group had sold a 13 per cent stake in the club for $400 million to China Media Capital, a state-backed media investment group that has been spending billions on football and Hollywood production houses. CMC had just bought the exclusive rights to the Chinese Super League for $1.3 billion, a huge figure that was more than twenty times the previous deal. Over the last two seasons those rights had generated just $21 million combined. As part of the deal the chairman of CMC, Chinese media mogul Li Ruigang, would sit on City Football Group's board.

While the deal was exalted by the Conservative British government as proof that the country was open to Chinese business, by Manchester City as proof of the club's global popularity and by the Chinese as a show of its financial muscle, others were less happy. 'This devalues our entire Hall of Fame. It's a corruption worthy of Sepp Blatter,' said the British Labour opposition politician Clive Efford. 'How will all those other players feel when they see Sun Jihai is up there with the rest of them? If you can purchase a place in the Hall of Fame then it is a distortion of the entire process.'

Still, Jacco thought that this influx of new money into Dutch football and ADO Den Haag was, on balance, a good thing: business was getting worse in Holland, unemployment was rising, he'd been out of work for almost a year after losing his last job in a company's IT department. China was new and fresh and growing – it represented the future, and the new money would inject new life into the club and maybe his part of the city too. More importantly, it might even help the club finally leave the shadow of Ajax. Den Haag was a one-team city, meaning that Amsterdam's top club – the club of Cruyff, Rinus Michels and Total Football – was the focus of ADO's hatred.

Wang Hui breezed into The Hague a hero and straight away went about trying to ingratiate himself with the fans. An agreement had been signed in March 2014 and Wang immediately tried to prove to the fans and the city just how passionate he was about football and ADO, despite the fact he hadn't actually paid for the club yet. Deadlines were missed in June, then July and finally in August. But investment was on its way, it was promised. Eventually the money did arrive, six months after it was due. Wang would turn up at the training ground and was pictured in a beanie hat and boots, joining in. 'I understand that Mr Wang can play decent football,' ADO's coach Henk Fraser joked after the training session. 'And [Dutch striker] Michiel Kramer has been injured slightly. So who knows?'

Despite their reputation for bluntness and treating anyone from money with a dose of contempt, ADO's fans had been won over quickly. They arranged for a huge banner to be displayed at the Kyocera: a large Chinese dragon with 'Welcome Wang' written on it. The new owner even met Mark Rutte, the prime minister of the Netherlands. Rutte had been in China heading up a trade delegation when Wang presented him with an ADO shirt. On the back was the number eight, considered lucky in Chinese culture. Underneath it was the name 'Rutten'. Someone had got the spelling wrong, although the prime minister took the mistake in good humour.

Wang would turn up for matches in an ADO top and scarf. Local TV cameras trained their lenses just on him for 90 minutes, watching as he jumped out of his seat when ADO scored, or slumped down if they conceded. 'The supporters were enthusiastic because it is not a club with a lot of money or success,' said Menno Tamming, an investigative sports journalist for Omroep West, a local TV and radio station that covers the goings-on at ADO in depth. 'You hear that a Chinese investor with a lot of money has come, and they promise the Champions League.' Tamming only met Wang once during that summer. Through a translator he was told that Wang had promised that 'ADO will be the biggest club in Holland. Bigger than Ajax. We'll win the Champions League.' Equally as promising was the huge market Wang said he had now opened up for ADO. There was a country with 1.4 billion potential fans out there, and Wang was going to unlock the door for ADO. All the club had to do, if it had the ambition and foresight, was to walk through it.

Jacco's supporters' club welcomed Wang's ambitious attitude with open arms. With all the packages for the food bank now collected, the bus was parked and the supporters filled a one-storey prefabricated hut next to the ground that served as the supporters' bar. 'About 20 or 30 supporters came to the stadium to meet him,' shouts Ruud Albrecht, the supporters' association's financial officer, trying to be heard over the deafening sound of Dutch techno being blasted out of the speakers by the pre-match DJ. Albrecht's first impression was positive. Wang gave a presentation and took questions, translated through his son Terry, outlining his ambitions for the club. 'Everyone asked each other later after he was gone: "What can we expect from this man?"' Ruud recalls. 'He was enthusiastic. But no one knew [whether] to be pleased or sad. Will the club lose our soul or is it a big step forward?' That has proved a perennial question whenever big money rubs against the roots of football clubs grown in the fertile soil of late-nineteenth- or early twentieth-century working-class culture. Success or heritage? For Den Haag fans, perhaps it wasn't a zero sum game, and perhaps Wang was genuine. Big-name players were signed that reflected the new and improved budget, including Mike Havenaar, a Japanese international striker whose father, Dido Havenaar, had played for Den Haag between 1979 and 1984 before leaving for Japanese football. There were high hopes for the 2015–16 season.

And then, all of a sudden, the money stopped. Two further payments had been missed, leaving the club with a €4.1 million shortfall. The Dutch football association, the KNVB, has strict rules on clubs' finances, far stricter than the English FA. Before the start of a season, every club must have its finances signed off if they are to receive a playing licence, and are graded in one of three categories, three being the best, one the worst. Category one clubs require the KNVB to step in and set the club's budget for them in order to allow them to play, a financially and morally ruinous position to find themselves in. Just a few months on from a summer of optimism, ADO was in danger of being placed in special financial measures and were languishing in their usual mid-table position. The future that Jacco and ADO Den Haag's supporters had been promised had turned out to be very different.

The supporters left their bar and moved through the wind and rain to their seats. 'Wang has to think very carefully, he is not doing the right thing,' says Marcel, a 50-year-old mixed martial arts instructor who was hurrying on his way to the match with his daughter just a few moments before kick-off. 'We are not a big club, we are an intense club, with intense supporters and we are serious about it.' Marcel was angry – he looked like someone who could rip a human being in two if he chose to. 'We are worried, we have the club at heart but I don't think he understands Dutch culture.'

What do you mean by that? I ask.

'Criticism,' replies Marcel. 'Responsibility for your actions. Maybe it is a culture difference.'

Criticism has been something Jacco is wary of. *Cultuurverschillen* – roughly translated 'cultural differences' – had been a word often used by the club and others to try to explain why there had been so many missed deadlines. Jacco was sceptical, but was playing the long game. 'There won't be any banners against Wang today,' Jacco says. No one wants to anger Wang and take away their one chance of being a contender. A new deadline for the following week, just before Christmas, has been set

to packed-out stadiums on tours in 2001 and 2005. By the time the Glazers had bought the club in 2005, Manchester United was well established as probably the most popular club in Asia: Manchester United restaurants, leisure complexes and museums were opened in Hong Kong, China and Malaysia; during a match in Malaysia on the 2005 tour the club signed a sponsorship deal with budget carrier AirAsia, whose owner Tony Fernandes had seen the value in having the club's crest on his plane's tail fins. The rights to produce club merchandise were sold in Thailand, Malaysia, Hong Kong and the Philippines.

English clubs were by no means coy about the true motives behind their regular trips to Asia, which would spark fierce bidding wars between broadcasters, corporations and even governments for the honour of having a club play in their country. By the summer of 2009 the pre-season pilgrimage to Asia was a well-worn path. That year Manchester United arranged a tour of China, South Korea, Malaysia, and Indonesia, whom the club were due to visit for the first time. One country they would not be visiting, however, was Vietnam, who had not secured a visit despite offering $2.47 million just to host a single game. 'Our tours to Asia are always special,' said the club's chief executive, David Gill, shortly before the club arrived in China. 'But our presence allows us to deal and have relationships with multinational companies.' Gill claimed that there was little profit in the trip, but that it gave the club greater leverage in future commercial deals. 'That presence enables us to have that extra income, which is then invested back into the club,' he added, although the consideration he mentioned last was perhaps most telling. 'Also it allows us to get closer to the fans.'

Even the club's outspoken coach appeared to be on message, despite the gruelling trips not being ideal preparation for the coming season. 'We know we will get terrific support in each of the locations and we will be going to put on a show for our millions of fans over there,' Sir Alex Ferguson told the club's official website. 'Indonesia will be a new experience for us and one I'm especially looking forward to.' One hundred thousand fans were expected at the Gelora Bung Karno Stadium in Jakarta, but the match was cancelled. A bomb attack on two luxury hotels in the capital – one of which was due to host the United delegation – had killed nine people. The tour ended in China, where United beat Hangzhou Greentown 8-2, Ryan Giggs scoring a hat-trick. A few days later the club were in Germany to play another two games, this time in honour of the car manufacturer Audi, who had been in business for a hundred years. By then the English Premier League was established as by far the most watched league in Asia, and was only challenged by the popularity of the NBA in China, and that was largely down to two unique factors: the endemic corruption in Chinese football, which had turned fans away from the local game in droves, and the emergence of Yao Ming, a huge basketball star in China and a major player in the NBA after his move to the Houston Rockets.

But that success saw the door swing both ways. Asian businessmen who had made their money in this rapidly developing economic environment also wanted to bask in the reflected glory and success of European and, in particular, English football. The first time most people in England had heard the name Thaksin Shinawatra was when the prime minister of Thailand attempted to purchase Liverpool FC in 2004 to become the first Asian owner of a European football club.

Shinawatra had risen to power in an unconventional way. Since the Second World War Thailand has had a difficult relationship with democracy, segueing between elections and *coup d'états*. The one constant since 1946 had been the country's popular head of state, King Bhumibol Adulyadej (or at least that was the case until his death in October 2016). As Thailand switched from civilian to military rule and back again, King Bhumibol was considered the one figure above the fray. Neither civilian politicians nor generals dared take him or the institution of the monarchy on. But Thaksin was a different type of prime minister – a populist with his power base in Thailand's rural north, away from Bangkok, centred in his home city of Chiang Mai.

Thaksin was born into a self-made, wealthy, ethnically Chinese family that acquired political connections. He joined the Thai Royal Police force before leaving to pursue a career in the fledging computer industry. That, in turn, morphed into a highly successful mobile phone corporation that made him a billionaire. He moved into politics, forming the Thai Rak Thai Party, and won a landslide election in 2001 by harnessing rural voters who had often been overlooked by the traditional Bangkok elite, putting the military's noses out of joint in the process. He was persistently dogged with accusations that he had acquired his wealth through corruption, nepotism and graft. Thaksin dismissed it all as lies told by disgruntled opponents.

Initially, Thaksin's policies of focusing on lifting the rural poor out of poverty and implementing a limited system of universal health care made him popular among the electorate. But then he decided that a boost was needed ahead of his potential re-election. Thaksin had seen first-hand the kind of power and adulation that English football could bring when he saw Manchester United come to Bangkok in 2001. Huge crowds followed the team wherever they went. Sir Alex Ferguson presented a grinning Thaksin with a Manchester United shirt, complete with his name and the number 52. Thaksin duly watched as United beat the Thai national team 2–1 in front of 65,000 people at Bangkok's Rajamangala Stadium on his 52nd birthday.

The English press were subsequently perplexed when it emerged that Thaksin wanted to buy a 30 per cent stake in Liverpool three years later. Who is he, they asked, and why would he want to invest in an industry that had traditionally been a financial black hole for most owners? Various reasons were offered: the club would promote Thailand internationally; the purchase would allow Liverpool's coaches to come to Thailand and improve the standard of football, and help Thailand to finally qualify for its first World Cup finals. Most improbably, one of Thaksin's advisers suggested that the purchase would inspire young people in rural areas with nothing else to do to stay fit and stay off drugs. 'Lots of our products need a brand and Liverpool is one that we can use on the world market,' Thaksin said, as the deal was being concluded. 'It's an established club with a lot of popularity in Asia.'

The Liverpool board approved the bid before the whole thing crumbled. Initially it had been assumed that Thaksin would be tapping into his own vast fortune to fund the deal. Instead it emerged that one plan involved using state funds to buy the club. One suggestion involved the setting-up of a state lottery to raise $250 million, effectively transferring wealth from some of the world's poorest people into the pockets of some of the richest. The deal collapsed.

But that wasn't the end of Thaksin. A year later he won re-election. Such had been the predominance of military coups in Thailand's recent history that it was the first and so far only time a Thai prime minister had successfully seen out a full term of office, let alone won re-election. Although his second coming did not last long. Thaksin returned to football in 2007 and purchased a majority stake in Manchester City for close to £81.6 million. There was uproar, not least over the persistent allegations of corruption and human rights abuses that had dogged his 15 years as a politician. The most damaging accusations, though, concerned the alleged summary executions of suspected dealers and traffickers in his so-called war on drugs, one of his first and most controversial policies since coming to power. Thailand had been gripped by a wave of methamphetamine addiction, something that had got so bad that the king even made a public appeal for the prime minister to do something about it – an extremely rare intervention in day-to-day politics. The response was laid bare in a 2004 Human Rights Watch report *Not Enough Graves: The War on Drugs, HIV/AIDS, and Violations of Human Rights*, which detailed how 'black lists' were drawn up of suspected dealers and traffickers and handed to local police. Thousands subsequently disappeared.

Similar tactics were allegedly used against an Islamic uprising in Thailand's Muslim-majority southern states. Human Rights Watch was up in arms when it was announced by the English Premier League that Thaksin had passed its so-called Fit and Proper Persons Test. The organisation wrote a letter to Richard Scudamore, the chief executive of the Premier League, deploring the decision. 'Our research and that of other credible organisations shows that Mr Thaksin's time in office from 2001 to 2006 was characterised by numerous extrajudicial executions, "disappearances", illegal abductions, arbitrary detentions, torture and other mistreatment of persons in detention, and attacks on media freedoms,' they wrote. 'By his government's own count [the war on drugs saw] more than 2,275 people killed.'

Scudamore didn't budge. It took Thaksin's own military to decide that, in their opinion, Thaksin was not a fit and proper person to lead Thailand. Seven months before his bid to buy Manchester City, the prime minister was toppled in a coup. He eventually fled into exile in 2008, and after initially hoping that mass protests against the military's move would pave his way home, he remained in exile, moving from country to country looking for a new home with a Montenegrin passport but with little success. Thaksin's reign at City lasted for a single, rumbustious season after he was forced to sell the club when his assets in Thailand were frozen. The club was sold in 2008 to Sheikh Mansour bin Zayed al Nahyan of Abu Dhabi. Overnight, the club was transformed into the richest in world football. Thaksin made a large profit on the sale, too.

Around the same time Thaksin was being removed from power, both in Thailand and later as chairman of Manchester City, another Asian businessman dipped his toes in football investment. While Thaksin at least had the prestige of political office, all that was known about Carson Yeung was that he came from Hong Kong and had, until relatively recently, been a top hairdresser to the stars. Yeung – the son of a vegetable seller who grew up on a public housing estate in Kowloon – had made a fortune seemingly from nowhere. Yeung had started trading penny stocks on the stock exchange while also training to be a hair stylist. He allegedly made his first millions opening a chain of salons in high-class hotels in Hong Kong, before ramping up his investments and, a decade later, emerging to buy Birmingham City. The deal initially fell through as Yeung couldn't prove he had the necessary money, before it was finally pushed through in 2009. The club was sold by its British owners – David Gold and David Sullivan, two businessmen from east London who made their fortunes in the British sex industry. 'I'm rich enough to have a company that buys a football club for £81 million. And to buy a house in London, my second home,' Yeung told the *Independent* in 2010 when asked how much he was really worth and why he would want to buy Birmingham City. 'I'm the first man from Asia, from mainland China, to get involved, and that will give me a head start [marketing a club] in Asia.'

The golden honey pot was – as ever – the vast and largely untapped Chinese market, which Yeung hoped he could ignite by emulating Yao Ming's move to Houston and enticing top Chinese talent to Birmingham. 'Obviously we're not going to just bring in a mediocre Chinese player. We will source the best Chinese player, in due course, and we're already looking for that player.'

The top Chinese players never arrived but Yeung did enjoy some success with Birmingham City – the club initially held their own in the Premier League and won the League Cup in 2011, before being relegated in the same season. Not long after that, Yeung was arrested in Hong Kong. The subsequent court case examined how he'd come to acquire such fabulous wealth. In 2014 he was found guilty by a Hong Kong court on six counts of money laundering to the tune of £65.5 million and sentenced to six years in prison. Shortly before the sentence was handed down, he resigned from all his positions at Birmingham City. He lost his final appeal in July 2016 and is now serving out his sentence in a Hong Kong prison. The club had faced transfer embargoes and the very real threat of being wound up. But, after seven years, Birmingham was finally sold to new owners, although it would be another leap in the dark with another unknown

Hong Kong investor. In October 2016 a Hong Kong based company called Trillion Trophy Asia bought the club. 'A line can formally be drawn under the old regime and we can continue to plan ahead for a brighter Blues future, off the field and on it,' the club said in a statement. And it was true; Birmingham's dreadful experience with Yeung had come to an end. Yet no one was entirely sure who Trillion Trophy Asia was, nor who the man was who would now control the club, Chinese businessman Paul Suen Cho Hung. 'Suen owns slightly over 60 per cent of the stock, making him one of the biggest single shareholders for several decades in Birmingham City's history,' said the *Birmingham Mail*'s Brian Dick. 'We don't know a lot about him, so there are still questions that need asking about this takeover process. . . . At least for the next couple of years they [TTA and Suen] will be in charge of events at St Andrews.'

Other wealthy Asian owners followed, with various degrees of success. There was Vincent Tan, the well-connected Malaysian billionaire who made his money in real estate and gambling, and who bought a 35 per cent stake in Cardiff City for £6 million in 2010. The Welsh club were steered into the Premier League for the first time in their history, but at a high price. Tan promised to pull his investment out of the club if he was prevented from changing the club's historic blue strip to red – a lucky colour in Chinese culture. There was also a demand to redesign the club's badge to make the most of a cultural symbiosis: the importance of the dragon in the national mythology of both Wales and China. The supporters were understandably outraged, but the move went ahead. The club was promptly promoted, but relegated the following season. In 2015 it was announced that, after languishing in the second tier ever since, the team's kit would revert to blue after taking advice from Tan's mother. 'My mother, Madam Low Siew Beng, a devout Buddhist, who attended Cardiff City Football Club to watch them play, spoke to me on the importance of togetherness, unity and happiness,' Tan wrote in a statement. 'Cardiff City Football Club is important to me and I wish to see it united and happy.'

Tan has, since taking over, spent more than £140 million on Cardiff City, but a gradual slide down the Championship doesn't appear to have put him off. In 2013 he bought Bosnian club FK Sarajevo. The club won the Bosnian Cup in his first season, ensuring that Tan received a significantly better reception from the home support in the Balkans than he did in South Wales. In 2015 he also bought Belgian club KV Kortrijk, as well as investing in Major League Soccer, with a stake in the new Los Angeles Football Club franchise, alongside fellow owners Will Ferrell, Mia Hamm and Magic Johnson. LA FC is due to join the league in 2018.

Also on the list of LA FC owners is fellow Malaysian businessman Ruben Gnanalingam, the CEO of port operator Westports Malaysia. He is also the co-chairman of west London club Queens Park Rangers, alongside Malaysian businessman Tony Fernandes, CEO of AirAsia, who was once a sponsor of Manchester United. Fernandes, nominally, was a West Ham fan but failed in his bid to buy the club from David Gold and David Sullivan – who in turn had sold Birmingham City and bought West Ham after the London club found itself in deep trouble when its Icelandic billionaire owners lost their shirts in the 2008 financial crisis. Fernandes turned his attentions to QPR. The club had just been promoted back to the Premier League, and Fernandes bought a 66 per cent stake from Bernie Ecclestone, the controversial Formula One mogul who had initially bought into the club alongside fellow Formula One magnet Flavio Briatore and steel baron Lakshmi Mittal, at the time Britain's richest man. Between them they had represented the richest club owners anywhere on earth. Yet despite hugely overspending, and contravening UEFA's new Financial Fair Play rules designed to rein in the largesse of spend-happy owners, success didn't follow. QPR were relegated in 2015 and, like Cardiff, have remained in English football's second tier ever since.

Possibly the most surprising purchase of all was that of Blackburn Rovers in 2010 by Venky's, a vast poultry business from India that supplied the likes of KFC and McDonald's back home and who bought the club for £23 million, as well as absorbing its £20 million debt. 'We expect to be the first Indian company to acquire a Premier League team and we are particularly delighted that the team is Blackburn Rovers, with whom we believe we have many shared values and ambitions,' said Venky's chair, Anuradha Desai. Buying the club, based in a Lancashire town with a large second- and third-generation Asian population, was part of Venky's ambitious plans to build a global brand: worldwide poultry domination piggybacking on the Premier League's success.

The club was bought from the Jack Walker Trust, named after the club's previous owner who had bankrolled an improbable Premier League title in 1995. Walker was the archetypal local boy done good. He left school at 14 and worked in his father's sheet-metal workshop either side of a stint in the British army, back when there was still conscription. But when his father died in 1951, Walker and his brother Fred set about transforming C. Walker and Sons from a backyard scrap merchants into one of Britain's biggest steel companies, Walkersteel, which he sold for £360 million in 1990. In semi-retirement he ploughed a large chunk of that fortune into Blackburn Rovers, a club that had experienced little success in his lifetime but of which Walker remained an avid lifelong fan, even if he had swapped Lancashire for Jersey's lax tax jurisdiction. He'd already spent millions on the club in dribs and drabs – a new stand here, a new Argentine midfielder there – but the spending accelerated after he took full control in 1991. Kenny Dalglish, who had taken a break from football after witnessing the horrors of the Hillsborough disaster, had been talked out of retirement to coach the team; £25 million was spent on players. The British transfer-fee record was broken when Blackburn signed Alan Shearer and again two years later when Chris Sutton was bought. For a fleeting few years, Blackburn's spending power terrified the established elite of Manchester United and Liverpool, forcing a hyperinflation in wages and transfer fees that continues today. The 1994–95 title, won on the last day of the season, was Walker's crowning achievement. He was, and to this day remains, a hero to the people of Blackburn.

In many ways Jack Walker was the missing link connecting the old world and the new. He had ploughed his money into his hometown club with little thought of profit or expanding any global brand. But he was also an accumulator of great wealth, a tax exile and a major beneficiary of the deregulation of the Thatcher era. In 1991 an article in *Management Today* named Walker as one of the UK's biggest corporate winners under Thatcherism before the early nineties' UK recession. The Walker brothers were part of a club of 'clever deal makers with an impeccable and infallible sense of timing. Many cashed in on their success by exiting just before the current recession began.'

When he died in 2000 after a long battle with cancer, there was genuine grief at the passing of 'Uncle Jack'. Ten years later, the trust seeded with his money and set up in his name sold the club to Venky's, but the move has proven to be a costly disaster. After sacking Sam Allardyce, a coach renowned as a Premier League survival specialist, Venky's hired his assistant Steve Kean. Kean had been recommended by his agent, who also advised Venky's on the purchase of the club. His tenure was a disaster. Kean's Blackburn Rovers side narrowly avoided relegation in his first season, and then finally managed it the next. Kean was fired and moved on to coach Brunei DPMM, who play in Singapore's S League, winning the championship in 2015. The club made a combined loss of £93 million over the following four years, while angering their fans with a string of decisions that you would expect from a company that has expertise in running a successful poultry business rather than a football club. By May 2016 Blackburn were shouldering debts of £104.2 million and had a livid fan base persistently calling on the chicken and livestock merchants to sell the club. The final indignation, after the firing of five coaches in five seasons, was the hiring of Owen Coyle, who once coached fierce local rivals Burnley. The anger even reached the British Houses of Parliament. 'Most Rovers fans have a serious lack of trust in the owners,' the then leader of the Liberal Democrat party, Tim Farron, told the *Lancashire Telegraph*. 'I hope that Venky's will either fully back Owen to get us back into the top flight, or else do the decent thing and sell the club to someone who will.' Coyle was sacked a few months later. In May 2017 Blackburn Rovers were relegated to English football's third tier.

English football has not been the only target for Asian investors in recent years. Peter Lim is a former stockbroker and sits at number 854 on the *Forbes* billionaires list, with an estimated fortune of $2.3 billion. One of his forays into football ownership wasn't for a club, but for a player. Or to be precise, a footballer's image rights. In 2015 Lim's company Mint Media purchased 50 per cent of Cristiano Ronaldo's image rights, with the other 50 per cent staying at Real Madrid. Lim had already dipped his toe into football club ownership, having spent €100 million purchasing 70.4 per cent of Valencia, a La Liga a club with no previous record of foreign ownership but one deep in financial trouble for years, and exasperated by plans to move from their iconic Mestalla Stadium. Lim had also purchased a 50 per cent share of Salford FC, a non-league team near Manchester. His business partners would include former Manchester United players Gary and Phil Neville, Nicky Butt, Paul Scholes and Ryan Giggs, who each held a 10 per cent share. In fact, Lim didn't stop there. He had met Gary Neville and co back in their heyday, on one of Manchester United's early tours of Asia. As with Thaksin and Tony Fernandes, he had been impressed by the economic leverage of Manchester United and the English Premier League.

But football still has a way of clouding the judgement of even the finest business minds. Lim installed Gary Neville as Valencia's coach. In December 2015 they were ninth in La Liga, five points off the Champions League places. Four months later Neville was sacked after going ten matches without a win, on the way losing 7–0 to Barcelona in the Copa Del Rey semi-final.

By the start of the second decade of the twenty-first century, Asian money and Asian entrepreneurs were in the ascendancy. But one thing was missing: the purchase of a truly elite, top-level European team – one of world football's crown jewels. That eventually came to pass in 2013, when Erick Thohir bought Inter Milan. Thohir was born in Indonesia to an already super-rich and influential family. His father, Teddy, was a titan of Indonesian business who died in 2016. Thohir junior used patronage and his family money to make large investments in Indonesia's media, betting on the almost limitless appetite for gossip and sport from Indonesia's growing middle class. Rupert Murdoch – a man who knew how to leverage sport to expand a platform – had also invested in Thohir's domestic operation, so it wasn't surprising when Thohir began accumulating sports teams. Following his first love – basketball – he became the first Asian businessman to part-own an NBA team when he became part of the $280 million consortium, alongside the likes of actor Will Smith, that bought the Philadelphia 76ers. He bought MLS club DC United too. By 2013 he had sold the 76ers and moved into Italian football, purchasing 70 per cent of Inter Milan for €350 million.

Where other Asian owners had been seduced by profit or glory, Thohir had seen an important truism in the game: that football wasn't just a money pit any longer. That it wasn't so much about the club, or the stadium or even the players and fans, but media – content; something more ephemeral and easily shared, like a TV series that never ends. 'Football is changing,' he said in an interview with the *Financial Times*. 'I want to use the US model, where sport is like the media business, with income from advertising and content, mixed with the consumer goods industry, selling jerseys and licensed products.'

Thohir was learning from the best. He installed Manchester United's former chief operating officer Michael Bolingbroke, and dared to vocalise something long suspected but strenuously denied: that players had been signed not purely on talent, but for their marketing potential in Asia. While that tag has unfairly followed the likes of Park Ji-sung, the South Korean international who was a hero back home and enjoyed a solid career at Manchester United yet always had to fight the assumption that he was in the squad to help expand the club's Asian appeal, few saw it coming from the other direction. There was hardly a murmur when Thohir later revealed that he'd signed Nemanja Vidić from Manchester United – who was at the end of his career following bad luck with a succession of serious injuries – because of his United connections and the potential to leverage that in Asia, calling the Serb defender a 'good brand for the Asian market'. This, it was made clear, would be an important component for any future transfer. 'I sit down with the management and ask, "Will this player help us compete on the field, and what about on the marketing side?"' he told the *FT*. 'It's like a credit committee in a bank.'

But Thohir at least knew a good deal when he saw it, and in 2016 he sold a majority stake of the club. Suning Holdings Group – the Chinese electronic retail group who had pumped millions into Jiangsu Suning in the Chinese Super League – bought close to a 70 per cent share of Inter Milan for €270 million. Thohir would retain 30 per cent of the club while Massimo Moratti, the long-time owner, would sell the last of his 29.5 per cent shares and have no role at the San Siro. It ended Moratti's 21-year association with Inter, where he'd spent over a billion euros on securing five back-to-back *Scudettos* between 2005 and 2010 as well as one UEFA Champions League title. 'I had a nice, cordial chat on the phone with the new chairman and his son, who is a very alert and nice lad,' Moratti told *Gazzetta dello Sport*. 'Like all fans, I expect this to relaunch the club, in their way with their decisions. But I am sure they have a relaunch in mind.' Thohir was the new chairman, although the new dawn of Chinese ownership had not led to immediate success on the pitch. Dutch coach Frank de Boer was sacked with Inter languishing in mid-table. They were later humiliatingly eliminated from the Europa League group stage too.

**

Globalisation has made almost every marketplace on earth accessible to all, regardless of geography or expertise. Some early investors in football from Asia were not necessarily looking just at the bottom line. Ego played its part but the need for love and popularity – adulation – is hard to quantify. So what else can explain why so much money from the East has been invested into the football clubs of the West? In countries like Thailand or Malaysia, where fortunes are built as much on patronage and access to power as any kind of business acumen, visibility matters. After all, what is given with one hand can be taken by another. Owning a football club means visibility, and visibility means insurance. Insurance means that a fortune could not be taken on a whim.

Almost every investment, on a business level, has been a failure in terms of how the asset was meant to function as its base level: how a team performed on the pitch, and how much profit it made, if any. Almost every Asian investor had made staggering financial losses. But as rich and powerful as these men and women are (or were) in their home countries, characters like Erick Thohir are small fry compared to the economic power of the Chinese government. Football club ownership ceased to be the preserve of privateers looking for a port in any future storm. It became a matter of global strategy, and a matter of national importance.

3.

On New Year's Eve, a few hours before the start of 2014, Premier Xi Jinping was seated behind a dark wood desk in his Beijing residence ready to deliver his annual address to the people. 'The year 2013 has been a special one for our country and people,' he began. And indeed it had, especially for Xi himself. He had just turned 60 and this was his first New Year address since officially becoming the President of the People's Republic of China. It was also something of a change of scenery. Instead of a dull address at a lectern, as had been the case for every address since the 1949 revolution that brought the Communist Party to total power in China, this was a far more intimate setting. A golden portrait of the Great Wall of China hung behind him. Bookshelves were crammed full of illuminating tomes. Pictures scattered the room.

Xi had spent most of 2013 trying to stamp his personality on his ten-year term at the helm of the world's most populous country and fastest growing major economy. He had embarked on a campaign of free-market reform alongside efforts to curb excess and corruption, especially among government officials. 'In 2014 we will take new steps on the road to reform,' he said, promising more change. 'Reform is a great cause that we all should strive for. And it calls for arduous effort. There is no harvest without ploughing.'

Xi Jinping's recent elevation to China's highest office had come as something of a surprise. He had held public office in an array of Chinese regions for over three decades but little was known about him. There were, however, several clues to be gleaned from three pictures that had been strategically placed behind him for the address. There was the picture of him as a younger man with his wife, Peng Liyuan, a famous folk singer who had a far higher profile than he did when the photo was taken, in 1987, outside a temple on Dongshan Island on their honeymoon. (Such was his anonymity that according to a *New Yorker* profile of Xi, a popular joke had been doing the rounds: 'Who is Xi Jinping? He's Peng Liyuan's husband.')

There was a second photograph of his father, Xi Zhongxun, who died in 2002, in a wheelchair pushed by his son with his family around him. Xi Zhongxun was a famous revolutionary who was a propaganda minister under Chairman Mao. He was later denounced for deviating from the ideological path during the purges of Mao's Cultural Revolution, which set a blazing, radical youth against the ruling elites over a destructive ten-year period. The *New Yorker* noted that he was sent to jail for, among other things, 'gazing at West Germany through binoculars while standing in the east'. He was partially rehabilitated and brought back into political life, but Xi Jinping's opportunities as a young man were drastically curtailed due to his father's pariah status. Today, in power, Xi Jinping is part of a class referred to as 'the princelings', the sons of the original revolutionaries, who believe they are the gatekeepers of the revolution, and the natural next generation of leaders in China – in short, a one-generation communist aristocracy.

But there was one photo particularly unusual for a Chinese politician to display. It was taken at Croke Park, Dublin, back in 2012 when Xi Jinping was still a deputy. Far from the usual poker-faced official photos of Chinese statesmen abroad, it showed Xi, front on, face fixed in concentration, volleying a Gaelic football as a cast of Irish dignitaries looked on from behind. Not only did the photo hint at youth and vigour, it also highlighted something else important in Xi Jinping's life: he was crazy about sport, and in particular football.

It had long been known that Xi Jinping was a huge football fan. He often discussed the game at the highest level when involved in bilateral talks in his previous role as deputy premier. When he visited Seoul in 2011, Sohn Hak-kyu, the leader of Korea's main opposition Democratic Party, presented Xi with a signed shirt from Park Ji-sung, the former Manchester United midfielder. Xi was also asked what his three wishes for Chinese football were. 'To qualify for another World Cup, to host a World Cup and to win a World Cup,' he replied.

The official story is that Xi Jinping inherited his love of the game from his father, who would watch both foreign and domestic games. But the new premier's fire for reform was stoked by an unlikely source: Watford FC and former England coach Graham Taylor. Xi was one of the 70,000 supporters who turned up at Beijing's Workers' Stadium to watch the final game of Watford's three-match Chinese tour in the summer of 1983. After two comprehensive victories for the Hornets, Watford won the final game, against the China national team, 5-1. 'The Hornets, who have made such a big impression – both on and off the field – in China, left their brand of attacking football indelibly stamped on the minds of the Chinese followers,' reported the *Watford Observer* at the time. 'In the magnificent Peking Workers' stadium, scene of their 3-1 triumph in the opening match last Wednesday, Watford again endeared themselves to the 70,000 enthusiastic spectators and the millions of television watchers.'

Watford, the report continued, 'were 2-0 up after only 17 minutes and despite substituting their goalkeeper, the "bewildered" Chinese went in at half time trailing 4-0 [following] a thundering left-foot shot from Kenny Jackett and other goals from [John] Barnes and [Luther] Blissett (2).' China pulled one back from the penalty spot before John Barnes scored his second. After the game, Taylor was far from complimentary about the quality of the hosts' play. 'When we beat them last week, they played impressively and well enough to have won. But they bored 70,000 people silly tonight,' he was quoted in a Chinese newspaper as saying. 'If they feel this is what they have to learn in order to be a top footballing country then I'm afraid they are sadly mistaken.'

Watford thought the tour was a resounding success. Elton John had joined the delegation, as had former FIFA president Sir Stanley Rous. Elton had spent most of the trip giving impromptu gigs in between visiting tourist spots like the mausoleum that held Chairman Mao's embalmed body. 'The morning sees our departure from Shanghai to Peking aboard an Ilyushin il-62 of China Airways,' wrote the club's then director, Muir Stratford, in a tour diary, 'with Elton spreading alarm and despondency about the plane's safety record.'

Watford's verve may well have left the club's 'brand of attacking football indelibly stamped on the minds of the Chinese followers' but it also left a different kind of lasting impression on Xi Jinping. In 1983 he had just been appointed deputy party secretary of Zhengding county, in Hebei province, about 170 miles southwest of Beijing. And he was furious at the humiliating result. 'Xi left the stadium angry and upset,' a friend of Xi's who had accompanied him to the match said in an interview with Chinese state media.

So when, in the autumn of 2012, he emerged as China's new leader, he began work to end the humiliations of the past. The result was the 'Chinese football reform and development programme' – a 50-point plan commissioned by Xi aimed at revitalising Chinese football. 'Since Comrade Xi Jinping became general secretary in the 18th Congress of the Chinese Communist Party (CCP), he has placed the development of football on the agenda in order to build China as a great sports nation,' read the opening line of the report. Many of the reforms are functional and straightforward, others borderline incendiary. On the one hand it calls for the mass building of football pitches, on the other it calls for the removal of government control from the Chinese Football Association (which, technically, is outlawed under FIFA's rules anyway). It also calls for academies to be set up across the country and for China to learn from more established nations about how to raise champions, while also urging that football is used to 'promote the spirit of patriotism and collectivism'.

'That is an incredible change,' says Rowan Simons, author of *Bamboo Goalposts*, a book on the history of football in China. Simons has lived in China for thirty years and has seen the game wax and wane, from the ashes of Mao's Cultural Revolution, which almost destroyed football (gatherings of more than ten people were banned, after all), to the false dawn after the 2002 World Cup that ended a decade later with the arrest of hundreds of officials for match-fixing and in the eventual dissolution of the Chinese league. But Simons has never seen anything like this. 'Everything in sport is controlled by government,' he adds. 'It is right at the top of the articles of China's sports laws.'

Xi ordered a committee of five working groups to examine the game and suggest radical reform. With football being given an official seal, investment in China's tightly controlled private sector followed. 'As soon as the plan came out, everyone was dissecting it and working out how they could contribute,' says Simons. What followed was an orgy of spending by China's richest men trying to ingratiate themselves with the party's elite. First, there was the re-emergence of the Chinese Soccer League as a global force, with clubs now owned by super-rich businessmen (supposedly above the need to make comparatively small sums in match-fixing) spending huge amounts of money securing the services of international players. These players were far from the stereotype of the past-their-best foreigner looking for one last payday that had typified much of the previous footballing exodus east. There was the Colombian international Jackson Martínez, signed by Asian Champions League winners Guangzhou Evergrande from Atlético Madrid for $32 million; Brazilian internationals Alex Teixeira and Ramires were bought by Jiangsu Suning for $38 and $25 million respectively, with Teixeira's fee breaking the transfer record for any player in Asia. The spending spree put Europe's powerful leagues on alert. Teixeira, in particular, could have been expected to play for any number of teams who appeared regularly in the UEFA Champions League, as many of his former Shakhtar Donetsk teammates had done. But even Roman Abramovich couldn't compete.

There was, for now, a new player in town prepared to pay over the odds.

a pretext to purge political opponents. A letter was briefly published on a government website in March 2016 calling on Xi to resign. The letter was quickly taken down, but such open dissent was previously unheard of in China. The response was brutal. Anyone who mentioned it was severely punished, not least dissidents living in the US and Germany who had commented on the significance of the unprecedented letter. Unable to punish the miscreants directly, the authorities instead targeted their family members back in China, even arresting elderly parents for their children's crimes. 'There is undeniably a reassertion of government control over the media and in all other aspects of life there is a recentralisation of control,' explained Simons of Xi's China. 'In the middle of this, football is told to be democratic.' But even in the apparent scale-back of government control where football is concerned, the state's hand is still the guiding force; the cue from which all action, private or public, financial or otherwise, is to be taken. When Wang Hui bought ADO Den Haag, it wasn't about ego. It was largely about access to the famous Dutch school of coaching. The purchase of European teams might have opened up China's huge market for the West, but, more importantly, it allowed Chinese access to European coaching, a key part of Xi's plan to rejuvenate football and take China to the World Cup finals again. 'I had a good impression when I spoke to him,' said Tom de Bruijn, a local politician who sits on the executive board of Den Haag's municipality, of his first meeting with Wang Hui. But that soon changed, especially after Wang went missing. 'You can't run a football club on a daily basis from Beijing. It is extremely difficult to communicate,' said De Bruijn, who explained that the club's supervisory board has a Chinese member who has never been seen on the premises. 'We don't know if he even exists!'

Shortly after purchasing ADO, Wang had arranged for several coaches to travel to China and help implement Xi's vision. The coaches were to be sent to a school in Beijing – not just any old school, but Xi

Jinping's former middle school. Chinese coaches would travel the other way too: Gao Hongbo, who had coached the Chinese national team and taken the country to its last major tournament, the 2011 Asian Cup, had been dispatched to The Hague. In China it was proudly reported that Gao – who was China's most experienced coach – was going to Holland to take charge of the team. He would become the first Chinese coach to take charge of a European team, offering further proof – if it were needed – of China's inexorable rise.

4.

Over the course of the 2015–16 season, Henk Fraser has approached the press in exactly the same way as ever – as if he were about to face a firing squad. It is Friday, the day before ADO Den Haag's league match against Willem II, and Fraser is going through a familiar routine in the club's press room. None of the assembled press ask questions about his players, injuries or tactics. They want to know about China, the money, Wang and, more importantly, about his job. Or, more precisely, whether his new assistant coach will be taking his job. 'I don't know, you will have to ask the club,' Fraser says, stony-faced, as he is asked another question about Gao Hongbo.

A few weeks earlier, Fraser had suddenly been informed that he had a new assistant, the former head coach of the China national team. The move came as a shock to him, the club and the journalists who followed ADO, none of whom had heard of Gao. At first the club refused to comment, leaving Fraser to deal with the barrage of inevitable questions. Gao Hongbo was unveiled by Wang in China. The club's website announced the move as a chance for 'knowledge transfer' from ADO to China, as per Premier Xi's football masterplan. Although Gao didn't get that memo and was keen to point out it was not just a one-way process. 'On the one hand I want to learn new things,' he said.

'But on the other hand, as an assistant head coach, I have to advise and see what can be done better.'

Every day for months Fraser was peppered with questions about Gao. Where is he? What does he do? Is he the head coach? Does Wang want to replace you with him? Every time he would offer a straight bat, with a club PR man by his side to deflect the most difficult questions. 'This Mr Gao will come here to collect knowledge,' the PR man announced tetchily to end the press conference. 'And with a folio full of knowledge under his arm, he will go back.'

That was in September 2015. Now it was December, and the facts on the ground had changed. The money had stopped, plunging ADO into their financial crisis. Wang had disappeared. The club had been forced to admit that they couldn't contact him. Gao Hongbo had disappeared too. 'Well, to be honest, I spoke to him occasionally. He is not part of my training staff because here in Holland it is important to arrange the paperwork. That is difficult,' Fraser said, sitting at a desk nearby after the press conference had finished. Fraser was born in Suriname and represented the Dutch national team on nine occasions. He is a young, up-and-coming coach, one of the few black coaches in charge of a top-tier European team. This 2015–16 season had been chaotic and stressful, but ADO found themselves where they had spent the best part of the past ten years: safely in mid-table. The distractions of Wang, the financial crisis and the arrival of a possible usurper had not changed much when it came to results at least. 'He is not part of my training staff, so I don't have an opinion on his coaching abilities,' Fraser says firmly. 'No, no, no. He was upstairs. He was here to get the Dutch way of working,' he adds. 'Most of the time he was upstairs in one of the units watching the way we train, talking to a lot of people.'

After months in the spotlight, and under intense pressure, Fraser was at least keeping his team of players together, and was still hopeful for ADO's future, in public at least. 'We had some hooliganism maybe

A few days later, Wang Hui was discovered alive and well, sitting in his office on the 22nd floor of a building in downtown Beijing. The Dutch media had been trying to track down Wang Hui with little luck for months to ask questions about ADO's financial problems, as well as others about Wang's own finances and backstory. With little verifiable information available, most of it had been taken on good faith. For them, his radio silence was a sign that all was not well. It would be a few months until I travelled to China, so I sent some questions to a Beijing-based journalist, Adam Wu, to see whether he might have better luck. He tracked Wang down within a few days. Far from being secretive or difficult, he invited Wu to the office of his United Vansen International Sports Company, which is on the same floor as his law firm. Inside, Wang was seated in front of a large bookshelf. A yellow and green ADO Den Haag pennant hung from one of the shelves, alongside trophies, flags and football shirts from clubs that had visited China in the past. 'I don't just do business,' Wang said. 'I love playing football too. Fans of ADO Den Haag also invited me to play football with them.'

ADO Den Haag wasn't Wang's first choice for a European club to buy. He had been in advanced talks with an Italian Serie A club before the negotiations broke down. When Wang found out that ADO was available it ticked a lot of boxes. 'The cost of the takeover was not too high and it would be a good start for us to familiarise ourselves with the European football business,' he said. 'Second, ADO Den Haag has a personal appeal to me. I was a law student back in college and in my law courses I first learned Den Haag as the place where the International Court of Justice locates. I had been admiring this city for a long time.' After meeting with Dutch legend Johan Cruyff in Barcelona, Wang was convinced that ADO was the club for him and, more importantly, would have the kind of coaches who would impress people back home. Two, he claimed, were sent to the Bayi School in Beijing. He also seemed pleased with the contribution of Gao Hongbo, who he said was now back in China. 'I think his participation in the coaching work [at

ADO] has taught him deeply about Dutch football. We haven't decided whether he will immediately go back to Holland.'

Wang seemed to understand the objections to a Chinese takeover. The Dutch league was more conservative than the English Premier League, he believed, and many people were – are – worried that the club would not be run professionally: 'That's why I said, after I buy the club, they can manage the club by themselves. All I want is to make this club better, not worse. Den Haag is the third largest city in Holland. I don't think the current performance of ADO Den Haag is compatible with the status and the significance of the city. Den Haag is also an international city. The club should be international too.' When the issue of the missed payments was raised, Wang wasn't complimentary about the club's management. 'The €12-million payment I've spent on the takeover has been made already, in January [eleven months previously],' he said, although this appeared to refer to the cost of the actual purchase of the club and not the money needed to keep ADO solvent. 'I said to them that I hope the club could do better and, to achieve that purpose, the club can show me their plan and proposal and I can invest accordingly. I want to clarify that it is not a "promise" because I don't need to promise anything to anyone in terms of investing more money into my own club.'

Wang was perplexed at the attitude of the board in the Netherlands. He had spent a large sum of money buying the club. He had cleared the debt. And he had invested in new players. To him, the requests for more money sounded like ingratitude at best, incompetence at worse. 'You shouldn't take my money for granted!' he said. 'When the club asks [for] payment from shareholders, it should think about how to make money on their own as well. You should think about how to improve your efficiency, how to save expenditure and spend the money in the right place. After we move in, we've opened the enormous Chinese market for you. You should think about how to make money there. Running a football club is just like running a company. Of course you can ask shareholders for liquidity for the short term, but you can't solely rely on this. You need to make money on your own.'

The problem, of course, was that the club had submitted a budget to the Dutch football association at the start of the season, which had three phases for investment. Missing those payments meant placing the club's finances under the control of the Dutch FA. As well as being a humiliation, it meant no transfers or investments could realistically take place. 'After I pay the takeover, the club is mine,' said Wang, who also wanted to downgrade the budget as it was clear ADO would not make the top five in the league that season. 'It is my business in terms of how much I will invest in the club. How can I promise my employee how much money I will invest in the club? It is invalid from a legal perspective.'

For the most part, even Wang put the disagreement down to cultural differences. He promised that the money would be paid but was incredulous at how Dutch clubs run their financial affairs. 'The club thinks in a very simple way. "You've said you will invest so you should invest." But they are intervening in the boss's decision-making process. You can offer suggestions. But now the circumstances are different and I need to adjust my strategy.'

**

A few weeks later, early in the New Year, ADO Den Haag's Kyocera Stadium is bathed in the harsh light of a low sun. Snow still covers the floor from the previous night's flurry as fans hustle to their seats for the early, midday kick-off. ADO v Ajax is considered one of Dutch football's highest-risk games thanks to past violence, not to mention the racist and anti-Semitic chanting. Ajax has long had a strong Jewish identity and Israel's Star of David flag is frequently flown on the terraces, even by non-Jews. But today the away section is empty: Ajax fans have been banned from travelling to ADO Den Haag matches for more than five years. Mr Wang isn't here either.

The money hasn't been paid and he certainly did not turn up for his proposed meeting with Jacco and the rest of ADO's supporters' group. The club have announced they will have to scale down their ambitions to balance the budget and prevent ADO from being labelled a category one problem by the KNVB. As has been the case for most of the past 35 years, Ajax win, 1–0. There are, however, no banners or songs against the owner. Any illusions that ADO Den Haag can still compete, with Wang's money promising a different future, are long gone.

Jacco is not happy. His team have lost against their most hated rivals, but this season it feels worse than before. This season they have let themselves believe. The money, the rich foreign owner, the new players and promises of a brighter future have not led to any improvement on the pitch. Worse, ADO's past has returned: a section of the home support could be heard making racist chants during the Ajax game. 'The monkey noises are something we haven't heard for a very long time,' Jacco says, downhearted. 'It's disgusting. You have several dark players yourself and you are screaming monkey noises, while [ADO's Dutch international winger] Ruben Schaken is standing next to you. Hey, who are you shouting to?'

At least Henk Fraser is still there. The club have given him a one-year extension as reward for guiding the team away from relegation, which would destroy the club. Although this perhaps has not gone down well in China. 'Well, Gao Hongbo, came to be Fraser's assistant. That went wrong and he didn't get a job at ADO. Henk Fraser re-signed his contract,' says local journalist Jim van der Vel, explaining why ADO's Chinese owners had disappeared. 'Mr Wang is angry at a few things.' For Van der Vel, cultural differences had played their part as well as a fundamental difference of where the two sides felt the money would come from in the future. 'Wang wants the education of players in China. That is the money maker in China,' he said. 'Here, he wants to be successful in Dutch and European leagues, with a full stadium. He makes money in China, he won't at ADO. No one has gained anything for being too loud against the Chinese owner. He is the legitimate owner of the club. Let's just hope he makes the payment. If he doesn't have the money, that is no problem. But please don't make any promises you cannot follow. Don't tell big stories.'

As the New Year turned into February, ADO Den Haag waited in vain for the promised money. In March, with still no end in sight to ADO's financial crisis, the KNVB placed the club into category one along with the other financial basket cases.

5. Xi'an, People's Republic of China

On any normal day the Shaanxi Province Stadium in the Chinese city of Xi'an hardly looks like a 50,000 capacity all-seater football arena. The stadium is found a few kilometres south of Xi'an's ancient citadel, whose walls protected what was once one of China's four imperial capital cities. The façade of the stadium is a riot of colours made up of neon signs and banners from hundreds of shops and market stalls advertising clothes and sports equipment. The drapes and notices ring the entire stadium, clambering up over each other for prominence across the grey concrete structure, obscuring its true purpose. A large line of people snake down a set of stairs, around the corner and into the distance, as young women in facepaint hand out red t-shirts. At the front, two ticket booths are open underneath a large blue banner that advertises the main event. In three days' time the China national team will play Qatar in what has become a must-win 2018 World Cup qualification match.

It has been a long time since an international football match in China has meant this much. The national team has been in the doldrums since its last, and so far only, World Cup appearance in 2002. Back then, the prospect of a football-mad China had every organisation with skin in the game – from FIFA to Manchester United – salivating at the potential of its huge market. But inept organisation and endemic corruption crippled football's rise. Qualification campaign after qualification campaign ended in failure, and interest faded as Chinese fans switched their attentions to the NBA where, in the Houston Rockets' Yao Ming, they had a genuine world-class sports star.

Basketball's dominance is clear, even at a Shaanxi stadium preparing for the big match. As workmen totter nearby on overly extended ladders trying to drape blue satin cloth over the shop signs and neon lights – a prerequisite so as not to offend Chinese football sponsors – football seems in short supply. Hundreds upon hundreds of young men and women are playing sport, but not a single football is present. Instead, rows and rows of concrete courts full of young people playing basketball stretch to the horizon.

Regardless, the China v Qatar match is due to be a sell-out, even though China's chances of qualifying for the final round of matches for the first time in 16 years are very slim. The national team is guaranteed a second-place finish behind a Qatar team who have won every single game – but to finish as one of the group stage's best second-placed teams China has to win against an unbeaten Qatar and hope that results in Australia, Iran and the Philippines go their way.

It is an unenviable set of circumstances for the national team's new coach. Gao Hongbo had been unveiled a few weeks previously after the Frenchman Alain Perrin, once of Portsmouth, was sacked following two politically embarrassing 0–0 draws with Hong Kong. Gao would be in charge for two games; two games that could save China's faltering 2018 World Cup campaign. The first had gone to plan, a 4–0 victory against the Maldives in Wuhan. 'I know the Chinese team is in a very difficult position. We don't just have to win,' Hongbo had said as he met China's media, hundreds of journalists, before training in Xi'an. 'What is pressure? I know pressure. And these players play in the Chinese Super League. They know pressure.'

This was, of course, Gao's second spell in charge of the national team. His first, between 2009 and 2011, saw China qualify for the 2011 Asian Cup in Qatar, only to be knocked out at the group stage before Gao was fired. When Gao took over in 2009, Chinese football was at its lowest ebb. The game was mired in a match-fixing scandal that involved the Chinese Football Association (three of whose vice presidents were arrested), referees, coaches and players. In one infamous case, China's most famous referee was jailed for taking over $100,000 in kickbacks. It was also revealed in court that CSL club Shanghai Shenhua had spent over $1 million alone in bribes to fix matches.

But now the situation was vastly different. Xi Jinping's intervention had sparked billions of dollars worth of investment in a short space of time. The most visible source of Chinese embarrassment was the failure of the national team. The investment had clearly come too soon to have much of an impact, yet China still had ambitions of being an elite player in the world game and no one wanted to disappoint the leader.

Gao was cautiously welcomed as the China team's last chance. His previous spell in charge had seen supporters criticise him for the team's dull style of football, and there were even unhappy fans after the 4–0 victory against the Maldives, given that China had 40 chances but only managed to convert four. But in Xi'an no one wanted to speak about Gao's recent experiences in the Netherlands with ADO Den Haag. 'The fans were not satisfied with the performance [in Wuhan], but after they went for signatures with the players and everyone was happy,' says Chen Yitong, a reporter for LeTV, who had followed the team's progress through qualification. 'Some of the staff think he [Gao] is a great man. He didn't make a success in The Hague and he came back.' There was scepticism, too, that bringing so many expensive foreigners into the game would have much of an effect on the Chinese players in the league. 'You say lots of money [has come into Chinese football] but they used the money to invite many foreign players,' says Chen. 'For Guangzhou Evergrande there are many foreign players and they can make some influence on Chinese players. But in other provinces, other teams' foreign players can't help the players. They are so-so.' Gao saw the influx of money as broadly helpful, but spent in the wrong direction. 'I do have some suggestions, if there is a lot of money coming through,' he offers. 'We need to spend more on youth study and education.'

Previously defeat and failure was to be expected, with many Chinese fans washing their hands of the domestic game and its national team. Now failure was unconscionable, and not just because of the money. The match against Qatar had attained presidential importance; it represented an opportunity like never before: for progress, for respect and, most importantly, proof of the leader's foresight.

A few hours before kick-off, hundreds of stalls line the route from the metro to the stadium, creating a sea of red flags, scarves and shirts, only broken by rising smoke from street vendors selling snacks and drinks. At least three separate branches of the security forces are here – the police, specialised riot police, and the army – to keep order. Inside the stadium 50,000 people are giving a deafening rendition of the Chinese national anthem. Earlier, Australia had beaten Jordan 5–1, meaning that at least one of the four results China needs has gone its way. The first half is loud, tense and full of errors. Qatar, who have already qualified, look off the pace and there for the taking. But the crowd has to wait for the second half for any goals. China hit the bar and see two world-class saves, all in ten seconds, before Guangzhou Evergrande's Huang Bowen fires China ahead from the edge of the box. The noise is explosive, but it isn't until the 88th minute that the result is sure, after Wu Lei scores a stunning second. In the Philippines, real drama is taking place too. In the last few minutes in Manila, North Korea have thrown away a 2–1 lead and are now losing 3–2.

When Gao Hongbo arrives to meet the press he receives a standing ovation, but still has no idea whether China have made it. 'I am still the actual manager of the Chinese team!' he says when asked whether he'll keep his job for the next round, as news filters through that Iran are beating Oman 2–0, guaranteeing China's progress. Another standing ovation follows. 'If we qualify the coaching team must stay together. But who will lead the team? We need to think about it.'

Gao Hongbo had made sure that China, and by extension Xi Jinping, had not been embarrassed by the national team's failure. 'China is developing fast and the Chinese government are paying more and more attention to football,' he says. 'If we develop like this, in two or three years we will be very strong.' Gao Hongbo left the Shaanxi Province Stadium, past rows and rows of troops waiting outside, knowing that he had done what was asked of him, but not whether it was enough to keep his job.

6. Guangzhou, People's Republic of China

If Philip K. Dick were alive today the city of Guangzhou in 2016 might have made a better setting for *Do Androids Dream of Electric Sheep?*, the source material for *Blade Runner*. The city is two and a half hours' flight south of Xi'an. If Xi'an symbolises China's imperial past, Guangzhou is its future: a sprawling megacity of 13 million people where the sun only ever seems to shine weakly through pollution and humidity. Skyscrapers dominate the city, covered in neon lettering in English, Mandarin and Cantonese; a grey smog envelopes the Tianhe Stadium. It is a few days after China's last-gasp qualification for the final round of the 2018 World Cup, and the Chinese Super League is about to return to action with one of the biggest games of the season: the Guangzhou derby between Guangzhou Evergrande and Guangzhou R&F. Nearly 40,000 people attend tonight's match, creating a constant wall of noise. A dozen choreographed flag bearers fly red standards as the game kicks off. Banners hang from every advertising hoarding: 'More Than A Team', 'We Are Not Just Dreamers' and 'Believe in Canton'.

Tens of millions of dollars of talent walk onto the pitch. Jackson Martínez is one, alongside former Tottenham midfielder Paulinho. They are coached by former World Cup winner Luiz Felipe Scolari. Before that they were coached by Fabio Cannavaro and before that Marcello Lippi. Since being bought by property tycoon Xu Jiayin's Evergrande Real Estate Group in 2010, over $100 million had been spent in five years. In 2014 the founder of China's biggest e-commerce site Alibaba – Jack Ma – bought a 50 per cent stake in the club for $200 million. It was a strange business direction in which to take his company. 'We are not investing in football, we're investing in entertainment,' Ma said after the purchase. Ma is the poster boy for the new, meritocratic state-run capitalism of twenty-first-century China. His parents weren't party cadres and he certainly wasn't a 'princeling'. Ma's mother and father were once folk singers and storytellers. He taught himself English and became a teacher. Much of his early life was defined by failure. 'There's an examination for young people to go to university – I failed it three times. I failed a lot,' he told Bloomberg. 'I even went to KFC when it came to my city. Twenty-four people went for the job. Twenty-three were accepted. I was the only guy [who wasn't].'

Ma had no previous investments in sport when he decided to buy into Guangzhou Evergrande. The club had a strong pedigree in Asia by 2015: they had already become champions of Asia twice and played Barcelona in the FIFA Club World Cup. While the world had just woken up to China's money, Evergrande had been spending freely for years. 'A lot of Westerners have got this wrong. The development of the league started before Xi Jinping. It has escalated with Jinping,' says Mads Davidsen, a Danish talent scout and coach who started his career in China with Sven-Göran Eriksson at Guangzhou R&F before moving with him to Shanghai SIPG. When Davidsen first arrived he would look for value in the domestic league. But as time went on, it was clear that the money and will was there to attract bigger names.

'My system now is that I put the players in bookshelves,' he says about his method of prioritising players. 'Shelf one, you have the best of the best, the Messis, the Ronaldos. We cannot touch these players. Shelf two: I can say we have been offered 11 top players from top European clubs. We choose not to sign them. It is a game-changer. We can now compete for EPL players. And, of course, the best in South America. China can now compete.' In the past, leagues in developing nations would only attract those looking for one last, big contract at the end of their careers. But that had changed. China was now an option for some of the best players South America had to offer.

Guangzhou Evergrande have had a slow start to the season, which has not done Scolari's mood much good at all. He's standing on the touchline screaming at his players, a Chinese interpreter is standing next to him relaying the messages in a meeker manner. On a hot, sticky Friday evening, Martínez looks a class above the rest, Paulinho scores the opening goal before, later in the second half, setting up Martínez to finally score the goal his efforts deserve. Guangzhou Evergrande win 2–0 to get their season back on track. The main draw has always been Jackson Martínez, who had starred at Porto but was moved on by Atlético Madrid within just six months of arriving in Spain. 'I'm really impressed . . . it's a league that is not as easy as people think,' says Martínez, standing by the exit door with his young son, who is also wearing a red Guangzhou Evergrande jersey. 'You can't compare this club [with Atlético] but the organisation always tries to do its best.' Money had dominated any discussion about his move to China, but Martínez insists that he had earned enough playing in Mexico, even back in Colombia, to look after his family: 'My mum and my two sisters and everybody else could live well. Not everything is about the money. It's about the opportunities.' Yet, unlike Mads Davidsen, he admits that China isn't yet at the stage where players would consider a move there while in their prime, even with the money. 'I'm 29 and about to hit 30. If I was 25 or 26 I wouldn't think of coming here, but because of the situation at Atlético Madrid, I couldn't play well, things didn't go as expected,' he says honestly.

'Everybody talks about money [but] my salary is not that high!' laughs Guangzhou R&F coach Dragan Stojković. The Red Star Belgrade legend has been coaching for years in Japan's J-League and his move to China is indicative of another powerful movement, coaches and players eschewing the traditionally powerful leagues in Korea and Japan and moving to the Chinese Super League instead. 'My life was very adapted to Asia in Japan,' he says. 'It is a good challenge. The league is strong. I think year by year they have a great future.'

A few weeks later Guangzhou Evergrande were top of the league but had also managed to get themselves knocked out of the Asian Champions League during the group stage – a disaster for a club who had hoped an appearance in the Club World Cup would again elevate them to where they wanted to be, alongside the world's elite of Juventus, Barcelona or Real Madrid. But that will take time, as will the hunt for a world-class national team. As Mads Davidsen points out, the maths is on China's side. What's missing is a true superstar to emerge. 'With 1.4 billion people you will produce world-class players,' he says confidently. 'What Chinese football doesn't have is a Yao Ming.'

**

A four-hour drive north of Guangzhou, the biggest football academy in the world is doing just that, searching for their own Yao Ming, sifting through China's vast talent pool looking for that mercurial, truly world-class Chinese football player. The Evergrande Football School was built 80 miles from the city, high in the hills and away from the smog that blights it far below. Just under 3,000 students live here, in a school that cost $R1.2 billion ($185.3 million) to build. It looks uncannily like Hogwarts: part stately pile, part Transylvanian gothic castle, but with close to 50 football pitches out the back, serviced by 130 teams of differing ability. A 10-foot replica of the World Cup greets you at the front gate. A plaque stands nearby, awarded by the *Guinness Book of Records,* just in case anyone was in any doubt as to the school's sheer scale.

'We get no money from the government,' Deng Sheng, a director at the school who speaks perfect English with a slight Australian accent, picked up from his years working there as a journalist, says keenly. 'This is not for profit. It costs between 50,000 and 60,000 RMB a year, and 25 per cent get help from our scholarship fund,' he adds. There is a computer room, Wi-Fi, gyms and a shop ('No Coke or rubbish food!' Sheng makes clear). The children who are still here lounge around on the steps outside their rooms playing computer games on their phones.

What is the aim of all this? I ask.

'To revitalise Chinese football,' Deng says, 'and to cultivate football stars.'

In ten years' time he hopes some of these graduates will play in the Chinese Super League. For Guangzhou Evergrande, obviously, but many players come from every corner of China – and many will return there, taking what they've learned too. We tour the school's silent corridors and classrooms, pictures of famous players pinned to the walls. The boys and girls live four to a room, each left neatly arranged with only a pair of shin pads on each bed to indicate each pupil's team: AC Milan, Manchester United and Barcelona. It is a national holiday – the day of the cleaning of the tombs – meaning most of the pupils have returned home to their families. But the football doesn't stop. Deng drives a sturdy electric van through the maze of walkways between green playing fields towards the school's main stadium. It takes 15 minutes to get there: a patch of red clay among fields of green, complete with bleachers and a huge electronic scoreboard that wouldn't look out of place in a national stadium.

The final of an under-15 tournament between some of Asia's best academies had just started, and Evergrande's team has made it through, against a team from Tokyo. Nearly all the pupils that have stayed behind have packed the stands for the match. At the front, next to the fourth official, the school's principal Liu Jiangnan is watching on his day off. 'The aim here is to improve Chinese football because Chinese football level is low in the world,' he says, keeping his eyes on the game in front of him.

'The foundations are poor. The younger people, the player, is very important to us. So this school trains the young people to be excellent players.'

For Liu, the influx of money into the school's parent club and into the CSL is a good thing. Much as with the early arrival of foreigners in the English Premier league in the mid-1990s, it is hoped that the successful imports can raise the technical ability of the players around them, and add a little glamour that keeps the attention of his pupils. Despite his attention on the game, the principal had never been a big football fan in his youth, preferring swimming and track and field. 'I don't pay much attention . . . to the English player[s]. I cannot remember who is the best,' he admits. 'I just know Beckham . . . he's gone to America, yes?' But he has a plan. 'In ten years China's team can be improved and become the strongest team in Asia,' he believes. 'Maybe in eight to ten years they can play for the Chinese national team. I have these dreams, for me.'

Liu has at least got good help to hand. The coach of the Evergrande team is shouting at his players in Spanish, the instructions relayed in Chinese, in what is turning out to be a bad-tempered match. In the bleachers, the coach's performance is being watched by Fernando Sánchez Cipitria, the director of training at the Evergrande Football School, who has been seconded from the Real Madrid Academy on an eight-year contract to train the Chinese stars of the future.

Fernando was himself a midfielder, with two caps for the Spanish national team. He was part of the famous Deportivo La Coruña team that won the Spanish league, beating Real Madrid, Barcelona and Valencia to the title in 2000. 'It was like Leicester City today!' he laughs, pointing out proudly that the northwestern city of La Coruña has a population of just 250,000. 'For Madrid, one part is the financial part, yes, but the other part is that they are looking for a connection with Asia,' he says frankly as to why 25 Real Madrid Academy coaches – a huge number – were present at the Evergrande Football School alone. It was a set-up that ADO Den Haag and Wang Hui could only dream of. 'China is the future and will have many famous players. It is important that we make this connection in Asia early.'

The aim, for Fernando at least, is for the players to move to Europe and prove their skills at the highest level. Only then will the rest of the world truly sit up and listen – perhaps whenever Chinese football's Yao Ming is finally, and perhaps inevitably, found. 'This is what European clubs want but don't have,' he says, pointing to the huge complex to our right. The match is coming to an end. It is 1–1 and headed for penalties. 'Technically and physically the players are very good. But the idea of football here, it is an old way of thinking. This is what we are trying to teach them, modern methods.'

Every penalty is scored with a precision that would embarrass the English national team until, finally, one player from Evergrande misses. Since I first arrived in Xi'an, it is China's only misstep. The Japanese players celebrate as the young Guangzhou players mooch back to the bench, distraught. Japan has long been the best team in Asian football, with the best league and the best academies churning out players that have gone on to thrive in Europe. Now Japan has a real rival, perhaps their oldest rival, breathing down their necks. 'Yes, they lost this time,' Sánchez says, as the teams collect their medals with Queen's 'We Are the Champions' blaring out from the speaker system, 'but China's time will come.'

But before China's time, another country acquired what every investor in European football ever dreamed of yet scarcely believed could happen in an age where the financial brute force of top clubs guaranteed that gatecrashers and outsiders were not welcome. With a fraction of the resources, and a fraction of the population, businessmen from one Asian country had managed to secure the English Premier League title. That country was Thailand.

7. Buriram, Thailand

Every map calls it something different, but everyone in town knows where to find the Thunder Castle. It is incongruous against its sparse tropical background; a jagged blue outcrop made of what appears to be huge plastic Tetris pieces, built in the middle of a vast unbroken concrete plateau next to a modern shopping mall.

In the guts of the stadium, underneath one of the stands, a high-pitched yelp is followed by the deep thwack of foot against leather as a few dozen Thai kick-boxers practise, shaded from the intense heat. Outside, the wide empty car parks and proximity of the only McDonald's within 160 kilometres of here give the impression of a small Florida town sleeping in the mid-afternoon sun, rather than a town just 50 kilometres from the Cambodian border, and home to Thailand's league champions.

Buriram United FC have won four Thai Premier League titles out of the last five and are the current champions. They are the country's most successful team, even though they didn't exist a few years ago and hail from a poor town far from the capital. The answer to Buriram's success is sitting pitchside. Newin Chidchob is the king of Buriram. He is one of Thailand's most powerful political brokers, and the head of a powerful political clan that has dominated the city and region of Buriram – some say the clan controls how the region of Buriram votes. As the former Thai prime minister Thaksin Shinawatra had built his political career on the votes and promises given to the rural population who lived around the city of Chiang Mai in the north of the country, so Newin's power centre was in Buriram in the east. From here he became one of Thailand's consummate political operators, switching between rival political clans and interests, occasionally being censored by the law along the way, until he sank his time and effort into football. He is also one of the closest allies of Vichai Srivaddhanaprabha, chairman of the King Power duty-free empire, a retail giant that reaped huge profits from its duty-free monopoly at Bangkok's main airport, and the owner of Leicester City FC.

Early comparisons were made between Srivaddhanaprabha and Thaksin Shinawatra, but the differences between the two are stark. One played polo, courted royal audiences and shunned the limelight; the other craved popularity and political power. One had bought a club and secured, against the odds, the Premier League title, while being showered with honour and praise by Thailand's revered king; the other had bought a club only to sell it a year later after his assets were frozen and he was forced to live in exile.

Yet the two men, along with Newin, are inextricably connected. Each followed his own path to success in Thailand's booming economy during the 1990s and each counted the other as an ally during periods of political and economic upheaval. To understand Leicester City's success is to understand how the fortunes of the three men have waxed and waned. It is also to understand why Thailand's super-rich are investing so much money in English football.

'My first memory of football is breaking my leg,' says Newin. He is sitting by the pitch, his wife close by. She is intensely monitoring the conversation. Newin turns up every day for every training session, his CEO says, whether it is for the first team or one of his youth squads. He had bought the club, then called Provincial Electricity Authority and based in Bangkok, in 2009 and moved it 400 kilometres east to Buriram. Despite being one of Thailand's best-known power brokers, Newin had been banned from all political activity after the 2006 coup that threw Thaksin from power. Newin threw himself into football instead. 'This [the region of Buriram] has the sixth highest population but it is in the top ten poorest in the country as well,' he says, when I ask why he bought the football club. 'It comes from my passion for football. I'm getting old and I didn't have anything to do [so] I bought the club to make Buriram more popular. To let everyone know in Thailand, and the continent, it is a destination.'

Newin was once one of Thailand's most notorious political operators. 'He has been the key politician since the early 1990s and he has a habit of betraying his party leadership and defecting,' says Dr Paul Chambers of the Institute of South East Asian Affairs at Chiang Mai University. 'He is from a very major family. Thaksin had a lot of popularity in northeast because Newin controlled the vote canvassers. When he lost Newin in 2008, it was not good for Thaksin.'

Newin was also a long-time friend of Vichai (King Power sponsors Buriram), and both were political allies of Thaksin. In fact, Newin defected to Thaksin's Thai Rak Thai Party in 2001 after having already had a hand in toppling one government in 1997 when he switched parties. He served as an MP for Buriram, a cabinet minister and confidant to Thaksin, until he was eventually ousted by the military. In the wake of the 2006 coup everyone around Thaksin had to make a decision, including Vichai, who had been awarded his lucrative duty-free contract under Thaksin's regime. 'Both Vichai and Newin had to make a choice,' says Dr Chambers of the post-coup period. 'Stay with Thaksin or see the way history was running and make that choice.' When Thaksin returned to Thailand briefly in 2008, Newin reportedly cried when he saw his political ally arrive. But it didn't last long. Knowing that the military was here to stay and that the options for Thaksin's return to power were fast vanishing, Newin turned on Thaksin and questioned his loyalty to the royal family before backing a military approved political party instead. Thaksin, Dr Chambers said, felt betrayed.

Vichai too had thrown his lot in with the military, after almost losing everything. His extraordinary wealth, estimated at $4.3 billion, came largely from winning the duty-free contract for the new Suvarnabhumi Airport, a pet project of Thaksin's that was bedevilled by delays and controversy, cost billions of dollars, but which Thaksin saw as essential to tapping into Thailand's huge tourism potential. King Power already had the concession at the previous airport, the smaller Don Muang Airport, but Vichai secured the contract for Suvarnabhumi during Thaksin's reign in 2004. When Thaksin was removed, the new military controlled regime moved quickly to invalidate the contract. The Airport Authority of Thailand accused Vichai of leveraging his political connections to ensure there was no competitive tendering and the deal was therefore invalid. It was a huge honey pot, but no one was under any illusion that the move wasn't political. The one airport alone generated $403 million in sales in 2007. After a lengthy battle, Vichai beat off the legal challenge, but it cost him millions more in back fees and taxes. At the same time he had been leveraging his influence within the new military regime. Many knew that corruption was rampant during Thaksin's reign, but the corruption in the military dictatorship was much more opaque. It was about aligning yourself with certain generals who shared similar business interests. 'If you want to do business in Thailand, these are the people you need to talk to,' says Dr Chambers. 'Business people who are associated with the military. King Power remains influential. The threat by the junta to break off some of the monopoly power of King Power didn't happen. Instead, the influential reach of Vichai saved him.' It could only have helped that Vichai was also working hard to raise money for several charities close to the king. In return, in 2013, Vichai Raksriaksorn was awarded the royal name 'Srivaddhanaprabha' meaning 'the light of progressive glory'. Vichai Raksriaksorn originally bought Leicester City; by the time Leicester were top of the English Premier League everyone knew the owner as Vichai Srivaddhanaprabha.

'For Vichai it is easy to follow the arch royalist path if you are making profits out of it,' said Dr Chambers. 'Thaksin is not the name of the game right now. For at least five years the military is likely to remain in power or close to power. With that in mind, if you are Vichai you want to be on the right side of history. King Power is an enterprise through which the interests of Newin and others are met. It is a big political economy.'

Newin took a different path. With direct political action out of the question, Newin fell back to Buriram and his football club. In fact, as Dr Chambers points out, many former leading politicos who suddenly found themselves banned or *persona non grata* by the junta turned to sport and football in particular, creating a new informal network of communication and influence. 'After the 2006 coup political parties were illegal. Whole groupings of politicians later became owners of football teams. Some other sports as well,' said Dr Chambers.

Newin's return to Buriram was just as colourful as his political career in the capital. He was known for his impeccable political connections but also for playing rough if he had to. He would regularly be seen with his motorcycle club, travelling around the country on his Harley-Davidson. There is a famous video that can still be found online of a rock concert and kick-boxing night that Newin had organised. A group of young men had been causing trouble; fighting other groups of Thai men and trying to rob foreign tourists. Newin sprang into action, ordering the men to be rounded up. Three were caught. Newin led the men into the kick-boxing ring where each man was forced to face a professional Muay Thai champion, who promptly beat them to a pulp in front of a braying crowd. Newin had dispensed justice swiftly and brutally. 'Sometimes, the police do not act the way they should, so we did,' he says, smiling a little.

His move into football club ownership had been an unqualified success. Aside from the titles that he had won, Buriram United were now regularly appearing in the Asian Champions League. In fact, as we met, Newin was preparing for the visit of another top continental team, Japanese champions Sanfrecce Hiroshima, for an Asian Champions

League match. Buriram were bottom of the group, but they had established themselves as one of the best club teams on the continent. The club had also, Newin believed, had a huge economic impact on the region. 'Some may buy [a football club] for football passion, some do it because it makes good business, but for me I am sure it is because I love football and I want to make the city better,' he says. 'For the first three years the GDP of the city has grown 32 per cent. So far from the first year, there has been 200 per cent growth, because I love football and I want my home town to be better. For me this is enough. I am more happy to see the whole city have better quality of life and good business in Buriram than to buy a European club.'

But Newin's closest ally had bought a European club, and the success of Vichai's Leicester City has touched everyone of influence in Thailand. 'He is a big smart businessman, he is a very big friend,' says Newin. 'He only knows how to make big decisions. Not small, only big. He is serious, a serious guy; he wants to make it big.' Leicester City's incredible season had created national pride, but it had also proved that successful football club ownership could build your own personal brand – while giving greater leverage in any politically motivated business disagreements back home. Vichai held the purse strings while Newin held the all-important block of votes that anyone needed if they hoped to get elected. Vichai's success in English football strengthened both their positions.

'As a friend and a brother I congratulate him for the success and we have to admit that it is a football miracle that has happened,' says Newin. 'This was a team that struggled last year and were almost relegated. They almost lost millions. Now they will go to the Champions League! It is good for football and for Thailand too.' The success has also challenged the traditional supporter base of the big clubs. 'Thais [traditionally] only support Liverpool, Manchester United, Arsenal, Chelsea, but now they support Leicester City because it is a Thai club owned by Thai people,' believes Newin, with the caveat that Buriram

United FC still have more of an impact in Thailand and are far more popular. 'Leicester's success is good because it shows more the role of Thais in global football but doesn't affect Thai football at all. We are close friends. He [Vichai] decided not to buy a club in Thailand so we don't fight each other. So he buys Leicester City in the Championship. Vichai is more about business abroad, but me: it is more on how to grow Buriram.'

Both men's careers in football ownership are going well. They have successfully negotiated the choppy waters of post-coup Thailand, retained their business interests and influence by lining up behind both the king and the military junta. Elections are again on the horizon, firstly for a new post-coup constitution, which has been heavily criticised by almost everyone outside of Thailand as being undemocratic for seeking to secure a permanent political advantage for the army. There has been a wave of arrests as the military have virtually outlawed any campaigning against the new constitution. If it is passed, new elections to choose a civilian prime minister are planned to take place in 12 months time. Newin says he is now out of the political game, but few in Thailand believe him. 'I don't act in politics any more because when I was a politician half of the country hated me,' Newin says. 'Half walk away from me. But now half walk towards me. I'm not Mr Newin any more; I'm Uncle Newin to the fans. I feel admired by fans. That is more than being in politics.' Remarkably, he says that he still speaks to his old ally Thaksin, even though they are now effectively political foes. 'As a friend,' he qualifies. 'Politics? I don't do that any more. It is hell. I'm not a sadist and I don't want to go back to that hell. So don't ask about politics. I'm not going back to that.'

**

Around ten thousand fans have arrived at the Thunder Castle to watch Buriram United in what is effectively a dead Asian Champions League rubber against Sanfrecce Hiroshima. One stand is filled with the

'Hardcore', the supporters' group of Buriram. They are an odd mix of young male fans who model their support on Western ultra groups, old women dressed in blue team shirts, and drummers. They do not stop singing throughout; haunting, tuneful songs that seem beautifully out of place in a football stadium. On the bench, Newin Chidchob assumes his usual place next to the coach to help direct the team on the pitch. With nothing to play for, the match begins as a dull stalemate, before Sanfrecce eventually break through and score at the end of the first half. A second goal kills the game, but the fans still sing their ethereal songs.

'Football has improved a lot in Thailand. I checked the club and facilities and thought, "OK, it's a big club who invest money in good players and good facilities,"' says the team's Brazilian coach, Alexandre Gama, who has spent most of his career in Asia but is relatively new to the workings of Thai football. He does not appear to be put off by the presence of Newin on the bench next to him. 'Here in Thailand I think all the chairmen sit on the bench,' he laughs. 'We exchange information. He respects me a lot and he knows why I am here. This is the new challenge for me. This belongs to him.'

Of more concern was China. Earlier, Buriram's CEO had complained that the new muscular Chinese Super League was making recruitment impossible. Any player from South America was now four times the price they were the previous season. Agents and players had hiked up their prices to take advantage of the new Chinese spending spree.

After the game Newin Chidchob kept his team and coaching staff in the dressing room for over an hour, leaving the press sweltering in the heat outside. 'He spoke a lot about the game, how we need to improve, like a coach,' says Andrés Túñez, a Venezuelan international who had played most of his career at Celta Vigo. 'He tries to improve us and give our best level.' For Túñez it was unusual to see an owner on the bench, but, 'Mr Newin is very good with us. He is with us every day. He always has questions for you. We are happy. He is a big, big man in Thailand, all people know him. He is like a father to me.' The transition from Newin Chidchob the canny political operator who would switch sides when it was expedient, to Uncle Newin, the paternal football club owner, was almost complete.

**

From the outside, Bangkok looks much the same under a dictatorship as it does under a democracy. Its streets and markets bustle with colour and noise; its roads are jammed with tuk-tuks, overloaded lorries and expensive sports cars. In the centre of the city King Power's headquarters dominates several blocks. Outside the front entrance, a huge portrait of King Bhumibol Adulyadej greets visitors. Over the course of the 2015–16 Premier League season the company have shown Leicester City's home matches on a big-screen TV, distributing free beer and noodles to attract huge crowds – a tried-and-tested method of the rich and powerful in Thailand, whether they are trying to cajole people to the opening of a mall or to vote in an up-and-coming election. English football has traditionally been the only game in town, a consequence of the FA Cup final being the only match shown on state TV for years, not to mention the tours by visiting teams that have shored up support for Manchester United, Liverpool, Chelsea and Arsenal.

As late as April 2016, the big clubs continued to dominate here. In the nearby markets selling Premier League bedspreads and fake replica kits, Leicester City pillowcases and home strips were still an oddity.

That weekend, Leicester were playing Sunderland in another must-win match. Singha Beer, who also sponsor a string of football clubs in England including Leicester City, had arranged for a huge event in a trendy bar complex a few miles away from the centre of town. Two huge outside screens were set up, and an army of staff dressed like American servicemen had been dispatched to deliver beer and fries to the crowd. But no one turned up. Thai New Year, *Songkran*, was around the corner, yet only a handful of people stayed to watch Jamie Vardy score twice and take Leicester another step closer to the title. 'Vichai is a super-wealthy guy, connected to military dictators in Thailand and making sure an underdog team in England win,' said Dr Chambers. 'It isn't such a Cinderella story.'

8. Paris, France

Thaksin Shinawatra watched Leicester City's remarkable Premier League campaign far from home. Powerless for almost a decade, the former Thai prime minister had not returned to his homeland since 2008, when the military junta froze his assets and vowed to arrest him on corruption and other charges the moment he set foot on Thai soil. What followed was a nomadic existence, looking for a country that would take him in. The UK revoked his visa, leading to Thaksin withdrawing his request for political asylum. Others didn't want to know. Instead, it was left to the UAE, and in particular Dubai, to offer Thaksin sanctuary, both for himself and what remained of his fortune.

But on this sunny May day, Thaksin Shinawatra is not in Singapore, or Beijing, or the Middle East. He is sitting in his hotel in Paris. He is staying in a plush suite with a low-key, private entrance and a Thai security guard – complete with earpiece and a dead-eyed scowl – that gives the impression that a head of state is being guarded inside. Thaksin is sitting on his sofa in an immaculately ironed white shirt, looking exactly the same as the fresh-faced billionaire who had shaken up Thailand's staid political scene when he entered the great game in the mid-1990s. 'I remember a state visit to London, and Prince Philip and I talked about the drug war,' Thaksin says as we sat down to talk. 'He surprised me. He told me I should decriminalise drugs. All drugs!' He laughs with a little shake of the head. Thaksin couldn't do that, of course, but he was amused by how an elderly member of the British royal family might in fact be a radical libertarian. Thaksin has many stories like this: moments when he was treated like a statesman, like an equal to the other rulers of the world.

Now he was in Paris, escaping the intense Dubai summer heat, taking it easy, spending time with his grandchildren and checking up on some of his new investments – small sums sunk into biomedical research and a few other stocks he declined to name before the conversation turned to his favourite topic: football. 'What happened with Leicester is the combination of a good coach, good team spirit and moral support from the owner. It is not about the stars and very expensive players and coaches,' says Thaksin proudly.

Thaksin knew the hard way the game that had to be played to survive in Thai business, and didn't bear any grudges at how his former colleagues and supporters had lined up behind the current regime. Business was survival, and survival was business. 'He is very Thai and has a [Thai] touch; he has a good touch with the players and coach, and they work together like a family,' he says of Vichai's regime at Leicester City. 'Also, he brings some Thai monks in to give a kind of belief, faith that you play better. And they really played better!' He quickly corrects himself, just in case anyone got the impression that Jamie Vardy had embarked on a spiritual awakening in Bangkok. 'They are not Buddhist! After they did a ceremony, they feel confidence. It is psychology. Everything is about psychology.'

We soon start talking about Thaksin's own football experience. 'You know Ranieri? I once interviewed him and decided to hire him,' he says, referencing his time as the first Thai owner of a Premier League club. 'But the agent said please change to Sven [-Göran Eriksson]. Because Sven was more famous at that time.' Thaksin liked the exposure being owner of Manchester City gave him. He could entertain his allies and brag in front of his foes. He could show his love for Thailand's king on the city of Manchester's big screens and broadcast it all around the world, infuriating the military in the process. But he says he bought

Manchester City for the purest of motives. After his failed bid to buy Liverpool, 'After I was deposed by *coup d'état*, I stayed in London. I love football. I was thinking about it in 2003 and then came Manchester City. And I really wanted to own a team. I was watching the Premier League for many years. And then I decided to buy it.'

Thaksin's 'stay in London' had of course been enforced. In September 2006, while he was in New York for the UN general assembly, tanks rolled onto the streets of Bangkok, the military declared martial law and suspended the constitution. It had been a long time coming. Thaksin had been embroiled in a multifaceted political crisis over the previous year that had seen him accused of everything from abuse of power to corruption and self-enrichment, and even of employing black magic to replace the statue of the creator god Brahma with one of his own. But his downfall wasn't at the hands of a shaman. A law was passed that allowed 100 per cent foreign ownership of Thai telecommunications companies. Within days, Thaksin's Shin Corp was sold to a company owned by the Singaporean government. Thaksin's wife and family made $1.88 billion on the deal while minimising their tax bill. The following uproar sparked protests for and against Thaksin, pitting different Buddhist sects, cities and regions against each other, largely splitting the urban, royalist middle-class anti-Thaksin factions against the poor, populous rural areas of Thaksin support. When the levee broke in September, Thaksin's rule came to an end.

By 2007 he was in London, thinking about the future. It was then that Thaksin had been offered 'two or three' other clubs to buy. But he liked Manchester City. He knew what kind of pull the Manchester brand had after being presented with a special Manchester United shirt back in 2001 by Sir Alex Ferguson. United were, of course, now completely out of his price range, even if he did have a fortune estimated by *Forbes* to be $2 billion back then. Still, City weren't just cheaper, Thaksin believed that the team perhaps distilled the spirit of the city better than its red half. 'In Manchester itself, the fans more support City than United,' he says. 'And City had a new and good stadium. At the time, the team was about to be relegated every season. And I thought, "If we gave a decent investment . . ." So I decided to invest.'

Thaksin bought the club in June 2007 for what is now considered a knockdown price: just £81.6 million. Even though he had passed the Premier League's infamously lax Fit and Proper Persons Test, there had been uproar over the persistent allegation of human rights abuses that international rights groups had levelled at him, connected to his 'war on drugs', the jailing of political opponents and the high body count from suppressing an Islamist uprising in the south of the country. It was already well known that the Thai junta's 'Assets Examination Committee' had requested that Thaksin's assets were frozen over 'alleged conflicts of interest, corruption and related offences in Thailand'. The committee was due to make its final decision a month after the sale, with Thaksin 'vigorously defending all such allegations'. The Premier League let the sale pass as Thaksin had been charged but not convicted of the charges in front of him.

Today, Thaksin bristles when asked about the allegations. 'When I was deposed by *coup d'état* the military tried to tarnish me by giving bad info out. They control the mass media in Thailand,' he states. 'They [the British press] believe one-sided, negative things. Then they have a bad impression from there . . . [the Thai military] formed a committee and investigated me. Those who died related to drugs was not that high. Maybe 2,000 was everything.'

Thaksin's unveiling was the stuff of legend. He had arranged for a bevy of Thai singers to perform in Manchester's Albert Square. Free Thai beer and noodles were handed out and Thaksin himself took to the stage. He was warmly received, but became a cult hero shortly afterwards when he took to the mic and butchered a rendition of 'Blue Moon'. By the time he was finished, he had been christened 'Frank'

Shinawatra. In an almost-perfect start to Thaksin's reign, City began the season with three wins out of three, including a 1–0 victory over Manchester United, a game that Thaksin says is his finest memory of owning the club. 'It was exciting because as an owner, when you sat in the stadium you play every ball. Your foot, *pssshht,*' Thaksin mimics kicking the ball by jerking his head forward and raising his knee. 'When you win you are very happy and when you lose you are *huuuur,*' Thaksin slumps in his seat as if a malfunctioning robot had been abruptly shut down. 'It is up and down.'

The human rights concerns melted in the background when Manchester City were winning. Thaksin's political career might have been sinking fast back home, but in Manchester he had found an alternative to that itch that politicians need scratching: universal adulation. 'You are proud when you stand on the stadium with a lot of fans,' he remembers. 'It is very similar to politics. If you make people happy you are proud of serving them.'

Yet Thaksin's reign was beset with problems from the start, not least with the prevailing English football culture. 'I was told, "Don't get involved with the manager as they have 100 per cent right to handle everything,"' he recalls, making the statement sound utterly ridiculous in the process. 'I said, "As a businessman, I invest, why shouldn't I have some say?" But the lesson with Leicester City confirms my belief that the owner should get involved, but not with a heavy hand: psychological support, moral support. The players are successful young men. Sometimes they can't handle themselves as they get paid a lot of money every week. Then back home they are very poor: mother, father, cousin asking for money. It is a lot of pressure.'

Matters came to a head when Thaksin returned to Thailand. His relationship with Sven had become frostier from the turn of the year. 'In the first half of the season the relationship was very good,' he says. 'I went back to Thailand, the team was getting worse. The football was not football at that time. I was watching from a distance and I was very upset. When I came back I said I had to talk to him in such a way that it turned a bit bitter, so I ended the contract.'

City fans were not happy, and the sacking effectively ended Thaksin's honeymoon period with the club, which had been bolstered by home and away league victories against Manchester United. But what really ended Thaksin's career was his wife's conviction on corruption charges. Rather than face the three-year jail sentence, the two fled. They would later divorce, with Thaksin staying on the road ever since. 'It was very unlucky for me,' he says. 'After I bought the club, I committed the investment and I have my assets frozen.' He lamented the timing in a way that suggested he hadn't really gotten over losing the club. 'To own a club in the Premier League you have to have deep, deep, deep, deep pockets. Not just one, but many deep pockets. It burns your money quickly. I feel very sad I had to sell. I had no money after they froze my money. I had to borrow here and there.'

He had to sell the club quickly. The club was costing him '£4 million a month' in wages and instalments on earlier player transfers. It was then that Thaksin heard that a member of the Abu Dhabi royal family had been on the lookout to buy a club. At that time, Thaksin says, Sheikh Mansour bin Zayed al Nahyan – a little-known member of the Abu Dhabi royal family who nonetheless held significant sway in the UAE government – had been trying to buy Liverpool but the deal was blocked. 'I approached the agent, a woman: "We are selling much cheaper than Liverpool!"' There is still no official figure on the amount of money Sheikh Mansour paid Thaksin Shinawatra for Manchester City, but it is believed to be around £150 million, a huge profit on his original investment, one that Thaksin readily admits (but refuses to confirm the specific amount). 'Good price, made a profit,' he says sharply.

Thaksin's time at City was over and his time in the political and football wilderness had begun. He would like to get back into football club ownership, he says, but the value of Premier League clubs now is too great to make a decent profit. He has been approached, he says, by a few Premier League clubs willing to be sold for free, if he was willing to invest, a deal that – in today's climate of exploding TV deals and buyers dominated by Chinese investors – sounds too good to be true. Value could be found instead in the second tier of English football, where Thai owners Dejphon Chansiri (Sheffield Wednesday) and Narin Niruttinanon (Reading) have moved in, both having made their fortunes in fish. 'We have no tuna in Thailand, but his family gets rich on tuna!' laughs Thaksin, referring to Chansiri's multibillion tuna-canning fortune as a sign of Thai business acumen. Yet one thing stays with Thaksin above all else from his time in charge of Manchester City, something he saw in the first few weeks of his ownership that seemed so alien, yet also reflected something uniquely English. 'When I went to work in the club, I saw a group of people and they wore all black, like after a funeral,' he recalls. 'I asked them, "What can I help you with?" They replied, "We are waiting for the official to put the ash of my husband in the pitch." My god, I never knew this before. He [the deceased] had been a fan for City of 42 years. He passed away and asked to put ash on the pitch.' Thaksin seemed as dumbstruck by that today as he had been nine years ago.

Thaksin's time has passed. He is 69 years old and probably too old for a political return to Thailand, although many feel his influence is still strong within the country. After the coup that removed him died down, the military promised to return to civilian rule, but not before trying to game the constitution and political parties to ensure that they still held the whip hand in Thai politics, but with the veneer of political legitimacy. The plan backfired. Instead, Thaksin's sister stood for election as head of the Puea Thai Party. Yingluck Shinawatra won the election in 2011. The military had suspected that another hand lay behind her Puea Thai Party, tapping into exactly the same constituency – the rural poor outside of Bangkok – as her brother had. In fact, many in Thailand saw her election as little more than a cover for Thaksin's own political ambitions and, more importantly, his route back to his homeland. Yingluck too was toppled by a military coup in 2014, creating the political climate in Thailand today – Thailand remains under military rule, with freedoms being restricted on an almost daily basis: censorship, the arrest of human rights activists and the use of 're-education' camps for people who disagree with the path that the government has chosen. I ask Thaksin about a news story I saw in Thailand concerning how the military had seized thousands of red bowls earmarked for distribution during the Thai New Year celebrations, each embossed with an esoteric message from Thaksin himself. The men caught with the bowls were sent for re-education. 'They have a lot of weapons: why are they scared of the bowl?' he says, chuckling to himself again. 'If my name pops up, they are scared. I am an old man. I have nothing. I have no gun. They should not be afraid of me. They should talk to me. I'm not asking for myself. I am asking for my people and the country.' If Thaksin's rule had taught others one thing, it was that if they wanted to retain their fortune, then they shouldn't enter politics. On the other hand, buying a foreign football club, especially an English club whose subsequent success could be hailed in honour of the king, will make you untouchable. At least, until Thailand's dangerous political sands shift once more. 'I think that might be a good strategy for him [Vichai],' Thaksin says. 'Being a business and then threatened by different camps of politics. And now he is a popular man because of the football club. Somehow it is an insurance policy. It is good insurance.'

Unlike Thaksin, none of the other leading businessmen in Thailand appear to hold political ambitions. 'He saw my lesson,' Thaksin continues of Vichai. 'He'll never jump into that! Politics is not good for a very successful businessman. You have a lot to lose. Politics in developing countries is good for those with nothing to lose. It is good for the people, but not politicians. They are jealous. You have more, and they think money is everything. Actually, money is not everything.' Thaksin's foray into politics might have helped him expand his fortune, but he has lost more than he made. In fact, the only thing that he can point to in terms of a healthy profit in recent years was selling Manchester City. 'In 1993, *Forbes* valued me at $2 billion. I was in the top 20 businessmen in Asia. At the end of '94 [when Thaksin entered politics] I voluntary declared assets of $2 billion. Now I have $1 billion left.' The cost of Thaksin Shinawatra's political ambition was $1 billion. Yet by studying Thaksin's blueprint the Thai super-rich have learned what works and what doesn't. What had once been seen as a route to securing power has now dovetailed with what is happening in China with its huge investment in European football. Football-club ownership is about sycophancy and wealth retention. A case could be made that, if it hadn't been for Thaksin's purchase of Manchester City, as flawed and as imperfect as that had been, Vichai Raksriaksorn would never have found a path to the East Midlands. But Thaksin did not attend Leicester's victory parade, even though he was a relatively short flight away by private plane. 'I congratulated him before,' he says, but it was impossible for Thaksin to show his face. It would be interpreted by the military regime back home as tacit support from Vichai for his old mentor, and tantamount to a business death warrant. 'I am a political target,' remarks Thaksin as we say our goodbyes. 'I do not want anyone to be in trouble because they are paranoid over me.'

Thaksin Shinawatra went back to work, checking his stock portfolio and dreaming of a route back home.

**

A few days later the victorious Leicester City team returned to Bangkok. They visited Phra Prommangkalachan, the 63-year-old monk at the city's Traimitr Temple, who had famously flown to the East Midlands to bless the stadium and the team, before arriving at the Emerald Buddha temple in Bangkok. An open-top bus parade set off, as thousands lined the streets to celebrate a title that was as much for Thailand as for anyone else. But perhaps not all was as it seemed. Allegations later emerged that large numbers of the crowd had been paid to turn up – at a rate of 500 baht, around £10 per person – and handed free King Power t-shirts, while the company's employees were also urged to attend. The 500 baht attendance fee was a common trick for getting numbers to attend political rallies on all sides of the Thai political spectrum. 'It's true we allowed King Power employees whose shifts ended – numbering 500 for each shift – to join the parade, but only if they wanted to,' a King Power spokesperson told the *Bangkok Post*, denying that the supporters had been paid to be there. 'Since they already had Leicester t-shirts it was only natural that they wore them on the occasion. It's the same in Leicester, where 240,000 residents wore the club t-shirt during the celebration.'

The club's historic Premier League title had come at an opportune time for foreign investors in the European game, especially in China. It proved that to compete with the likes of Manchester United you didn't need to spend like Manchester United. With the right coach, the right mix of players and just enough luck when it comes to injuries, perhaps any team could be moulded into champions, and deliver the kind of publicity and brand recognition that any owner craved.

The final stop of the Leicester City tour of Thailand was a visit to King Bhumibol Adulyadej's sprawling palace complex in central Bangkok. The world's longest-serving monarch was 88 and in poor health. At the palace, Leicester City's coaching staff and players all kneeled in a line. In the centre, Vichai Srivaddhanaprabha, alongside his son Top, presented the Premier League trophy to the palace, and placed it in front of a portrait of the king. In October, King Bhumibol died. A month of mourning was announced. The football league was cancelled with three matches to play and Muangthong United were declared champions. Buriram finished fourth, although the Brazilian coach Alexandre Gama was sacked shortly after I had met him, replaced by Afshin Ghotbi, the former coach of the Iranian national team.

There was a genuine outpouring of grief for a beloved royal. Stocks of black clothing ran out as Thais dressed sombrely to mark his passing. At one point, the Thailand v Australia 2018 World Cup qualification match looked like it would be cancelled. When it was finally agreed for the game to go ahead, the authorities declared that no cheering was allowed. That too was rescinded, before Thailand went on to secure an emotional 2–2 draw at the Rajamangala National Stadium in Bangkok.

No one knows what will happen next, but they know who will replace King Bhumibol. Crown prince Maha Vajiralongkorn has a reputation as a playboy who has shown little appetite for the public service his father embodied. Although none of his shenanigans (including appointing his pet poodle as air chief marshal) can be reported in the Thai press, he is deeply unpopular and commands none of the respect his father did.

It will be the military and its powerful business allies who will control Thailand's future. All eyes will be on the elections now delayed until at least 2019, to see when, or if, civilian rule returns. But the military has learned its lessons from the past. In the hope of preventing a rerun of Yingluck Shinawatra's triumphant campaign, a new political party is being formed under the aegis of the current, civilian National Council for Peace and Order. 'Thanks to his massive wealth and strong connections, Vichai is seen by some as having the potential to be the "last piece in the jigsaw" needed for the ruling National Council for Peace and Order (NCPO) to retain power via a new political party,' reported Thai newspaper *The National*. Alongside the deputy prime minister and defence minister general, Prawit Wongsuwan, and another political leader, Anutin Charnvirakul, was a familiar fourth name: 'Newin Chidchob, the former Cabinet minister and political broker who owns Thailand's leading football club Buriram.'

9. *The Hague, The Netherlands*

John van Zweden's shop Behangparadijs can be found just below Den Haag's Laan van Meerdervoort, where the houses are built on clay rather than sand. As you would expect from a man who made his fortune in interior design, John van Zweden's Wallpaper Paradise (the English translation of his shop's name) is beautifully appointed. Packets of laminate flooring are neatly stacked next to displays of upmarket wallpaper. It is also unmistakably Anglophile: a London taxi, coloured white rather than its mandatory black, takes pride of place in the centre of the shop, next to a red British telephone box. A dartboard hangs on the wall next to the tills. 'I sponsored Barney, and was best man at his wedding,' he says. 'Barney', Raymond van Barneveld, is one of Holland's most famous darts player, a rare foreign champion in an unashamedly English sport.

Van Zweden is a big man in his fifties with an unwrinkled face and a thick shock of white hair. He is wealthy, but would never consider himself *Hagenaren*, from north of the Laan. 'My old shop was in the south,' he says quickly. 'That shop was in the real Haag.'

That shop was his father's, which Van Zweden took over and expanded, making his fortune in the process. His mother still works for him, greeting customers as they walk in. He talks bluntly, with a slight English accent, and wears a yellow and green bracelet on his wrist. He has several tattoos visible on his right arm in honour of his two loves: ADO Den Haag, the team he has supported since a young man and now sponsors, and Swansea City, the club in which he owns a 5 per cent stake (or he does for a few more weeks at least). 'I used to have a London bus parked outside too, where you could go and see the wallpaper,' he says as he gives a tour of his shop, past the rolls of Barcelona and ADO wallpaper, and a Swansea City edition that sells surprisingly well this far from the south coast of Wales. 'That bus took up a lot of room, the neighbours complained,' he says, as if its absence still bothers him somehow. 'So I sold it. For a profit.'

Profit is something that Van Zweden has done well in accumulating in recent years. As a young man his life nearly went off the rails after running with the notorious Den Haag hooligans of the 1980s. He was arrested in 1984 after a particularly violent match between Den Haag and Ajax at the old Zuiderpark stadium, when an explosive device was thrown into the away end, injuring several Ajax fans. Van Zweden spent time in prison for a crime he says he didn't commit. 'I wasn't an angel, but I saw who threw it – a Chinese man or a Korean, I think – who we never saw before or since,' he recalls. He tried to stop the mystery man from throwing his 'bomb' but was too late. The security cameras placed him at the scene, and he went to prison for eight months. 'I looked out of the tiny window of my cell, and what could I see? Ajax's stadium! I went on hunger strike.'

The strike didn't last long. The guards took pity on him and allowed his worried mother to visit him in prison to deliver home-cooked chickens. He spent the rest of his time playing ping-pong and watching TV. When he was released, he vowed never to return and threw himself into his father's business, which would eventually give him enough money to become a sponsor of his beloved ADO Den Haag, as well as buying a stake in Swansea City in 2001 for just £50,000, back when they were in the fourth tier of English football, in danger of both relegation and bankruptcy. Van Zweden had fallen in love with Swansea after becoming a pen pal of a Swansea City fan at 16 in a bid to improve his English. By the time he was an adult he was travelling to Wales almost every weekend to watch the Swans play. Decades later, and with the club in deep financial problems after the disastrous ownership of an Australian consortium that had alienated the fans, he bought 5 per cent of the club after remortgaging his house without his wife's knowledge. 'I got an angry phone call from her when she found out,' he says. 'I didn't tell her. But she found out when a BBC journalist knocked on my door and asked for more information on who the new co-owner of Swansea City was!' Now the club was valued at £100 million and on the verge of being sold to a consortium of American businessmen. 'She's more than happy now!'

But Van Zweden's first love is ADO Den Haag. He is now the fiercest critic of the club's Chinese owner and is deeply unhappy with the fate that has befallen his club. 'If that Chinese does not want to sell, then it will be the end of ADO Den Haag at the end of this season,' Van Zweden had said in a TV interview shortly before we met. 'The problem with that Chinese, I find, is that he just does not follow up on his promises – which has resulted in our club, that has existed for 110 years already, being destroyed.'

Finally, after months of waiting, 'that Chinese' had paid at least some of the outstanding money owed to ADO. Spring had arrived and Wang returned to the club and two million euros were paid to lift the immediate financial clouds and take ADO out of its category one status. But it had done little to assuage the club's fans. As the season had progressed there had been regular protests against Wang Hui. Anti-Wang banners had appeared in the stadium and the club's director Jan Willem Wigt – who was popular among the supporters and with whom Van Zweden worked as an informal advisor – was fired, allegedly for the loss of face that Wang had suffered after going public about ADO's money issues last December. Henk Fraser had, after successfully fighting off what many saw as an attempt to install the Chinese national team coach Gao Hongbo into his job, remained as ADO coach and took the club to a steady 11th-place finish in the league. The season before, they had finished 13th. For all the drama, the promises and all the faded dreams and upset, the club had improved its league position by just two places. With ADO's safety secured, Fraser left the club and signed as coach of Vitesse Arnhem.

The first Van Zweden had heard of the sale of the club to a Chinese investor was when a local football journalist invited him to his office to tell him about the new owner. 'I tried to stop it every minute of the day,' says Van Zweden. 'I tried to stop him because I didn't trust the guy. I was completely right. This guy is an idiot . . . he made a fool of himself when he came to the stadium and trained with the first team. That is mental.'

As it started to dawn on the club that the money might not come as planned, Van Zweden was recommending that the club be bought out by a consortium of local businessmen, the preferred option for Den Haag's municipality, which had never come close to fruition. Despite frequent calls for local investment, no one put their money where their mouth was. Instead, ADO's supporters were told to understand that the new working relationship between club and owner would take some time. There were big differences in how business was done in China and in the Netherlands. 'That is a word I don't want to hear – "cultural differences",' says Van Zweden, still visibly angry talking about it. 'If you come here to my country, you have to understand the rules. Yes, you're a Chinese guy but you bought a football club here, you know how it works. If you want to be treated with respect you need to earn respect. When the club finally spoke to him, he said, "All you want is money." Yes! Because that is what you fucking promised us! And when you don't pay the money we can't pay the fucking bills, so what the hell are you doing?!'

A few weeks later, 14 years after remortgaging his house without his wife's knowledge, John van Zweden would no longer be a co-owner of an English Premier League club. Swansea City had finally tied up a £100 million deal to sell a 60 per cent stake in the club to an American consortium led by Jason Levien and Steve Kaplan, two men with vast experience of extracting value from US sports franchises in Major League Soccer and the NBA. Van Zweden might no longer have a seat in the boardroom, but he was now almost £5 million richer: 'When I invested in Swansea we had nearly no fans on the terraces, it was a hell of a lot of money, and I thought I had lost the money. But we escaped relegation and then it was all the way up for the Swans.'

Part of the success, Van Zweden believes, was the ownership structure that meant 21 per cent of the club was owned by a supporters' trust. Fan ownership no longer meant amateurism, or only keeping your head above water in the lower leagues: Swansea showed that a fan voice could be melded with success and profit, while also keeping ticket prices down – the key bugbear for many who fear that the reliance on TV and international finance dilutes a club's connections to its community. It was Swansea that led the way in lowering ticket prices for away fans with their 'Twenty is Plenty' campaign. 'The first time I went into the boardroom, as a North End boy, it was OK as there were not many big names. Soon as we reached the Championship it was a different world. Suddenly you are having dinner with Sir Bobby Charlton, or Elton John or Vinnie Jones – or brunch with Princess Anne. For a normal wallpaper guy from Holland this is a bit strange.'

And yet there was something slightly contradictory regarding his opinions on foreign investors. Van Zweden bemoaned the foreign influence in ADO, yet had forgotten that he had invested in English football as a foreigner. On the one hand, Van Zweden had been scathing about Wang Hui and his stewardship of ADO who, aside from staying in the Eredivisie, could not have had a more disastrous first season. On the other, he conceded that foreign investment is necessary to keep a club competitive in the top division. 'There is no choice, we cannot bring this club forward,' he said of his decision to sell his stake of Swansea to an American owner. 'Half a year ago I would say, "No, we don't need it." But we sacked our manager and nearly had a relegation battle. It was really frightening.'

That close call, he says, convinced him and others at the club that now was the time to sell to a new owner with deeper pockets, even if that money came from the east coast of the US. 'If we went down, we could not take this club forward. Now we have a group of Americans who own more clubs. We met these guys. Nice guys. Yes, it's an investment, but they want to take the club forward. And we thought, "This was the time."'

ADO, meanwhile, would continue with its Chinese ownership intact for the next season. The experience had led to some soul searching in Dutch football. Unlike English football, long used to foreign owners coming in and buying clubs – sometimes successfully, often less so – there was only one other foreign-owned club in Holland: Vitesse – Henk Fraser's new club – run by Georgian and then Russian businessmen connected to Roman Abramovich as, controversially, a feeder club for Chelsea FC; and something of a laughing stock in Dutch football for their continuously changing roster of players, typically only around for a season at a time. Attendances had collapsed from the recent glory days when former Dutch international and former Southampton coach Ronald Koeman was in charge.

The only reason Wang Hui had been allowed to buy Den Haag in the first place was down to a legal sleight of hand by the club's previous Dutch owner.

When Mark van der Kallen saved ADO from bankruptcy in 2007, the municipality insisted that – given the city's huge investment in the stadium – it should get the final say when or if the club was subsequently sold. Van der Kallen agreed, but later helped to draft the new statutes governing any future sale. The evening before the vote on the new statutes went to the municipality, a dense 40-page document arrived. Of course, there wasn't enough time for the whole thing to be properly scrutinised, and the paperwork was voted through. What the municipality didn't know was that an extra provision had been slipped in. Sure, the municipality could stop any potential sale of the club, but only if they could find a buyer willing to match the offer. The city only discovered the clause when Wang tried to purchase the club. 'What were they thinking? That somebody would come and put his money in it without the possibility to earn it back? Or only with the approval of the municipality?' Van der Kallen said in a 2016 investigation, *Waiting for Wang*, on Dutch broadcaster KRO-NCRV. He showed no remorse. 'Why not just stay in it for the rest of your life?' Van Zweden, too, didn't see anything wrong in this. He considered the original clause one that would make it impossible for Van der Kallen to sell the club. 'The owner wanted to sell it, and fair play to him,' Van Zweden says.

Several more customers have now entered his shop, far too many for his mother to handle by herself. John van Zweden says his goodbyes and goes back to work. Before he did I ask whether he would invest any of his newfound wealth into ADO, and help realise the dream of a local owner for what is an avowedly local club. 'No way!' he replies unequivocally. 'You saw what happened with Twente and Munsterman,' he adds, referring to the recent case of Joop Munsterman, a self-made publishing millionaire from the city of Enschede near the German border, who bought his hometown club and bankrolled them to the Champions League with former England coach Steve McClaren in charge. But when the club subsequently lost the title to Ajax on the last day of the 2010–11 season, finishing second, and then missing out on the Champions League group stage after losing a playoff against Benfica, the debts and wages became unmanageable. To compensate, Munsterman entered into a third party ownership (TPO) agreement with a sports investment vehicle based in London and Portugal called Doyen Sports.

TPOs allowed outside parties to essentially loan clubs money against the future sale of their top players. Some clubs, like Porto, had benefited hugely from these financial instruments, but when the Wikileaks-style website focused on football finance, Football Leaks, released copies of Twente's TPO agreement, it was clear that a desperate Munsterman had ceded too much control to Doyen, giving them an automatic say on some transfers if an offer was made at the right price. This was clearly a step too far in terms of third-party interference for the Dutch FA and FIFA. TPOs were banned, as were Twente from European football. Initially the club was also relegated, but later reinstated into the Dutch league. Munsterman had to step down after going from hero to zero over the course of two years. 'I know

Munsterman and he is a good guy. It all went wrong and if he comes to FC Twente the fans will kill him,' says Van Zweden, as he is about to serve his next customer that afternoon. 'I don't want that to happen to me and Den Haag. I will never, ever invest in my football club.'

Jacco van Leeuwen, meanwhile, had come to terms somewhat with the new era of Chinese money. We met one lunchtime at a café in the city of Utrecht, in the centre of the Netherlands. He was dressed smartly, in a crisp white shirt and trousers. 'I have a job interview in one hour, finally!' he says. It was for a job in a firm's IT department near Utrecht's Stadion Galgenwaard. Jacco wasn't exactly overjoyed to be so close to the home of FC Utrecht, one of ADO's fiercest rivals, whose fans have almost as uncompromising a reputation as ADO's, but he had been out of work for over a year now, and his employment benefit was about to run out. 'And I have alimony to pay, ha ha!' he laughs. It was a bright spring day and life was looking up for Jacco. For one, he had finally met with Wang. After the money was paid in April and the club was back on a solvent footing, Wang had returned to The Hague to mend fences and sack his chairman Van Wigt.

'At this moment, the fans are happy,' Jacco says. 'What we need now is a period of silence in the club.' Not everyone, however, was happy. When news got out that Wang was in the city a group of 50 ADO fans headed to his hotel to, as Jacco tells it, 'have a word with him'. In the end they were stopped by the police before they could confront him. 'He gave a good presentation, and I was surprised how good his English was,' Jacco said. Convinced that Wang was now on the right track, Jacco still believed that there was only one way to truly win over the fans. 'There is one answer to every question: money,' he says. 'If he pays, we win a Cup or get into Europe, we will build a statue to Wang! That is how it works in football.' The first step, though, was building up confidence. The meeting had reinvigorated his belief that, next season, ADO wouldn't face the same problems and that the money to cover 2016–17 would come through. Wang had promised to invest four million euros in the club to buy better players. After everything, ADO Den Haag in the summer of 2016 was in exactly the same place it had been the previous year, with exactly the same promise of exactly the same sum of money. 'The biggest mistake when people buy a club is to expect to earn money,' Jacco believes. 'It is impossible to earn money. Unless,' he adds, 'you are John van Zweden.'

But Van Zweden's profit from the sale of Swansea came from a booming TV money deal. Dutch football has gone backwards in recent years, its best players picked up for relative peanuts by mediocre Premier League teams with vastly superior purchasing power. The final indignation was the Netherlands failing to reach the 2016 European Championships despite the tournament's expansion to 24 teams, which made it virtually impossible for the big teams not to qualify. But the Oranje somehow managed it. Still, at least John van Zweden had his adoptive Wales to watch in the finals. Jacco was simply looking towards next season, with one eye on whether Wang came through with his promise. 'If he doesn't, we'll kill him.' There is a short pause before he breaks out into laughter and leaves for his interview. It was a success. Jacco got the job.

**

A few days later, ADO Den Haag's press officer called. After trying to arrange a meeting in Holland for the best part of a year, Wang wanted to meet for an interview to give his side of the story. 'You cannot tell anybody he is in the city,' said the press officer, the same one who had been desperately trying, and failing, to stop the Dutch media asking searching questions about the club's financial position. He was, it was clear, worried that another group of fans might discover Wang was back in Den Haag and try to storm the hotel again. 'Come to Den Haag and wait in the centre. We will call you.' I found a smart café in the city's pretty centre, and waited.

There were parallels to be drawn between ADO's experience and another Chinese purchase. The fans of French club Sochaux were now in open revolt against their Chinese owners after narrowly avoiding being relegated to the French third tier. Worse was to follow. The chairman of the company that now controlled the club, Li Wing Sang, had gone bankrupt. 'We don't understand Peugeot's decision to sell the club to this investor,' said Fabrice Lefèvre, president of one of the French team's supporters' clubs. 'It took us just a few hours and a few clicks on the web to find enough bad things to make us strongly doubt this sale.'

Both purchases had appeared to operate as a forward operating base for China's plans – a chance to learn from mistakes and rectify them – and as a foretaste as to what fans might expect when the brave new world of Chinese business comes to town. After all, by the summer of 2016 European football clubs were being bought by Chinese companies on what seemed like a weekly basis. Perhaps the issues at ADO and Sochaux were simply teething troubles, rather than an unbridgeable cultural gap. Or perhaps the problems were indicative of the more fundamentally awkward coupling of globalised wealth and hyper-localised assets like football clubs. A Chinese consortium, Rossoneri Sport Luxembourg, led by businessman Li Yonghong, finally prised AC Milan out of former Italian prime minister Silvio Berlusconi's grasp; Aston Villa were bought by Chinese owners; Nice in France and Granada in Spain were next. Wolverhampton Wanderers were purchased by the Fosun Group, a Chinese conglomerate, for £30 million (Fosun's chairman, Guo Guangchang, is worth over £4 billion and is China's 17th richest man); West Bromwich Albion were sold for £175 million to Yuni Investment, an investment fund controlled by Lai Guochuan, a 42-year-old businessman who made his first billion in a landscaping company. The club became the first in the Premier League to be bought outright by Chinese owners; today all the major West Midlands clubs are in the hands of Chinese owners. Swansea City's sale to an American consortium was even hijacked by a late Chinese bid, although it was sold to its current American owners in the end.

Even more intriguing was a proposal by the Dalian Wanda property group, owned by China's richest man, Wang Jianlin, part-owner of Atlético Madrid, to usurp the UEFA Champions League with a brand new competition with an expanded format that would see more big-name teams playing each other, and fewer teams from smaller nations appearing. Much like the Americans who had invested in European football after making their money in the NFL, MLB and NBA, the Chinese also see the benefit of dispensing with the meritocracy of promotion and relegation in order to sustain a group of legacy franchises through an effective cartel to protect owners' investments. The idea received a lukewarm welcome, but it is out there now, a pincer movement from China and the US that could change European football forever – assuming, that is, the investment is sustained. Many in China have seen this all before, when football was flavour of the month after the 2002 World Cup finals before collapsing under the weight of corruption. 'This is just a political phase,' explained the author of *Bamboo Goalposts*, Rowan Simons. 'Once the president reaches his final few years, if the new president is not a football fan all the investment will fade away and come to nothing.'

Back in The Hague, night began to fall, the café closed, and Wang Hui had decided not to come after all.

PART FOUR, THE MIDDLE EAST:

Princes and Sheikhs

1. Comilla, Bangladesh

In the early morning, before daylight and before Dhaka awakes and clogs its broken arteries with traffic and smog, the road from Bangladesh's capital city to Anamul and Razaul Hoque's village can take just over an hour by car. But today it takes four. It is April, and mangoes are ripening on the trees that line the dirt road that winds through the lush green Bangladeshi countryside, near the city of Comilla, next to the country's eastern border with the Indian state of Tripura.

The road thins and veers to the left, through a deep ford, before emerging at the Hoque brothers' small farm, set in front of picturesque paddy fields that stretch to the horizon, dotted with roaming cows and chickens. It is beautiful. It is also one of the poorest places on earth. Inside, Anamul and Razaul – dressed in tight-fitting shirts and wraparound *lungi* (a kind of sarong popular among Bangladeshi men) – buzz around collecting glasses, water and small, sweet bananas picked from their own trees.

The two received a flurry of visitors when they first returned home from Abu Dhabi, the capital of the United Arab Emirates, two years ago, but no one has come by for a while. They have started to think the world has forgotten about them. The two are friendly but guarded, as if they have seen this all before. 'We tell people our story, and they say they will help. But they go away and it doesn't change anything,' says Anamul, the elder and more talkative of the two, as he offers me a seat on his bed. He pulls a chair close to sit opposite. 'We have become forgotten.'

The two brothers grew up here, in a place that offers little way out of the grinding poverty of everyday life. Subsistence farming is all that is available. 'The environment here was good but the only business here is farming and we have a big family and it wasn't enough,' he says. So Anamul and his brother decided to follow a path that millions of Bangladeshis follow every year. They became migrant workers, doing the jobs in the rest of the world for a price that no one else could stomach: builders, labourers, cleaners, maids and drivers. And the most popular place to head, where there was always work, was the Middle East – especially the Persian Gulf states that had grown rich quickly off of oil and natural gas: Saudi Arabia, Qatar and the place Anamul and his brother would call home for seven years, the UAE.

'My cousins were in different countries, Qatar and UAE, so it influenced me to go abroad,' Anamul says. The brothers' father had also left home looking for work, spending decades in Saudi Arabia and Libya, living and working in tough conditions to send money home. He has long since passed away, prematurely, but his remittances built the house we are sitting in. For the young men here, it was a clear choice: permanent hardship, or a few years' pain to earn enough money to free their family from the cycle of poverty. 'I'm married, I have children, it was tough to meet their needs,' Anamul says. 'I was unemployed. So I decided to go abroad and earn lots of money.'

Bangladesh is a country that is both sprawling and overcrowded; abundant yet poor. It has a population of 160 million, making it one of the most populous on earth. After the partition of India in 1947, two distinct territories were formed: West Pakistan and East Bengal, later renamed East Pakistan. The military and political power resided in

West Pakistan, which spoke Urdu, while in East Pakistan they spoke Bengali. After decades of attempted suppression by West Pakistan of the Bengali culture, East Pakistan won its independence in the brutal 1971 Liberation War, in which as many as half a million people were killed, and became Bangladesh.

Years of military rule – and periodic coups – followed before democracy was finally installed in 1991. While huge strides have been made in literacy and life expectancy since 1991, Bangladesh is still one of the poorest countries in the world. According to the Asian Development Bank, 31.5 per cent of the population – close to 54 million people – live below the poverty line, surviving on less than $2 a day. The country's biggest domestic industry remains the textile business, where Western multinationals make many of the clothes found in high-street chains, paying knockdown wages. But Bangladesh would collapse without its single greatest contributor to the country's gross domestic product: the export of its people. Or, to be more precise, the import of their pay cheques.

Remittances – money sent home from workers abroad – are worth $15.32 billion to the Bangladeshi economy, which is close to 7 per cent of the country's entire GDP according to the IMF. Unofficially, it is closer to 10 per cent. Every year half a million people leave Bangladesh looking for the jobs that don't exist at home, in the hope of securing their families' futures. So, with the encouragement of his family already in the Gulf, and with the knowledge of his father's own self-sacrifice – and the house that his remittances built – Anamul decided that he too would leave for the UAE. His brother travelled later.

The global profile of the UAE has developed largely thanks to its investments in sport, and in particular Manchester City, owned by a member of the Abu Dhabi royal family. The club's success has helped to promote a vision of the Gulf state to the world – of a progressive, Western-friendly, pro-business beacon of stability in a turbulent neighbourhood. The reality of life in the UAE for Anamul, his brother and millions of others was very different.

'There was an agent. He took me to the agency. An interview, a medical test then took my passport and money and said they'd give me the visa,' Anamul recalls. Every Bangladeshi who is working in the Middle East finds their job through an employment agency. It cost Anamul 'two lakh, 10,000 taka', around £2,000 – an absolute fortune in Bangladeshi terms (one lakh, a unit of counting from India, equals 100,000 taka). He found the money by selling off most of his land and borrowing the rest from friends and family. 'With interest,' he points out. He was soon on a plane and on his way to Dubai for a job as an electrician with BK Gulf, a joint venture between local firm Dutco and Balfour Beatty, a British engineering giant that trades on the FTSE 250. 'I didn't know anything about the conditions before going there,' he says. 'I was a little excited because I was going to my new country for a new job, but worried as I was leaving my family.'

Life was hard for Anamul in the UAE. Migrant workers who arrive in Gulf states are subject to something called *kafala,* a system that places the responsibility for each worker in the hands of his or her employer. It means 'sponsorship' in Arabic and gives the employer, or the company, incredible power over those who work for them. It means that people cannot change jobs without their employer's permission, and in the cases of Saudi Arabia and Qatar workers can't even leave the country without their employer's permission. The system has been derided by human rights organisations as a form of modern-day slavery that has facilitated large-scale labour abuses across the region, including the UAE. At the airport Anamul's employer took away his passport. He'd work 12 hour days, six days a week. He lived in a labour camp, six to a room, separated from the rest of the country, earning $200 a month. There wasn't enough food or water. Temperatures in the summer reached 50 degrees and didn't dip far below that in spring or autumn. There were hundreds of Bangladeshis working alongside him, but he soon noticed a hierarchy of both wages and treatment. 'Indians, Sri Lankans, Filipinos, they all got treated very well and paid more,' Anamul realised. 'Everyone was in a comfortable situation apart from the Bangladeshis.' The Bangladeshi workers were paid the worst money, given the worst accommodation and treated more harshly by their Indian bosses. 'Everyone complained about their wages,' says Anamul, which were two-thirds of what the agent had originally promised. But it was too late to go home: he had no land left and owed a huge amount, which he was still trying to pay off. Going home would mean his family lost everything. Anamul had no choice but to stay – until a potential way out presented itself. In 2013 he was moved from Dubai to work on a new project in Abu Dhabi, the country's capital, a two-hour bus ride away.

Abu Dhabi was investing billions of dollars of its remaining oil wealth in becoming a world-leading cultural hub, through sport, the arts and education. It had secured a Formula 1 Grand Prix and built a state-of-the-art racetrack. It was building outposts of both New York's Guggenheim and Paris' Louvre museums. The country's deputy prime minister had bought and transformed English Premier League side Manchester City into champions. And now a deal had been signed with New York University to build a new campus in Abu Dhabi – a project that would be overseen by Mubadala, a sovereign wealth fund of Abu Dhabi. Its CEO, Khaldoon al Mubarak, would sit on the NYU trustee board back in New York as well as overseeing one of his other main jobs, as chairman of Manchester City FC. The Abu Dhabi government sweetened the deal by offering $50 million.

The move was highly controversial in the US. 'It is arguably an oppressive regime, which has been accused of torturing political prisoners, looking the other way at abusive labor conditions for migrant workers and discriminating against homosexuals,' wrote *New York Times* financial columnist Andrew Ross Sorkin. 'By selling a degraded clone of itself to the highest bidder, NYU is doing irreversible damage to US universities as a whole,' Sorkin quoted from an Abe Greenwald article in *Commentary* magazine.

Still, the project went ahead, and Anamul was sent to it with a promise of more money. His brother, too, joined him at this point. 'I was very happy that I would get double salary,' Anamul says. 'But when I started I found that no, we didn't make any new agreement. They said it was "processing". I decided to go to BK Gulf head office. The manager was from India. I met with him. They told me several times it would happen. But there was no contract with the company.' The money never arrived. Instead, the worst-paid workers – almost all from Bangladesh – became more and more disillusioned with the bad wages, poor conditions and terrible treatment. Eventually, someone had enough and organised a strike. Unionisation and strikes are both illegal in the UAE. 'Someone had printed leaflets and left them in the toilet, saying there would be a strike,' Anamul recalls. 'We didn't know who had organised this, but we knew it was happening.' One morning, there were more leaflets at the camp. The workers refused to board the bus to the site. The next day representatives from the company came by and asked them what the workers wanted. The workers wanted 65 dirhams extra a month, about £13. 'The company refused,' Anamul says. 'There was bargaining among the Bangladeshis and the company people and then some photographer was there who took some photos.' It was to be the two brothers' last day of freedom in the UAE. The next day the police and special branch arrived looking for the ringleaders and arrested anyone they found in the camp. In total, 300 men were taken to the police station. 'They took me!' Anamul fumes, still angry about it. 'They took everyone whether they were involved or not, and they took us to the jail.'

Inside prison they were beaten, denied lawyers and not given food or water. 'In the jail some Arabian-dressed people – we don't know who they were – they took us into several rooms. They wanted to know the leader,' Anamul says of his time inside. 'Truly, even now we don't know who was the leader. They slapped us, but didn't beat us that much.

They took our signatures on a blank piece of paper. They told us to sign it.' After signing the blank piece of paper, the two brothers spent the next ten days in jail, bruised, hungry and thirsty. As Bangladeshis they were treated worse than other prisoners. Finally, someone from the company building NYU's new campus on Saadiyat Island, off the coast of Abu Dhabi, came with their passports. They were being deported.

2.

Just as with Abramovich's purchase of Chelsea in July 2003, football made another financial leap forward in September 2008. When the Abu Dhabi United Group announced its purchase of Manchester City, some commented, tongue in cheek, that perhaps they had bought the wrong club.

Few outside of the Middle East had heard of the man behind City's purchase: Sheikh Mansour bin Zayed al Nahyan, a key member of the royal family of Abu Dhabi, the capital city and most powerful emirate of seven that make up the UAE. The Nahyan clan were also the world's second-richest royal family thanks to their access to the seventh-largest oil reserve in the world; their fortune was estimated to be as much as $1 trillion. Sheikh Mansour was one of 19 sons sired by Sheikh Zayed, the UAE's revered first president who founded the nation after British colonial rule in 1971 and persuaded the heads of the six other royal families that would make up the UAE – Dubai, Sharjah, Fujairah, Ajman, Ras al Khaimah and Umm al Qwuain – to bury their dislike for each other and unite. Mansour was the half-brother to the next UAE president, Sheikh Khalifa bin Zayed al Nahyan, who took the position when Sheikh Zayed died in 2004.

Until his decision to purchase Manchester City, Sheikh Mansour was known for his role in helping to run the UAE. As the son of the former king, he held vitally important positions within the ruling royal family. He was the Minister for Presidential Affairs, a position that essentially advised the president on matters of state. With reporting on the royal family heavily restricted in the UAE, little information was publicly available. Although a telegram sent by the US embassy in Abu Dhabi to the CIA and US Secretary of State in 2004 – later released by Wikileaks – filled in some of the gaps. Sheikh Mansour had studied English at Santa Barbara Community College, California, in 1989, before returning to the UAE to gain a degree in international affairs in 1993. 'He speaks English well,' read the cable, entitled 'UAE: Biographies of New Cabinet Members'. 'But his academic record was poor.'

The cable also revealed just how crucial Sheikh Mansour's role in the country's politics was. As was the case throughout the country, trusted members of the Al Nahyan family had been placed in charge of various sovereign investment vehicles set up to diversify the state's oil wealth. Sheikh Mansour was appointed chairman of the International Petroleum Investment Company (IPIC), at $70 billion the UAE's second-largest sovereign wealth fund, dedicated to investing in the energy sector. He was also part of an important Emirati clique that became known as 'Bani Fatima', one of the former leader Sheikh Zayed's six sons born to Zayed's favourite wife, Fatima, who enjoyed an elevated status.

Equally as important, 'Sheikh Mansour was a powerful behind-the-scenes player in controlling access to Sheikh Zayed through the President's Office,' the cable read. 'Press clippings have announced that Sheikh Mansour, as Minister for Presidential Affairs, will be Sheikh Khalifa's chief adviser in all issues.' He would later be appointed deputy prime minister of the UAE in 2009. His brother is Sheikh Mohamed bin Zayed al Nahyan, also one of the six Bani Fatima, and the crown prince of Abu Dhabi. Sheikh Mohamed bin Zayed controls the UAE's armed forces and will be the next leader of the UAE. In fact, he's considered by many to already be the *de facto* leader of the UAE after Sheikh Khalifa had a stroke in 2014 and hasn't been seen much in public since. 'Long before that,' Bloomberg wrote in a 2014 profile, 'MBZ [Mohamed bin Zayed] was the prime mover on security, and the point-person for Washington.'

With so much on his plate, you would think there wouldn't be enough time in the day for Sheikh Mansour to purchase and run a top-level English football club, but the sale went through with a team headed by a young Emirati businessman who had become the face of football's new economic world order. While Sheikh Mansour had built a powerful career from working behind the scenes, Sulaiman al Fahim was the exact opposite. He was in his early thirties and a brash real-estate investor who had his own TV series called *The Hydra Executives*, a thinly disguised copy of *The Apprentice*. Al Fahim took the Donald Trump role, but with added chintz. He'd replaced the catchphrase 'you're fired' with 'impress me'. When it emerged that he was brokering a deal on behalf of ADUG for Manchester City, Al Fahim made a slew of boasts about the new owners' wealth and desire to sign the most expensive players in world football. 'Ronaldo has said he wants to play for the biggest club in the world, so we will see in January if he is serious,' Al Fahim said shortly after the purchase. 'We are going to be the biggest club in the world, bigger than both Real Madrid and Manchester United.'

When City's shell-shocked fans arrived at the City of Manchester Stadium for their first home game as a newly knighted, genuine footballing superpower, many wore tea towels on their heads, aping the Gulf's traditional male headdress. Some waved wads of freshly minted £20 notes, the Queen's face replaced by Al Fahim's grin, the number 20 replaced by 500 billion. In those crazy, whirlwind few days, Al Fahim was the embodiment of English football's newfound economic confidence: arrogant and unstoppable. 'I always feel like I'm a kind of bulldozer, a fully insured bulldozer,' he said after the sale. 'If nobody likes it, it starts moving – even if there are cars in its way, it has to crush the cars and move. I can't stop. If I have an idea, I have to do it.'

A few weeks after the purchase of Manchester City, I met Al Fahim in Dubai. He was at a property show, promoting several developments that his company Hydra were investing in. He arrived with his sycophantic entourage, wearing traditional Emirati dress: a blue *kandora* (a long, ankle-length, dress shirt) and white headscarf. After we sat down, and his staff had told me how much money he had made that year, he discussed the biggest deal of his life and how he had suddenly, and briefly, become one of the most famous men in football. 'I was the one who did the deal, I was the one who closed the deal,' he said. 'And then I find myself as chairman, as owner, even our official press release said I was the owner. It was nice, I like it. I like it when they put my picture in the news!'

The question was, why did Sheikh Mansour buy the club? Although he already owned a club – his local Abu Dhabi-based team Al Jazira, who play in the UAE league – his low profile and the kind of aversion to publicity reserved for the truly super-rich seemed to suggest that ego wasn't the key driver to owning Manchester City. One clue lay in the open letter he wrote to City fans after the purchase, in which he set out modest aims for the club, dampening down the fury and excitement that had followed Al Fahim's whirlwind few days fronting the deal. He also made clear that he was buying the club in a personal capacity, and not as part of one of Abu Dhabi's many investment vehicles or government agencies. Instead, profit was given as the prime motivator: 'In cold business terms, Premiership football is one of the best entertainment products in the world and we see this as a sound business investment.' Of course, this raised more questions than answers. Why would one of the richest men in the world invest in an industry that involved huge outlays of money for a tiny return on that investment? There were far more promising investments in the world than English football clubs. Although there were other benefits, not least one-upmanship in the intense competition between the UAE's two most powerful emirates.

Until the discovery of oil in 1953, the Trucial States, as they were then known, were a loose alliance of poor Sheikdoms that stretched from Oman to the eastern Saudi coast under treaty protection offered by the British government. By the 1960s the British had concluded that they could no longer afford the military upkeep of protecting the Gulf, starting a process of decolonisation that saw the seven royal families, alongside Qatar and Bahrain, negotiating a loose federation, which quickly fell apart. With the British treaty about to run out in December 1971, Qatar and Bahrain both declared independence in the summer before the deadline, while the rest came together to form the UAE, with Abu Dhabi – as its richest, most populous emirate – as capital. That act of statesmanship was attributed to the skill of Abu Dhabi's ruler, and the UAE's first president, Sheikh Zayed, who modernised the country using its extraordinary oil wealth. Its citizens were given generous benefits: housing, education, even money when they got married. The flipside was: there would be no democracy. That was the deal. The country would be, essentially, a huge patronage network; a state that gave generously to its tiny number of citizens. Absolute loyalty was expected in return. Meanwhile, Sheikh Zayed's thirst for greater centralisation of power meant that tensions would remain between the two royal families of the two biggest emirates: the Nahyans of Abu Dhabi and the Maktoums of Dubai.

By the 1990s, and shorn of any foreign policy obligations, not to mention the other responsibilities of state, Dubai focused on trade. Under the effective rule of its young, Western-friendly ruler Sheikh Mohammed bin Rashid al Maktoum (who oversaw Dubai's remarkable transformation while his shy brother Sheikh Maktoum bin Rashid al Maktoum was technically in charge until his death in 2006) marketed itself to a global audience as a glitzy place to live, buy property and holiday – despite being part of a rigidly Islamic legal system, and whose summer months were too hot to even step outside in. It was a necessary economic move. Abu Dhabi had most of the oil – 95 per cent of the country's oil reserves, which in itself made up between 7 and 9 per cent of the entire world's oil reserves – and the real power. Dubai's oil reserves were tiny in comparison and would soon run out. By 2006 just 6 per cent of Dubai's economy was dependent on hydrocarbons. Dubai had been so successful in its global promotion that, as Al Fahim explained, people thought Dubai was a country in itself. It had achieved this type of international exposure with the help of sport, especially sponsorship of club shirts and stadiums, and even the FIFA World Cup, through Dubai government-owned and controlled companies like Emirates Airlines.

Abu Dhabi, by comparison, was seen as staid: Dubai's quiet, boring older brother. The place where the country's embassies were situated, but little else. So when the leader of Dubai, Sheikh Mohammed – a man who loved horseracing and had spent millions of pounds building the Godolphin racing stables in Newmarket – attempted to purchase Liverpool FC in 2007 through a sovereign investment vehicle, Dubai Investment Capital, it was seen as the next logical step: soft power and promotion through football. Sheikh Mohammed, the absolute ruler of Dubai, vice-president of the UAE and one of the richest men in the world, had seen the benefits of owning a football club and using it to enhance 'Brand Dubai'. But the deal floundered as the negotiations dragged on. 'We had quite a few false starts with people claiming they could introduce us to senior sheikhs and it turned out they couldn't,' said Rick Parry, Liverpool's then chief executive, in an interview with the *Liverpool Echo*. 'It wasn't that uncommon to go for two days and come back not having met anyone at all. We spent so much time kissing frogs and wasting time.' Parry had been convinced that the purchase of Chelsea by Roman Abramovich had changed the game. The huge amounts of money spent transforming Chelsea into champions – with little regard for profit or loss – had never been seen before. Where Jack Walker's spending on Blackburn Rovers, unmoored by the usual economic rationale but tethered to his deep love of the club, shook England's big clubs, Abramovich terrified the likes of Liverpool. And Parry wanted to compete. But after 18 months of negotiations, and with Liverpool feeling that DIC's chairman Sameer al Ansari was dragging his feet, the club instead turned to Tom Hicks and George Gillett. 'I dearly wish that the rulers of Dubai had been committed to the project. We flew out to Dubai around October [2006], ostensibly to meet the Maktoum family, and lo and behold we didn't meet any Maktoums,' said Parry, later defending a decision that almost brought the club to its knees thanks to its two American owners. 'To say we should have gone with DIC is complete and utter nonsense. That would have been a disaster too.'

Parry was right. The world was careering towards a global financial meltdown, triggered by a banking scam involving toxic mortgages in the US. When it hit, and asset prices tumbled, Dubai was hugely exposed. The emirate had largely relied on real estate and debt to fuel its great leap forward, while Abu Dhabi had the actual money in the bank from years of high oil prices. Dubai's economy collapsed and a humiliating bailout had to be brokered with Abu Dhabi. The UAE president, Sheikh Khalifa, convened a meeting between Dubai's Sheikh Mohammed and Abu Dhabi's Sheikh Mohamed bin Zayed over which projects should be scaled back in the capital to save Dubai. A deal was agreed. In return Sheikh Mohammed agreed to name his prestigious new building project – Burj Dubai, the tallest building in the world – the Burj Khalifa. Meanwhile, Abu Dhabi went on a spending spree, sensing there were bargains to be had. The biggest was Barclays Bank. While the British banking sector needed a huge government bailout of £500 billion, Barclays sought overseas investors instead. Sheikh Mansour agreed to invest £3.5 billion and Barclays was eventually saved without the need of British taxpayers' money. There was some confusion over whether Sheikh Mansour invested in Barclays personally or whether it was on behalf of Abu Dhabi's IPIC sovereign fund. Either way, the profit on the deal was anywhere between £2.25 and £3.1 billion. DIC, the investment vehicle that tried to buy Liverpool, had fallen on hard times and could no longer service its debts. In April 2016 it was announced that DIC would close once its remaining assets were sold.

But Abu Dhabi had watched the attempted purchase of Liverpool closely. 'It's a very good opportunity for Abu Dhabi to be in the Premier League. Everyone here loves the Premier League,' Al Fahim said of Sheikh Mansour's successful purchase. 'Man City is one of those clubs that has real big fans in the UK. It's not just about buying the best, most profitable club. Football is a passion but you have to buy a club people will really love. And then you need to make a plan to get it into the top five.' By now, though, Sheikh Mansour had grown tired of Al Fahim's notoriety, and he was quietly moved off the project, replaced by Khaldoon al Mubarak, the CEO of Mubadala, another Abu Dhabi sovereign wealth fund charged with diversifying the economy away from oil. He had a long history of political connections too: as a member of Abu Dhabi's 14-person Executive Council and chair of the Executive Affairs Authority. His father, Khalifa Ahmed Abdel Aziz al Mubarak, the former UAE ambassador to France, was assassinated in 1984 by the Abu Nidal Organisation, run by the eponymous Palestinian terrorist who fought any compromise with Israel.

The younger Mubarak rose quickly and by the age of just 27 was appointed to Abu Dhabi's Executive Council after the death of Sheikh Zayed in 2004. A US embassy cable to Washington, later released by Wikileaks, gave a brief biography of this unknown appointee. 'He is said to be very close to Sheikh Mohammed bin Zayed,' it concluded. At City it was felt a steadier pair of hands was needed, although Al Fahim denied he was moved on, insisting that he was only ever there 'to bring this opportunity and to bring it in time, in less than three weeks'. He had nothing but praise for his replacement. 'I don't like to interfere,' Al Fahim said. 'Mubarak, he knows the players. It depends on the management. They are focusing on the ten-year plan. They are looking for good, talented British players. I hope, what's his name? Mark Hughes and Gerry [sic] Cook and Khaldoon Mubarak pick good players.' He signed off with a typically grand flourish. 'I have to go and pick up Antonio Banderas at 2 p.m.,' he said, 'in my Lamborghini.'

A few days later City finalised the purchase of Brazilian international Robinho for a then staggering £32.5 million, just before the transfer window shut. When it opened again in the following January, the club spent another £50 million. Over the course of eight years, Sheikh Mansour has achieved his goal: the club have won two Premier League titles, played regular Champions League football, transformed the stadium, the facilities and the surrounding area. The cost has been huge: more than £1 billion spent, with UEFA having to intervene to prevent billionaire owners from bankrolling clubs to success in such a short time – what then president Michel Platini called 'financial doping'. Financial Fair Play (FFP) was brought in to try to limit the amount of money clubs lost so that they spent only what they earned. In 2011, and with UEFA implementing FFP, City made the largest single season loss in the history of English football, £197 million. The club had handed coach Roberto Mancini a huge war chest to invest in Champions League success. Nearly £160 million went on players alone: including £27 million on Bosnian striker Edin Dzeko, £26 million on Spain international David Silva and £24 million on Mario Balotelli. So the stadium's naming rights were sold, and in 2011 the City of Manchester Stadium, a government-funded project built for the 2002 Commonwealth Games at a cost of £112 million, became the Etihad Stadium, named after the national carrier of the UAE, for a price of £400 million in a ten-year deal that included shirt sponsorship and the building of infrastructure and youth-team projects around the ground. UEFA, which had rules preventing excessively inflated contracts, accepted the deal. Etihad Airways is wholly owned by the Abu Dhabi government. The president of its board of directors is Sheikh Hamed bin Zayed al Nahyan, half-brother of Sheikh Mansour. He sits on the Executive Council of Abu Dhabi alongside Manchester City chairman Khaldoon al Mubarak. Despite the obvious connections back in the Middle East, UEFA eventually approved the deal as representing market value. At the time, that looked fanciful, but the TV-funded economics of English football have continued to defy gravity. 'If we accept a case for City's shirt [sponsorship] deal being worth £20 million now, it could be £40 million in 2021. Or more,' argued football finance expert Nick Harris. 'What if it stepped up each year over the next decade, from £20 million to £22 million to £24 million to £26 million [and incrementally all the way up] to £37 million to £40 million? That's £293 million – just for the shirt deal.' If anything, he argued, City may have undervalued the potential for growth. 'Suddenly £20 million a year on average for the shirt (or £200 million over ten years) doesn't look so outrageous.'

The problem was that, for all the glitz and positive images of the UAE – of stable, prosperous, Western-facing, forward-looking cities like Abu Dhabi and Dubai – the reality was very different for the majority of the population. While oil and, to a lesser extent in the UAE, natural gas, provided the country with very deep pockets, it would take manpower to realise the sheikhs' grand ambitions. That involved importing huge amounts of migrant labourers, mainly from India, Bangladesh and Pakistan, but also from the rest of the region, to build the skyscrapers, malls and airports that they dreamed of. These workers would toil in tough, unforgiving conditions, in 50-degree heat. They would live in labour camps, with guards at the doors, living six, eight, ten to a room in often filthy conditions. The labour camps themselves could be bought and sold in the classified ads at the back of local newspapers. On their one day off each week the labourers would often be banned from the malls and hotels they built, even when there was no other public space to go to. But it was all an inevitable and necessary step towards development, residents told themselves. Workers were here because they made more money, wired remittances home and then left when they'd built their new family homes back in their villages.

For many labourers, drivers and maids, the *kafala* system that was meant to make that happen turned out to be an illusion. Among all the wealth, migrant workers were often paid less than $200 a month. Like Anamul and his brother, they lived in isolated faraway camps, were treated like third-class residents, and would have their passports taken away by their employer so they couldn't leave. It was illegal to strike or to change job. And the labourers would often be deeply in debt having borrowed money to pay the recruitment consultants in their home country, making it impossible for them to leave, creating a form of indentured slavery. They were, effectively, trapped in jobs no matter how badly they were treated. 'Agencies charged the men fees of up to $4,100 – nine times the average income of some workers' home countries,' said an early Human Rights Watch report on migrant labour conditions in the UAE. 'To pay the agencies' fees, workers borrowed money from relatives, raised cash by selling their farmland, livestock and homes, or took out loans from money lenders often at high interest rates. UAE law prohibits employers from working with agencies that charge workers recruiting fees.' And besides, many of the workers were illiterate, and found they had no bargaining position at all when it came to their contract. 'Workers are effectively working in conditions of forced labour: they were fraudulently lured to work in the UAE, had to work in order to pay off debts incurred to obtain their job, cannot flee the country because their employers have confiscated their passports upon arrival in the UAE and threatened them with illegal penalties if they quit their jobs,' Human Rights Watch said.

The vast majority of labourers are unskilled, moving heavy objects from one area of a building site to another for up to 12 hours a day, six days a week, in temperatures that most people would find difficult to walk in. Unexplained deaths caused by heart attacks among seemingly fit young workers rocketed. In 2004 the embassies of India, Pakistan and Bangladesh in the UAE sent 880 bodies of construction workers home from Dubai. Yet Dubai only officially recorded 34 construction deaths. By 2006 the UAE authorities vowed to get a grip on a problem that was staining their country's reputation. Sheikh Mohammed, the ruler of Dubai, ordered his labour minister to enact a series of legal reforms based on Human Rights Watch's scathing report and subsequent recommendations.

Meanwhile, Sheikh Mansour was now shaking hands with some of the world's most powerful men in his role as one of the UAE's deputy prime ministers – and gatekeeper to the president. He would be the man to greet statesmen when they came to Abu Dhabi, whether it was Chechnya's warlord-leader Ramzan Kadyrov or Hamas' political chief Khaled Mashal. Sheikh Mansour had acquired the deputy prime minister role in a bizarre fashion. In 2009 a court case in the US led eventually to the release of an extraordinary video tape. In it Sheikh Issa bin Zayed al Nahyan, a son of Sheikh Zayed and a half-brother of Sheikh Mansour, was seen torturing an Afghan grain merchant, beating him with wooden planks studded with nails, before running him over in his SUV, then raping him with an electric cattle prod and finally setting fire to his genitals. All this, while police officers can be seen standing nearby. Then US secretary of state Hillary Clinton said that she could not 'describe the horror and revulsion I felt when witnessing what is on this video . . . I could not watch it without constantly flinching.' After initially ignoring the tape, the UAE authorities eventually announced that Sheikh Issa would stand trial over the allegations – the first time a member of the royal family had been so publicly defenestrated. The UAE president, Sheikh Khalifa, fired Sheikh Issa's two brothers from the federal cabinet, both of whom had been deputy prime ministers. No explanation was given for the sackings and Sheikh Mansour was promoted in one of their places. Sheikh Issa was eventually acquitted by the UAE court on all charges. Instead, the court found the man being tortured in the video, Bassam Nabulsi, guilty of blackmailing Sheikh Issa after 'he and his brother had secretly injected Issa with drugs, thus rendering him incapable of having responsibility for his actions'. They sentenced Nabulsi to five years *in absentia*. 'I am feeling nauseous. It is really sarcastic. These people, the more they lie, the bigger the hole they are digging for themselves,' Nabulsi said after the verdict. 'They act like Al Capone in Chicago in the 1920s. No one can stop them.'

Sheikh Mansour, meanwhile, was soon taking on meatier roles and had also taken charge of two key projects, according to files released by Wikileaks. The first was to end the trafficking, detention, mistreatment and torture of underage camel jockeys. The second, revealed in a cable written by the then US ambassador, detailed how Sheikh Mansour had indicated that tentative steps towards democracy were taking place and that Khaldoon al Mubarak had been sent out to the villages and towns of Abu Dhabi to talk to tribal leaders about introducing limited suffrage. But all talk of democratisation ended abruptly in 2011.

The Arab Spring had begun. A wave of protests toppled leaders in Tunisia, Yemen and Egypt – and sparked civil war and the rise of Isis in Syria and Iraq. The chaos terrified the Gulf states: autocratic, absolute monarchies that could only keep power by essentially bribing their nationals with fabulous oil-funded benefits in return for their consent to rule. For the Gulf autocracies, the Muslim Brotherhood was, according to the UAE's crown prince Sheikh Mohamed bin Zayed, an 'existential threat'. The Muslim Brotherhood is a global

Islamist organisation born in Egypt in 1928. Mohamed Morsi, a Brotherhood-aligned candidate, won Egypt's first post-Mubarak presidential election in June 2012. Seven weeks later the UAE's ruler, Sheikh Khalifa, passed 'Federal Decree No.5', a media law that could be so widely interpreted that virtually any opinion the government disagreed with could lead to jail or a million-dirham fine (around £200,000). One article of the law banned any electronic communication 'deriding or harming the reputation, stature, or status of the state, any of its institutions, its president or vice president, the rulers of the emirates, their crown princes or their deputies, the state flag, national safety, its motto, its national anthem, or its symbols'. Another outlawed Emiratis from speaking to 'outside groups', a reference to human rights groups and foreign journalists highlighting the UAE's behaviour.

In their 2014 report 'There Is No Freedom Here: Silencing Dissent in the UAE', Amnesty International described how rights and freedoms had significantly fallen away since the Arab Spring. 'Activists who dare to challenge the authorities or speak out in favour of greater democracy and government accountability are thrown into jail,' the report stated. In other cases, there was an even more insidious form of punishment: 'The authorities have arbitrarily withdrawn individuals' UAE citizenship, depriving them of the rights and privileges associated with that status in the UAE and rendering them stateless.' Dr Ahmed al Zaabi, a former university professor and judge who was one of the so-called UAE 94 – a group of lawyers, activists and teachers, some with Brotherhood connections, some not, who had been arrested – detailed how he was tortured in jail. '[I have] some signs of beating on my left foot sole and bruises on [my] nails. Officers in the State Security beat me. They tied my feet with a machine that lifts feet . . . to make me confirm what they have written in their report. I was blindfolded and I did not see who inflicted the injury or who beat me.'

Any semblance of reform was sacrificed in the name of national security. After Morsi's election in Egypt, the UAE allegedly threatened to revoke trade deals with the UK. The regime's fear of the Brotherhood was such that outlandish claims were made in an effort to steer the UK government away from Cairo. Shortly before Sheikh Mohamed bin Zayed flew to London to meet British prime minister David Cameron in 2012, he was briefed by Simon Pearce, a board member at Manchester City. The paper written by Pearce, according to the Guardian, advised Sheikh Mohamed bin Zayed to tell Cameron that the BBC had been infiltrated by the Brotherhood and that the prime minister should rein it in. It also laid out a series of inducements for British businesses if they played ball, and punishments if they didn't.

Even after Morsi was removed in a 2013 coup, the UAE remained unhappy with the UK government, believing it to be soft on the Muslim Brotherhood. The UAE had already excluded BP from an important oil deal in Abu Dhabi and pulled out of a £6 billion deal to buy 60 Typhoon fighter jets. That prompted Cameron to order a review in to the Brotherhood's activities, to be undertaken by the UK's former ambassador to Saudi Arabia Sir John Jenkins. His first stop was Abu Dhabi to meet Manchester City's chairman Khaldoon al Mubarak, now Sheikh Mohamed bin Zayed's right-hand man and at the heart of the UAE government. 'The UK will need to consider the political implications when three of its most important allies in the region [Egypt, Saudi Arabia and the UAE] have taken a clear decision regarding the Mbs [Muslim Brotherhood],' the Guardian reported Mubarak as saying. 'Difficult conversations we've been having, will become far more difficult. We are raising a red flag.'

The former ambassador evidently failed to convince Mubarak. A month later the contracts of dozens of British military advisors were not renewed. Mubarak seemed to prefer dealing with a former British prime minister rather than a current one. Tony Blair

Associates had a reported £5 million deal with the UAE government to help advise governments in developing countries. He had also cultivated his contacts in China to secure several deals with Chinese sovereign investment funds.

A few months later, however, David Cameron and Khaldoon al Mubarak were all smiles again when they welcomed Chinese premier Xi Jinping to Manchester City in 2015 and later announced the sale of some of the club's shares to Chinese investors.

**

At the same time as Cameron, Xi and Mubarak were in Manchester, Iyad el-Baghdadi was still coming to terms with the home he had gained, and the home he had lost. Iyad came to prominence during the Arab Spring. His Twitter and Facebook posts – written in English and Arabic and often perceptive and morally compelling – had built him one of the biggest followings in the UAE. He ran an IT company and was a start-up consultant before forming a media agency in Dubai, hiring 'Lebanese, Indians, Arabs, Hindus, Buddhists, Christians' who would, come the Arab Spring, start translating many of the videos coming out of Egypt to a wider audience. 'It felt like the moment my entire generation were waiting for,' he says. 'Before the Arab Spring we never thought that protest could dislodge a dictator. Only violence. So when Tunisia fell that is when we thought everything could change. So I jumped in. I used my resources, editing and translating videos to try to explain our story to the world.'

Iyad was not an Emirati, even though he had spent all his life in the UAE. His father had moved to Dubai to work as a doctor. They were stateless Palestinians, but the UAE in the mid-1970s needed people like Iyad's father. He grew up in a multicultural environment, as more and more nationalities moved to the UAE to take advantage of its tax-free status and growing economy. But his family would never become citizens. Although there is a naturalisation law that allows for foreigners to become a national if they have lived in the UAE for 20 years, never committed a crime and speak Arabic, applications are rarely ever successful, unless you are a sportsman.

But Iyad was not an international footballer. He was a businessman and activist. Being a resident, as 90 per cent of the population are, didn't bestow the same rights as a typical citizen's rights in the West. Your resident permit could be revoked at a moment's notice, even if you were born in the country or had lived there for decades – a handy self-censorship tool for anyone who even thinks about speaking out. 'The insecurity only happened after the Arab Spring,' he recalls. 'And then I started to feel stateless.'

The day after Egyptian president Hosni Mubarak was ousted following continuous protests in Tahrir Square, Iyad was invited to a meeting with a high-level security figure with close links to Sheikh Mohamed bin Zayed. 'He said, "I just need to tell you you are already on the radar. There is a roof and your head is at the roof."' The situation rapidly deteriorated in 2012. 'It seemed the decision-making of the country was taken over by a security clique,' says Iyad. There were mass arrests and deportations, even among well-educated and well-connected Emiratis, some with royal connections. Many Iyad knew: 'These guys were mostly Muslim Brotherhood types. But many were not. Lots were just reformists who submitted a list of demands to the government. A very polite letter wanting reforms. The response was to strip them of their citizenship and put them in jail for ten years. The general effect is fear. Everyone knows any dissent, even opening the question, is not tolerated.'

For a long time Iyad continued to tweet and speak out. But eventually, in 2014, they came for him too. 'I was heading to work and the immigration department said they wanted to talk. I'd been expelled,' he recalls. 'It was not completely surprising [but] I was shocked it would come so soon. The guy said, "You have to go back home." And

I said, "What home?! I live here! I've lived here longer than you have!"'
It was then Iyad was told he was being taken straight to jail. 'There was
no process. No case. No one's testimony heard.'

They sent him to the infamous Al Sadr deportation prison in Abu
Dhabi. There were hundreds of men, mainly from southeast Asia, who
were all being processed for suspected labour violations. 'The worst
thing is to be a Bangladeshi in this jail,' says Iyad. 'If you are Arab, you
are kind of privileged in a UAE jail – you are not being spat on. But if
they mistake you for a non-Arab . . . There is a lot of racism against
Bangladeshis. The Arabs had ten people in a cell; Bangladeshis, 50.' He
witnessed regular beatings and intimidation. Indians, he explains, were
treated better, as they would send a man from the embassy to check on
their citizens. No one from the Bangladeshi embassy ever showed up.
'There were many incidents of violence,' recalls Iyad. 'There was a day
shifting us from one cell to a next. There was just a lot of abuse, lots of
kicking, punching, spitting. Complete impunity. One guard, talking
to another guard, said, "All Bengalis are animals." When the police
behind the counters heard a slap, they would cheer. That was the noise
they wanted.'

By the second week Iyad knew he had to get out fast. As a stateless
Palestinian he might never leave: 'I needed to get out or I'd be in jail for
ten years at least.' In the end, with his family seeking his release, and
Iyad using every contact he could think of, he applied to leave for
Malaysia. It was the only option as it is the only country in the world
that offers visa-free travel to Palestinians. When he arrived in Kuala
Lumpur he was denied entry and had to live in the airport for three
weeks until the Palestinian Authority could issue him the correct
documents. All this time, his wife, who was seven months pregnant,
was waiting to see him in Malaysia. The last time she had seen him was
saying goodbye the morning Iyad had left for work months previously.
His son was born healthy. His dad is now in Norway, applying for
asylum. Iyad had been targeted, he believes, to scare people away from

expressing any opinions or calling for any reforms. 'There is an atmosphere of fear all across the UAE,' he states. But he believes that the rulers' actions will also be counterproductive. The system only works if Emiratis continue to receive cradle-to-grave funding, which is unsustainable in the long term and counterproductive in creating citizens who think for themselves. 'The UAE is a classic rentier state,' says Iyad. 'Ninety-nine per cent of the private sector is non-Emiratis. The political economy is rigged against them. It is easy to get a government job that pays you loads. And it's risk-free. Why start a company when you can get a government job? In the UAE, for Emiratis, the government is your boss. Not only your ruler, but also your boss. What they are terrified of is this: what happens when the government is not your boss too?'

In the UAE everything is connected and nothing is by chance. Business, investment, security and power are all intimately linked. The UAE is one of the least democratic countries on earth. Torture and arbitrary arrest are rife. Workers' rights are trampled on. Citizenship is used as a weapon of punishment. Non-citizens are kept insecure and compliant. At the top are a tiny inter-related elite of royalty whose funds all come from the same place. And in the centre, forming a very different impression in people's minds, is Manchester City FC, which Human Rights Watch believes is helping to launder Abu Dhabi's reputation and to 'construct a public relations image of a progressive, dynamic Gulf state, which deflects attention from what is really going on in the country'.

Iyad knows only too well what is really going on in the Emirates. After 40 years of service in the UAE, his parents were given what he describes as a 'soft expulsion'. The hospital suddenly declined to renew his father's contract and none of his friends could help. There was no explanation. No process. No recourse. 'He's not doing well,' says Iyad of his father, who barely talks any more. 'We are talking to a psychiatrist.'

3. Dhaka, Bangladesh

The armed guard carrying the pump-action shotgun was quick to his feet, and out of the darkness of the lobby where he had been sheltering from the midday heat. The office of *Daily Prothom Alo* in the centre of Bangladesh's capital, Dhaka, has long needed protection. It is one of Bangladesh's most read and most outspoken newspapers with a circulation upwards of four million. Upstairs, inside an empty newsroom, Shariful Hasan is sitting at his desk following up on a lead. He is young, in his early thirties, with unruly black hair, and wears a *kurta,* a traditional top that stretches to his knees, over blue jeans. His mobile phone rings almost constantly, with calls from around the world placed by desperate people in desperate situations.

It is Friday, and should be a day off. But Shariful's phone still rings day and night, from Qatar, the UAE, Malaysia or Thailand. 'Look at these,' Shariful says, pointing to the rows of folders and documents filed behind his desk. 'I've been following the migrant story for nine years. I have all the case studies. Some of these even the government doesn't have.' Each file is a story of someone's exploitation, of someone stuck in a foreign country with no one to turn to. So they turn to Shariful. 'At midnight you are sleeping, and I'll get a call from a worker in the Middle East,' he explains. 'They are crying, saying, "Please, I am in great danger. Do something for me." It is my duty. We have to do something. Their calling doesn't bother me. But when my phone rings I am afraid that it is another Bangladeshi being abused. When they call, I know they are in danger.'

His phone rings again, but this time it is a Bangladeshi TV crew, looking for information about a case of female domestic workers abused in the UAE, the big issue he is working on right now. Such was the level of abuse that Sri Lanka, Indonesia, Uganda, Kenya and Tanzania all banned female workers from seeking employment in the Middle East. Bangladesh, meanwhile, saw it as an opportunity.

According to Bangladesh government statistics, in 2015 20,952 female workers travelled to Saudi Arabia for work. In the first three months of 2016, already 20,036 have left. 'The government get the remittances. According to the World Bank, Bangladesh is number seven in the world. Your reserve is strong. The government is happy.' Over the past nine years Shariful has reported on some of the worst that humanity has to offer. He had stood on the edges of mass graves in Malaysia, full of murdered Bangladeshi migrants who would never be identified. He's visited women seeking shelter in embassies to escape abusive employers. The worst cases have all come from the same region. 'If I was to categorise,' Shariful says, 'the worst conditions are in the Middle East.'

**

Bangladesh's independence coincided with the rise of the Gulf states' oil wealth. Following the 1973 OPEC oil crisis, when the Gulf's oil-producing nations led an embargo, the price of a barrel of crude oil quadrupled. The UAE, Saudi Arabia and (later) Qatar had money to burn and an almost-insatiable appetite for migrant workers – the men who built the towers, pumped the gas and cleaned the malls, while the women were employed to keep the home and tend to the children. Today, Bangladeshi workers are among the largest groups of migrants in all the Gulf, yet as Shariful's row of files show, they are often treated with contempt. Numbers are fluid, but according to the UN over seven million Bangladeshis are living abroad. Well over two million can be found in Saudi Arabia and the UAE.

At first, workers found themselves moving to the Middle East thanks to an informal network of recruitment. A worker in Abu Dhabi or Riyadh would be asked about vacancies at his company, and then recruit friends and family, in effect becoming a recruiter himself. Back home, they were not viewed favourably. 'There was a large degree of antipathy from the state towards migrant workers,' explains Dr

Chowdhury Abrar, director of the Refugee and Migratory Movements Research Unit at the University of Dhaka. 'They were viewed as the lucky ones who had got to the Middle East, even though a good number came back empty-handed and endured all kinds of harassment – not being paid wages, not being placed in their jobs, being arbitrarily deported.' Migrant workers were also depicted in Bangladeshi popular culture as being silly, frivolous individuals with their heads in the clouds. They were often portrayed negatively in teleplays on Bangladeshi television, labelled *Dubaiwallahs*: men who were obsessed with improving their status and would, among other things, demand that the recruitment fees be paid for by any marriage dowry. But the government soon changed its opinion – or at least changed how money was transferred home – as soon as the scale of the money being made was understood. 'The government has been very interested in harnessing the remittances sent by migrant workers,' says Dr Abrar.

The entire system of getting to the Middle East is built on a pyramid scheme of corruption and exploitation, and it works like this. A potential migrant worker is likely to be from a rural area, poor and illiterate. He will need to sell land or borrow money, or both. A fixer is found to do that for a fee. Now in debt, a middle man from his village will arrange for him to first get a passport. 'In theory anyone can get a passport,' says Dr Abrar. 'But I need a police verification. And the policeman will take his sweet time and it may take months for him to sort it out. He may demand money. I am an illiterate worker, so I might struggle. So I need a middle man to make sure that a police report is lodged in my favour.'

Then a visa is needed. That requires a recruitment consultant, who buys the visas and then sends out another middle man to the countryside to find the workers. All in all, there may be 'four or five tiers' according to Dr Abrar, with each tier needing to be paid: 'It is paid as a package but the money is distributed along the line.' The cost for a visa to Qatar is between 350,000 and 400,000 taka, around £3,500. According to the IMF's projected 2016 figures, per capita income in Bangladesh is just over £1,000. There is no guarantee of a job at the other end either. Agencies regularly take the money from 200 people, even if they only have 20 visas. 'They pay the money back,' believes Dr Abrar, 'but by then they have earned interest in that time.'

Corruption is rife. The going bribe to secure a messenger's job in Dhaka, the lowest entry-level job in Bangladesh, is between 300,000 and 400,000 taka. It requires a little more to secure a job as a police constable. Government jobs are even more costly. One university graduate, who requested not to be named for fear of harming their employment chances, had passed two of the civil service's gruelling entrance exams. Next came the interview stage, which wasn't really an interview at all. When potential recruits meet the examiner for their face-to-face interview, they will be expected to hand over a bribe of 1.2 million taka, around £12,000. The monthly salary is 20,000 taka, around £200. 'But you make it up elsewhere,' the graduate explained. By making it up, they mean by extracting bribes when the next person is hired, with smaller bribes further down the food chain. And the cycle continues. 'Bangladesh is one of the most corrupt countries in the world,' says Dr Abrar. In Transparency International's 2016 Corruption Perception Index, Bangladesh is ranked 145th out of 176.

If the worker makes it to the Middle East, they then face the myriad other problems (the heat, non-payment of wages, treatment as a third-class resident, appalling conditions of work and accommodation). But unlike other countries, the Bangladeshi embassies are slow to help. 'They do not stand up for the migrants with as much strength and support as they should,' says Dr Abrar.

Why? I ask.

'We are always fearful as a country if we speak too much about rights and good treatment of migrant workers we would lose the labour market,' he replies. 'We negotiate from a very weak position without realising that they *need* our labour force.' Dr Abrar has witnessed the conditions in the fastest growing destination for migrant workers in Bangladesh, Qatar – a major destination because of the huge building projects surrounding the 2022 World Cup finals (according to government figures, 211,000 Bangladeshis left for Qatar in 2014 and 2015, almost half of the entire number of visas issues for Qatar since 1976) – 'I visited and there is a large number of Bangladeshi workers unemployed, unpaid, who have paid hefty amounts to go, and then there's no job,' he says. For officials in Gulf states, this problem is largely down to the middle men, but for Dr Abrar that doesn't make sense. The governments in the Middle East have to issue the visas. Someone, in those governments, he says, is getting very rich: 'These are countries where the state is all powerful. If they do not allow [the middle men] to operate, they can't. There is a collusion of state agencies and private companies and the middle men. They are in a state of denial. It is a royal family and big companies involved in recruitment. There is, of course, collusion.'

In Bangladesh, however, the recruitment industry is a powerful lobby. It is effectively responsible for as much as 10 per cent of the country's GDP. 'They have MPs, they fund political parties, one minister makes his money from fleecing workers,' says Dr Abrar. Meanwhile, the workers themselves – some of the poorest, most vulnerable people in Asia – continue to leave for the Middle East, believing that they will be the lucky ones and that these scare stories won't happen to them. 'When they see a house being built by a successful migrant, who in two years is able to send his kids to a good school, he gets carried away with the demonstration effect,' Abrar says. 'They forget the other three failures in the village.'

Yet for Shariful at the *Daily Prothom Alo*, the effect of this corrupt, dysfunctional, impossibly byzantine system isn't about growth statistics or skills and training policy. It is about the body bags and ruined lives.

He goes to the Hazrat Shahjalal International Airport every week. Every day its departure hall is full of thousands of hopeful workers leaving for a new life in the Gulf. Every week, Shariful has stood and counted the bodies as they have returned: eight to ten bodies every day from the Middle East; every year more than 3,000 dead – 15,000 since he started counting. 'The people going to the Middle East, they are not just remittance machines. They are human beings. They have a life. They have their respect,' he says, now close to tears. 'When he is going, he's only thinking, "I've paid five lakh [500,000 taka, around £5,000]. I need to earn that money." What happens? Heart attacks. Heart disease. Aged 32, 33? How can a man of 25 die of a heart attack? Why? He is working 18 to 20 hours under pressure, working in the heat, worried about money. And his owner is not a good human being.' Shariful's voice breaks as he lists the indignations he has seen and reported on. He has been threatened several times for his work, especially in exposing the links between politicians, businessmen and the powerful recruitment agents, all of whom he believes are in business with the governments of the Middle East. 'There are many powerful groups there,' Shariful says. 'And the condition of democracy and the free press is well known.'

There has at least been one positive change. The 2022 World Cup has seen a positive effect in Qatar, he believes. Workers are now choosing to go there rather than the UAE. 'Compared to the UAE and Saudi, Qatar is in a good condition,' Shariful reckons. 'They are sending the wages of workers into bank accounts. There's a toll-free number to call [to report labour violations]; a human rights office. If you make a complaint, they investigate the case. They are taking actions, which is absent in the UAE. Because of the focus of the World Cup, everyone is looking at Qatar.' Qatar still has problems, he knows, not least the criminally low wages paid by one of the richest countries in the world, but Shariful is hopeful this will focus attention elsewhere, on countries that have got away without any real scrutiny: 'The whole world is focusing on Qatar . . . but we need to focus the same on the UAE.'

The blame, for Shariful, Dr Abrar and others, is a difficult thing to place. There are so many fingers in so many pies that it is hard to pin it on any one actor, or any one country.

'Who is responsible is the critical question,' says Shariful. 'I would blame the person violating the rights first. The person who is doing the torturing, he is responsible. And then it is his government who is responsible, because if he tortures and they are not taking action they will keep repeating their actions.' While the narrative in the West, and in the Middle East, has been of migrant labourers toughing it out for a few years to return home as heroes, building homes and educating their kids so they don't have to follow suit, the reality is rarely even close to that. Instead, so many people come back broken that Shariful believes it is having a significant effect on Bangladesh's psychological health, and could even be contributing to the growing Islamic radicalisation in the country: 'When the dead bodies come back to Bangladesh, they were usually the only people earning, so the whole family is in a worse condition. His children, for their whole life, know their father died in the UAE. Ask the people with long-term conditions. They spent their whole life in the Middle East, psychologically alone. Long term the country gets the remittances, the reserve is strong. But what happens in 20 years, when those millions come home?'

We had spoken for over an hour, with Shariful's phone ringing every few minutes, almost as many times as the building's power cut out and his computer screen went blank. He led me out to the street, past the armed guard who now nodded with a smile, and pointed towards a row of identical motorbikes, although it was clear which one was Shariful's – the one with the sign 'PRESS' printed on the visor, a brave move in a country where free thought and expression had become increasingly dangerous. He handed me a helmet and asked me to get on the back. His bike slalomed through Dhaka's gridlocked streets, where traffic moved at the pace of tectonic plates, even at the weekends. 'You will have to meet Noyon,' shouted Shariful. 'He has a story to tell.'

**

The office of Ovibashi Enterprise can be found in Bosila Garden City, which is known as a new suburb of Dhaka but already looks worn and abandoned. It sits next to the Buriganga River that skirts the southwest of the city, and which was once Dhaka's most important waterway for trade and transport. Today, the river is almost extinct after the many tanneries and factories that line its banks further upstream have spent years pouring thousands of tonnes of effluent directly into its waters.

Mohammed al Amin Noyon's one-storey building stands alone, away from other buildings, a short walk from Bosila's main mosque. Children play in the dirt road outside, while men with long, henna-dyed red beards walk past on their way to pray, eyeing us suspiciously. Noyon unlocks his front gate and invites us into his office, which consists of two large rooms and a squat toilet. One room is full of packets of spicy nuts, noodles and a candle-making machine covered in yellowish wax at the back; the other has a desk, two chairs and a wall full of pictures of Noyon with a selection of local dignitaries and UN apparatchiks. 'We make all these products, and give jobs to the men who come back,' says Noyon, a short, balding, muscular man who seems to be constantly cheerful. 'This is our slogan,' he says, pointing to a long phrase in Bangla pinned to the wall. 'It means, "I'm a man. I can do it. I will do it. I have to do it."'

Do what? I ask.

'Break free of exploitation,' he replies, handing me a packet of the nuts that his small company makes, prompting me to taste. On the packet is written: 'No Slave in Foreign Countries!' and 'Proper Work Can Change the Fate of the Country.' The nuts are so spicy I almost choke on the first handful. 'Our main aim is to give an occupation to the returned and spread the message through the country,' says Noyon. 'These people can make a change to the country. Against the traffickers, they can raise the voices.'

'Ovibashi' means 'migrant' in Bangla and the organisation had been set up to advocate for migrant workers, both as a way for workers trapped in difficult situations abroad to contact the authorities and let them know about their plight, but, more importantly for Noyon, as a way of helping the men and women when they arrive home. They will often return, Noyon says, damaged both physically and psychologically. He calls the returning workers 'survivors', and they have no one to turn to in a system that he believes is rigged from the start, carved up between the (legal) agents, traffickers who work illegally but whom make the system work, and the politicians who protect Bangladesh's most important industry. 'Agents have a licence from the government but traffickers are the representatives of the agency and they go to the villages to collect the workers,' he says as we sit down in his sweltering office. 'They are very powerful and have good communication with political leaders. Sometimes I feel afraid; I have been threatened every day when I am dealing with a case.'

Noyon has, over the past five years, helped thousands of people to put their lives back together. He decided to set up Ovibashi after he had been sold as a slave when he went abroad after being offered a job working in Malaysia. 'Someone offered me a good job with a handsome salary and I thought, "Why not?" I paid the money, made my passport, and in 2007, with 128 people, we went to Malaysia,' he recalls.

Almost immediately it started to go wrong. When he arrived at Kuala Lumpur airport, the men waited for two days with no food until finally someone came, but it was clear they were not happy.

Instead, the man split the group into three and bartered them with another group of men. Money changed hands. It was then Noyon realised they had been sold into slavery: 'We were forced to work two months in the jungle. Insects, snakes, we were given one meal a day.' Noyon quickly became the spokesperson for the group and organised the men. They told the boss that if he didn't free them they would all commit suicide. He responded by locking them in one room for five months. 'One night we broke the window and escaped,' Noyon says. They made it to the Bangladesh embassy and complained that they had been unpaid and held against their will. Noyon didn't get the response he was expecting: 'They said it was our fault. We were to blame. We were wasting the country's and company's money! They told me to get back to the company. So I organised a hunger strike outside the embassy.' They were released when a Malaysian human rights group intervened, but only after one of the men had died of a stroke. He was 26 years old. Eventually, some of them went home, but the promise of being paid their wages and their recruitment fees hadn't materialised. So Noyon organised the men to stay at the airport once they landed in Dhaka for three days to protest. It forced the government to finally take some action, and the men got their fees back, at least. 'After all of this, I realised that there are thousands of Bangla cheated like me,' he says. 'So I decided to start working to help them.'

The work is slow and dark. Everyone has a harrowing story, and can attract the attentions of the police and politicians. Every time Noyon takes up a case, he receives threats. The police, he says, harass him. The worst offenders in terms of the treatment of the workers are the Middle East: Saudi, UAE and Oman. His business is small, and can only employ ten people at a time – a drop in the ocean considering more than half a million people left Bangladesh for work in 2015. But for the men Noyon has put back to work, it has saved their lives. Abu Sayed Khan is 47 years old but looks two decades older. He has dark skin and wears a long, pointed goatee beard and frequently weeps when he tells his story. He ended up in Iran via Oman and Dubai. He was tortured, with his family listening on the phone; he was abandoned in a jail in Bandar Abbas. 'A man from the Bangladeshi embassy turned up in jail and said, "You can go home,"' Khan recalls. '"But you need to give me 65,000 taka [£620]."' He broke down in tears for the third time. In the end, his family had to pay. 'I didn't think I'd ever come back. It is like losing everything. My family didn't speak for several months. We didn't think we could go back. I can't express how it felt like.'

Khan met another Bangladeshi in jail who has a similar story. Elias Hossain is in his mid-thirties and had travelled, legally, to Dubai to work as a carpenter. 'They took me out into the middle of the desert and paid 50 dirhams a month [around £10],' he says. He was working as a carpenter at a gas plant but, after ten months of isolation and pitiful pay, he complained to the recruitment agency back in Dhaka. They arranged for him to move to a different job in Oman. A bus came to collect him with 70 Bangladeshi workers, which drove to the nearby emirate of Sharjah. They gave each man a white baseball cap with the company's name on it. From the border with Oman, they were forced to march day and night across mountains and desert to get to the coast. 'One of us died,' Hossain says, but the traffickers told them not to touch the body. So the group moved on, leaving the dead man where he lay. 'His name was Raju from Noakhali [a province southwest of Dhaka]. He was 31,' Hossain later tried to find his family with what little information he had, but could not. They were taken by boat to the Iranian coast, where they spent 12 days hacking their way through what they described as a 'jungle' before they reached a house run by one of the traffickers, who demanded 10 lakh, about £10,000. When they told the traffickers they had no money they were beaten and tortured. When Hossain refused to give them his parents' phone number, they pulled out his fingernails. Hossain raises his hands, showing his now gnarled and ruined fingertips. Next they used a hot iron on his body. He gave them his parents' phone number, and the traffickers let them hear the torture they were inflicting on their son. After two months, his brother finally managed to scrape the money together and they were kicked out and later arrested – which is when Hossain met Abu Sayed Khan. Both eventually made it home via Pakistan, but only after officials at the Bangladesh embassy had demanded more money.

As Noyon explained, abused migrant workers who return are shunned as failures, for bringing the family into disrepute. Khan's family shunned him for many months until, slowly, relations thawed. Elias Hossain's family took him back, but their sacrifice had almost bankrupted them. 'My brother was there to meet me at the airport,' he recalls. 'He had sold his house to pay the men. I was sick. He paid for my treatment.' Both Hossain and Khan spent months in hospital recovering from their injuries. But it is the psychological injuries that take the longest to heal. Justice, too, is far away. Both men have lodged complaints against their recruitment agencies. 'The police started to harass me!' says Hossain. 'They said, "Why are you doing this? They have a good reputation. Show your papers against them or shut up."' Of course, there were no papers that could prove their torture, just their scars and broken skin. But that wasn't enough for the police. 'In the end I gave up,' he says.

The sheer scale of the problem makes anything hard to change. When the three men tried to raise awareness of their experiences, they were criticised by politicians and members of the powerful recruitment lobby. 'These men [potential migrant workers] are from rural areas and are illiterate,' Noyon says, locking up his office so that he can go and pray. 'The recruiting companies can convince them. They tell them they can fulfil their dreams, that this country won't do anything for you, but abroad is a paradise.'

At the end of 2014, the three men again tried to tell Bangladeshis about their experiences, at a conference organised by several

European-based NGOs. Khan and Hossain told their stories, about the torture and extortion, about the blurred lines between legal and illegal recruitment, about the huge sums they had lost that crippled both their mental and physical health. But, according to a report in the *Dhaka Times*, it fell on deaf ears: 'When asked about the measures being taken to compensate victims of such scam, Expatriates' Welfare and Overseas Employment Minister Khandker Mosharraf Hossain said those who raised the allegations had all used illegal measures to travel abroad, so there was nothing that could be done about them. Some NGOs were exploiting these migrants for their own business, he claimed.' When pressed on the exploitation, the minister – who has since been moved to another ministry – did not react well: 'At one point during the conversation with the *Dhaka Tribune*, Mosharraf became enraged and cursed the migrants who used illegal measures to travel abroad, saying the government repeatedly told all migrants that the government would take care of them if they chose to travel through a legal way.'

**

In the lobby of the Bangladesh Association of International Recruiting Agencies, an organisation that represents the interests of Bangladesh's recruitment industry, hangs a large, colour portrait. It is a picture of the country's current prime minister, Sheikh Hasina, being greeted warmly by the president of BAIRA. Inside, dozens of workers buzz around, carrying stacks of papers from one office to the next, where the papers are signed and then moved to the next office. Sitting in the biggest office, the only one with air conditioning, is Abdulla al Baquee, secretary of BAIRA. He runs the organisation, after spending a long career in Bangladesh's civil service before retiring.

He is friendly and offers me a seat. A young boy pours me a cold glass of filtered water as Al Baquee complains about the unfair reputation that the recruitment companies he represents have acquired.

'A recruitment agency gets a demand from the employer, they get a request from their government, submit it to our embassy to verify and check,' he explains. 'Then it comes to our agency, the recruitment agency looks for the people that migrate. They sign an agreement with the worker.'

With so many people telling me horror stories, and with so many different groups highlighting how flawed and corrupt the system is, I was interested to see just how the business itself explained the huge numbers of people who lost out. The people who Al Baquee's members represented were building a prosperous new future for the UAE but seemed to get little in return. 'They have some problems,' he concurs. 'But it is not for all the recruitment agencies. It changes man to man.'

BAIRA represents the interests of over a thousand recruitment agencies. 'We represent the good ones . . . and bad ones!' he says, laughing. For Al Baquee, the system is working well. It is an industry that the country should be proud of, that is vital to the economy and which does not get the credit it deserves. The problems, he says, come from around the edges, and are mostly to do with corruption. People working in the agencies, he explains, sometimes arrange for workers to leave for jobs, off the books. 'They think their cousin or brothers can work in Saudi Arabia and they say, "OK, come through me." The payment he is talking about is much more than agency asks. It is corruption, but this is not more than 5 per cent [of recruiters].' The biggest problem for recruitment agencies, according to Al Baquee, isn't the corruption, or the poor treatment of workers, it is the migrant labourers' often unrealistic expectations of what life will be like in the Middle East.

The workers, he believes, do not read their contracts properly. 'If the employer pays less salary or doesn't fulfil his conditions as written in the contract paper it is the employer [at fault],' he explains. 'But if after six months he [the worker] wants to improve himself . . . You are in Dubai, it is hot. After six months you want air conditioning in the room. In your original contract it says just that they will give you a room, and not AC . . . they have some problems,' he shrugs, as if there is nothing he or his members can do about such an outrageous demand in the 50-degree Gulf summer heat. BAIRA are trying to get their members to change this, not by paying more or ensuring that workers are given the bare minimum conditions for a decent life, but in terms of informing them (with 'orientation classes') of just how bad 'social conditions' will be when they get to the Middle East.

The main problem is the government's reliance on overseas remittances. Not only does overseas work reduce the burden of the state to build an economy that provides jobs for its young, the huge inflow of money counts in its balance of payments. Healthy remittances mean a healthy current account for the country. In Bangladesh remittances are second only to direct foreign investment in terms of incoming capital. If the government wasn't so dependent on remittances then maybe it would dare to challenge the importing country over its treatment of workers. It is the 'weak bargaining position' Dr Abrar had spoken of: 'Saudi Arabia stopped recruiting Bangladeshis,' he said of the 2008 ban enacted by the Saudi government, who claimed that rising crime was attributed to the huge Bangladeshi community in the country. The Bangladeshi government intervened and pleaded with the Saudis to reverse the ban. 'After having many dialogues between the two, it was open again in February last year,' says Al Baquee. There was a further condition to be made. 'They [the Saudis] said, "You allow us to have household women workers, then we will open twelve other categories [of job],"' Al Baquee explains. 'So Bangladesh had to open this. We are on the back foot.'

Abdulla al Baquee was decidedly old school. He wore his grey hair in a side parting and had spent his entire career in government bureaucracy, viewing complex human issues through the prism of forms to sign and approvals to garner. Foreign NGOs, he believed, were picking on the problem, but there was little anyone could do if the Saudis or the UAE didn't sign International Labour Organisation resolutions. He had, however, noticed a change in Bangladeshi society in recent years that might explain why so many workers were having problems, when 20 years ago there didn't seem to be so many issues: 'I am from the older generation, but this generation, there are addiction problems of our society.'

I asked him what he meant.

'Rich people's sons have become addicted to drugs from boyhood. So what will they do? After a certain age they don't have education or facilities so their father, mother sends them to other countries as migrant workers. These people make the problems.'

So, young people are addicted to drugs and are responsible for the problems? I clarified.

He nodded.

I asked about the women who claim they were abused.

'No, these are rumours,' he said firmly. 'Within the last year, only three women telephoned me from Saudi Arabia and said they were in trouble.'

What type of trouble? I asked.

'One said she had been beaten by her master,' he said, before quickly moving on. 'The other two: one said, "I like to sleep. They don't give me time to sleep." The third was complaining about the food: "I can't take their food."' He opened his arms in exasperation. 'So, yes, there are rumours . . . yes, there are sexual assaults because Saudi people think, "I paid for her clothing, her food, her accommodation, so she is mine. I can use her." But it is improving. The Saudis insist they are taking initiatives to look after these matters.'

But, for the drug-addled, malingering youth sullying the good name of Bangladesh's recruitment agencies, there remains little choice.

The private and public sector cannot provide anywhere near the jobs needed for Bangladesh's young. The recruitment agencies are their only hope, and in the process have become the biggest industry in the country. 'Corruption, it is in every country. I don't think the fair recruiting agencies are involved,' he said, pointing out that it was their job to weed out those that don't follow the rules, before getting back to his big pile of forms to sign. 'This is the biggest contributor to GDP, so it is very important.'

A security guard accompanied me to the street, back past the portrait of the prime minister and the BAIRA president. This time, I noticed that he was holding a bunch of flowers. It wasn't clear whether he was giving them as a gift, or receiving them.

4. Comilla, Bangladesh

Anamul and Razaul Hoque were finally deported from the UAE in October 2013. Razaul listened quietly throughout as his brother explained how the two had ended up back in their village in Comilla, penniless, and were still coming to terms with what happened. 'We had no idea about the strike, we were in our room when the company came to the ground floor,' he said of the day the police took them. 'All of a sudden the police threw everyone in the police van. We had no idea what was happening.' They were still owed back wages, gratuity and other money, but none of it was paid.

Part of their hope was in the nature of the project. They had hoped, as an educational institution, that the New York University – overseen by Manchester City chairman Khaldoon al Mubarak – would hold itself to higher ethical standards. In fact, such was the uproar from donors and alumni when the tie-up with Abu Dhabi was made public – primarily on the issue of the poor treatment of migrant workers – that

NYU issued a 'Statement of Labor Values' in 2009, updated with specifics in 2010. These included a promise that 'Employers will fully cover or reimburse employees for fees associated with the recruitment process, including those relating to visas, medical examinations, and the use of recruitment agencies, without deductions being imposed on their remuneration', as well as making it clear that 'Employees will retain all of their own personal documents, including passports and drivers' licenses'. There was also a further promise that 'Foreign employees shall receive employer-funded air travel between the UAE and their country of origin', which was at least true in the case of Anamul and Razaul, given they were not made to pay for their own deportation.

The clear contradiction between the statement and reality came to light in 2014. A *New York Times* report laid out how workers from the same block Anamul and Razaul had lived in, Labour Camp 42, had been arrested after a strike, beaten and then deported. It also detailed the appalling conditions in which the men who remained in the UAE still lived: in isolated, dirty labour camps, their movements controlled by security guards, living eight or ten to a room, even though the NYU statement said that there should be 'no more than four individuals in any bedroom'.

But the *New York Times* discovered that inside the 'squalid quarters, the bedrooms are so crowded that the men must sleep three to a stack – one on the upper bunk, one on the lower bunk and one below the lower bunk, separated from the floor by only a thin pad for a mattress'. Everyone had the same issues: huge recruitment fees, long hours, unpaid overtime – and discriminatory treatment based on race or nationality. Mott MacDonald, an engineering company, was hired by NYU to audit the site and the workers' facilities. Their 2013 report uncovered none of these violations, nor the strikes or forced deportations.

After initially trying to blame subcontractors, NYU issued an apology to the workers who had been mistreated and launched an inquiry into what happened, to be headed by forensic investigator Nardello & Co. Their report backed up virtually all the claims for mistreatment, although it cast doubt on whether the poor conditions at the NYU site were the actual cause for the strike, which contradicted what Anamul and Razaul had said. (Neither was contacted for their opinion.) It concluded that thousands of workers were not covered by the guidelines because the rules were changed in Abu Dhabi, giving smaller companies an exemption. One company that benefited from the loophole was Mubadala, the investment vehicle run by Manchester City's chairman Khaldoon al Mubarak. (In 2017 Sheikh Mansour's IPIC merged with Mubadala, creating the Mubadala Development Company. Mubarak stayed on as CEO, Sheikh Mansour as vice president.) Mubarak also sits on the NYU board of trustees and, as chairman of Abu Dhabi's Executive Affairs Authority, 'has direct responsibility for NYU's branch campus'.

The report also found that NYU had not paid back recruitment fees as promised. It had narrowed its definition to those 'directly employed' on the site. Given the myriad companies, jobs and subcontractors, that amounted to just a few dozen people. Daniel Nardello, the chief executive of Nardello & Co, claimed that determining who should get a refund was almost impossible given how unreliable recruiting agents are. 'It would be like getting a receipt from a loan shark,' he said.

But rather than go after the violators, the UAE authorities went after those who had spoken out against the abuses. An NYU professor who specialises in labour rights was banned from entering the UAE after being quoted criticising the authorities. Worse was to happen to Sean O'Driscoll, the freelance journalist who co-authored the *New York Times* piece. He was followed, possibly by having his mobile phone traced, as he researched his story. Later, after its publication, he was told to write a rebuttal of the allegations in the local UAE newspaper where he worked. He refused and was called into the Abu Dhabi police chief's office.

Rather than have him arrested, the police chief thought that he could turn him into an informant: 'They said that from now on I was to be put on the payroll for the police and that I would be spying on foreign journalists coming into the UAE. I'd write a monthly report for the police and pass it on. I was to take foreign journalists out for drinks and figure out what they were doing in the UAE, and report all this back to the police.' O'Driscoll refused. He too was banned from re-entering the UAE.

Despite the fallout, and the promises to be paid back the money, Anamul and Razaul have not seen a single taka; not for their unpaid wages nor for their recruitment fees. It has been a year since NYU's 'Nordello Report' was published. They have spoken to countless human rights groups and local journalists. And they have been contacted by a UK law firm which has launched a class-action lawsuit for the workers on the NYU site. The brothers laid out the letters they had received on Anamul's bed, although they could not read them. They were documents instructing the law firm to sue BK Gulf's UK partner Balfour Beatty. 'They say they will get me what I'm owed and some of the money they will keep,' Anamul says of the papers. 'The company made a contract with me. I didn't know that much about it. I signed here.' Every few months a man who speaks Bangla calls from London to update Anamul on the case. Movement is slow. Meanwhile, life also moves slowly for the brothers. They have two tiny parcels of land left, all that was left of their father's land that wasn't sold for the recruitment fees. 'We are both completely unemployed,' says Anamul, his young son now playing at his feet. 'We grow rice, some other vegetables to survive.'

Do you regret moving to the Middle East? I ask him.

'I have regret,' he replies. 'At present I have no bank balance. No savings. You're thinking, "You go abroad to make a large amount of money and establish a business and have a good life with my family." And that didn't work.' The two brothers walk me to my car. They will stick to the legal case, but they have little faith that they will see the money they are owed again. Anamul is more worried for his five-year-old son.

What happens when he is old enough to work and the only option is to move abroad? Anamul will do everything in his power, he says, to stop his son from travelling to Abu Dhabi.

Through the window of the car, Razaul hands me two mangoes he has just knocked down from the top of a tree with a long stick. 'Why did they take my eye scans and fingerprints when they deported us? We don't know if we are even banned,' Anamul had said as I was about to leave. After everything he and his brother had gone through, after all the abuse and terrible treatment, it seemed like a surprising thing to say.

Why, would you go back? I ask.

'If it is the right offer, of course,' he replies before the car bumps back down the dirt road, through the ford, and past the lines of mango trees. 'What else can we do?'

**

There are always more people leaving the Hazrat Shahjalal International Airport than arriving. Hundreds of men queue out of the door, waiting to pass through security. The departures boards are full of low-cost airlines heading for cities in the Middle East: Abu Dhabi, Dubai, Sharjah and Muscat, to name a few. The night before, over a final dinner, Shariful had explained how he would wait at the airport to count the bodies as they returned home. Statistics were impossible to come by through official channels. It did not suit the interests of the Bangladesh government, the country where the worker died or the embassy in that country to keep accurate records. So Shariful did the best he could. His phone kept ringing, even late at night. 'No one is fighting for our people,' he said. 'I've seen mass graves. I've seen them, hundreds of bodies. They will never be identified.' This is what motivates him to keep going, in the face of acquiescence. 'You have a mother somewhere back home, waiting for her son.' I thought of Raju from Noakhali, his body left on an Omani mountainside, and the mother who will never know what happened to him.

Like any day, the vast majority of people waiting in line at the airport are migrant workers seeking a new life. There is excitement as the workers approach the front doors. It has already been a long journey, getting the paperwork and money together. Each man and each woman represents walking credit; labour that has been lent in lieu of everything their family owns. At the immigration desk, the men look blankly at their departure cards. One young man, with a mouthful of crooked yellow teeth, thrusts a form into my hand and points to it. He can't read or write and needs help. I fill in his form. Inside his passport is a one-month, short-term work visa for Qatar. He nods in appreciation and hands me three more forms from his friends. All are on one-month short-term work visas for Qatar. None of the group can read or write.

Walking to the gate for my flight to the UAE, I walk past the next flight to Doha. A long line of migrant workers snakes to the end of the hall. Two dozen workers are dressed in identical, green corporate polo shirts. Above their left breast is the logo of Greenland Overseas, one of Bangladesh's best-known recruitment agents. 'We are all excited, because we have jobs in Qatar,' says Arman, a migrant worker in his late twenties, in impeccable English. He is on his way to Doha to work for the Bin Laden company on the Lusail site, the centrepiece of Qatar's 2022 World Cup development, where the final will be held. 'I know this company. It is a big company, a big name in the construction game. So I am happy. We are happy we are joining this company.' And they were. Arman said he had been promised a wage of 2200 Qatari riyals, around £450 a month. From that, he would be charged £10 a month by Greenland for their recruitment fees. 'My target is ten years. That is my maximum, and my minimum is five years.' We exchange phone numbers just before he leaves to board the plane. 'You know, I like your Beckham and Wayne Rooney. You look like him,' he says.

Like David Beckham? I reply.

'No!' he laughs. 'Rooney, you have his eyes.'

5. Abu Dhabi, United Arab Emirates

The highway to Saadiyat Island, just 500 metres off the coast of Abu Dhabi, is wide and empty. The five lanes disappear into the distance as we pass beaches full of paragliders enjoying the late-afternoon thermals as the sun sets. In the middle of the highway, every few hundred metres, we pass portraits of Sheikh Khalifa, the official ruler of the UAE.

Saadiyat means 'happiness' in Arabic, and the island has been built to create one of the most luxurious neighbourhoods in the region, making it one of the most luxurious neighbourhoods in the world. The Frank Gehry-designed Guggenheim Abu Dhabi will open here, as will the Middle Eastern arm of the Louvre, drawn up by Jean Nouvel, alongside the Norman Foster-designed Zayed National Museum. Gary Player will design a golf course and already completed is the Abu Dhabi campus for New York University, designed by Uruguayan architect Rafael Viñoly. It is a place that exudes tranquillity: wide grey stone boulevards are lined with green trees and glass and wood walkways; fountains gurgle at the centre, meaning you can always hear the soothing sound of running water. Multinational students pass by, some wearing Islamic dress but most not. No one is in a rush.

There is no plaque to the men who built this state-of-the-art university – nothing to commemorate those who were injured, nor those who had demanded better wages or conditions; nothing to commemorate their lives, or their families' lives, or the struggles in leaving home and moving thousands of miles in order to build this campus.

Inside, it is cool and quiet. One white space is dedicated to a student's exhibition called 'Men at Work'. It's a collection of photos documenting the many 'Men at Work' signs you will find across Abu Dhabi's many building sites. In the centre of the exhibition is a pair of headphones. 'Walking around Abu Dhabi I became taken with construction scarecrows,' the artist narrates. 'There are no Men at Work in this gallery, and it would be a disservice to deny them their credit, their presence.'

In a lecture hall next door, a talk is about to begin: 'The Rise and Rise of Gulf Cities' by Sultan Sooud al Qassemi, an Emirati who is one of the best-known Twitter personalities in the Gulf (followers: 503,000) and who has frequently flown close to the sun in terms of what is considered acceptable. One editorial he wrote in 2013 asking whether it was time to offer a route towards UAE citizenship for foreign residents saw him fêted abroad, but criticised at home. ('He is on very thin ice,' said Iyad el-Baghdadi, the Twitter activist who was expelled from the UAE despite spending all his life there. 'The difference is that he is part of the Sharjah royal family. You have to talk about the government in terms of what you hope it will be. There is a lot of that in Saudi Arabia as well. He's at the edge of what he can talk about. I was more reckless, maybe brave . . .' he trailed off. 'But he's still there and I'm here.')

Al Qassemi isn't broaching any tough questions in the brand new lecture hall. He is talking about the UAE's success and the West's jealousy; how the UAE and Qatar have run rings around their leaden-footed former colonial rulers. He points out what he considers to be the erroneous criticism of labour-rights abuses at the site of Guggenheim Abu Dhabi, and mentions, approvingly, how activists protesting at the Guggenheim in New York had led the museum to cut off all contact with labour and human rights groups. Al Qassemi deems criticism or coverage of rights transgressions as Western 'pushback'. And at the centre of changing people's opinions about the region is sport. 'In 2022, Doha will be the most mentioned capital in the world,' he says, highlighting the extraordinary power of football to raise the Gulf to another political level. 'When you put yourself in the public sphere, be prepared for pushback . . . whenever there is pushback, they get creative.' The ideal creative response to 'pushback' involves purchasing trophy assets in the West, he states – like banks or Harrods or football teams such as Paris Saint-Germain and Manchester City. 'Is it an insult to call a team a trophy asset?' he asks. The crowd, mainly of Western academics, laughs.

He is right, of course. Football has provided a handy distraction from criticism in other areas. When the arrests of the Emirati activists and teachers were taking place, human rights groups highlighted the gap between what was happening in the UAE and how Manchester City were promoting a very different face of Abu Dhabi. There was relatively little written about labour-rights abuses in the UAE, compared to those in Qatar.

The oil-rich royal families of the Middle East quickly learned that sport was a crucial soft-power tool. Manchester City's purchase, and its subsequent repackaging as a forward-operating base for Brand Abu Dhabi, is a case in point. 'Buying a club buys you cheap advertising space to promote your brands – from airlines, to tourism, to construction companies – it also buys you leverage with the press, who need access to your players and your stadium, and it allows you to talk breezily about Abu Dhabi values and draw people's attention away from the fact that your record on human rights is grim and worsening,' explains Nicholas

McGeehan, a Gulf expert at Human Rights Watch. McGeehan had set up his own NGO, Mafiwasta, to raise awareness of the plight of migrant workers, before being banned from entering the UAE in 2014. 'The UAE's involvement with Man City is not about any love of football, it's not because they think City will turn them a profit, and it's not because of any emotional attachment they have with the club or the city.'

A far easier issue to unpack was the connection between what the UAE government does and what a football team represents. Sheikh Mansour claimed in 2008 that Manchester City was a private business matter. But private business matters largely do not exist in Gulf royal families. They belong to a small, tightly woven and tightly controlled network of patronage. Everything is given and nothing is earned in the traditional sense. 'This applies not only to the UAE but to other rich Gulf emirates,' explained Iyad el-Baghdadi. 'To me it's very clear. The majority of these figures could not have become independently rich if it wasn't for them being royals in an oil-rich absolute monarchy. There are examples of people who were smart entrepreneurs, but these figures are few, and they tend not to be at the centre of power. So no, the wealth of the ruling family definitely cannot be described as "private" wealth.'

The power structures of Gulf autocracies are opaque. Given Sheikh Mansour's apparent lack of interest in going to the Etihad Stadium, it has led some to suggest that his brother may well be the true power behind the throne, in more ways than one. 'The evidence suggests the club is being run by a coterie of individuals close to his brother, the Crown Prince Mohamed bin Zayed al Nahyan,' said McGeehan. 'It's his people – Khaldoon al Mubarak and Simon Pearce – who run Man City and MBZ is directly responsible for the post-2011 crackdown, and the institution of a brutal state security apparatus which has tortured and forcibly disappeared critics, opponents, or anyone unlucky enough to fall under suspicion of having relationships with groups that MBZ considers enemies of the

UAE, principally groups linked to political Islamist groups like the Muslim Brotherhood.'

Before the end of Al Qassemi's talk, I slipped out and drove back along Sheikh Khalifa Bridge, back into Abu Dhabi. There was a football match on that evening, an Asian Champions League match between Uzbek champions Pakhtakor and Al Jazira, the other football club Sheikh Mansour owns. There were perhaps twenty fans in the state-of-the-art, 40,000-plus capacity stadium, named after Sheikh Mansour's brother, Sheikh Mohamed bin Zayed. The club has become, according to one journalist who declined to be named, 'the worst run team in the league'. Very few fans turned up to games. One solution, I'd been told, was bussing in hundreds of labourers from Africa, the Philippines and India to fill the stands and generate an atmosphere. But none where here today. On the pitch, former Stoke and Southampton striker Kenwyne Jones tried his best in a turgid game, which Al Jazira lost 3–1. A week earlier, Manchester City had beaten Paris Saint-Germain in the quarter-final of the UEFA Champions League in, effectively, the real Gulf derby – Manchester City, owned and funded by the Abu Dhabi royal family in the UAE, against Paris Saint-Germain, effectively owned and funded by the state of Qatar.

A few minutes' drive away, in the south of the city, the workers labouring on Abu Dhabi's many building sites were returning to their accommodation. They live in specially built cities, a long way from anywhere else. Cooking in many of them is banned, so the men eat packets of cake or processed cheese, sitting on the kerb outside. Tall walls topped with razor wire surround each camp. Security guards stand at the entrances, checking for ID and logging who is coming in and who is coming out. CCTV cameras roam the horizon outside. The UAE claims it has improved its labour-rights record, and on paper it has. It passed a reform law giving workers the right to change jobs without their employer's permission. An article in the *Economist* claimed that this law alone had led to a rise in the wages of labourers, as firms paid more for workers at the end of their contracts in a bid to keep them. But Nicholas McGeehan is sceptical. 'The UAE has tweaked its labour system in recent years and it has made some changes that look quite good on paper,' he said, specifically pointing out the new job-change law. 'The problem is that the laws aren't backed up by institutions that can enforce them. So while we can talk of progress on some issues, this exploitative and abusive system is still very much in operation.'

Outside one of the camps in Abu Dhabi, a group of Bangladeshi men were trying to use the ATM but were having no joy extracting any money from it. Two Nepali men, who worked as security guards (they claimed) were returning home after going to buy their dinner. 'We can't cook here, we can't go as we please,' said Niraz, whose t-shirt has a big marijuana leaf on the front. 'If you come inside the camp the police will come.' I jumped back into my car. The taxi driver, from Sri Lanka, wanted to leave quickly. 'I could never live here,' he said. In the rearview mirror I could see the security guards had rushed out, looking for the car of foreigners asking questions. 'It is like a prison.'

6. *Doha, Qatar*

It was not even 8 a.m., yet a fierce sun was already beating down on the football pitch in a southern suburb of the Qatari capital, Doha. The Qatar Football Association's technical committee centre was quiet and still. The only sound came from outside its perimeter walls, past the thin white minaret that guarded its entrance. A group of men from India had started a full-sized game of cricket on a large circle of scrubby sand next door, with a roll of lino cut and laid to act as the wicket.

It was a Friday and the roads of the city were empty as the mosques filled with worshippers, but soon the noise began. A group of 50 men came out into the sun and began to suddenly bang drums and other musical instruments, singing African folk songs. They were wearing a mix of football jerseys – counterfeit Manchester United and Real Madrid shirts by far the most popular. What looked and sounded at first like musical instruments were in fact metal dinner trays and empty cooking-oil cans being banged with soup ladles. 'We are singing to God!' shouted one man wearing a blue t-shirt with the words 'Bnot Herzliya Israel' (a women's basketball team) on it in Hebrew and English. They were singing, he explained, in a Ghanaian dialect. 'Praise be to God!' he shouted as the group of 50 circled around and around the deep-green coloured football pitch just as the players began to arrive.

The men playing cricket nearby had gotten used to their early morning games being played to an unusual, and unusually loud, soundtrack. Every Friday morning over the past few weeks, hundreds of men would turn up by bus and start banging their makeshift drums. They had come for the weekly football tournament, which saw teams made up of labourers and other low-wage migrants represent their companies for the chance of reaching the final of the 2016 Workers' Cup. The tournament had begun a few months ago, with 16 teams playing in four groups. The final was to take place in a few weeks' time, at the Hamad bin Khalifa stadium nearby. There would be a big cash prize, as well as mobile phones and cameras for the victors.

But today was the semi-finals – a chance for the workers to get away from their isolated camps and meet other people on their one day off a week. So hundreds of fans, from camps as far away as 50 kilometres from Doha, had got up at dawn and travelled by bus to support their teams. The first game of the day would take place between Taleb Group, a local real-estate development company that employed thousands of people, and Larsen & Toubro, a Danish–Indian conglomerate.

Like most other Gulf states, Qatar is a small but immensely rich absolute monarchy that has boomed in recent years. Its population is far smaller than that of the nearby UAE – just 2.3 million people, of whom only 10 per cent are Qatari. The rest are migrant workers, subject to an even stricter form of *kafala* that also requires an employer's permission before any worker can even leave the country. Hundreds of thousands of migrant workers from India, Nepal, Bangladesh and other south and southeast Asian states have complained of the same forms of abuse as elsewhere in the Gulf: non-payment of wages, awful conditions, a high fatality rate among young men working in the incredible heat. There were other risks too. A few months later, 11 men working on a luxury waterfront development that included a Hilton Hotel were burned to death when their camp caught fire.

Like the UAE, Qatar has invested heavily in sport – and especially in sponsoring and buying football clubs – as a way of rebranding the country in the West. But unlike the UAE, Qatar has been under intense, largely unflattering scrutiny over its labour practices, thanks to a success that even Abu Dhabi couldn't have bought: winning the right to host the 2022 World Cup finals. The Workers' Cup – sponsored by the Qatar Stars League – was deemed a chance to show the world another face.

Still, the players appreciated the shop window. 'This tournament will make people know that we are footballers, and not just labourers,' said Jerry Ayitey, a player for the Taleb Group's team, as he arrived wearing his gold and black vertically striped kit. 'I'm a striker, but we don't have a defence,' he added, 'so I have to play in defence.' Jerry didn't sound too happy about that, but at least he was playing again. He had been in Qatar for 11 months working as a stonemason. Before that, though, he claimed to have played top-level football back home in Ghana. 'A connection from the company came in Ghana, they needed workers,' he said, of how his move to the Middle East materialised. At first he was convinced he was moving to Vietnam to play football there but says he was ripped off by a Bulgarian agent who promised him $4,000 a month to play in his preferred striker role. Instead, he paid $2,000 and ended up on a building site in Doha, playing at left-back for his company team. 'The salary is not good. It is the same wages as Ghana! And we work almost ten hours a day, live six to a room,' he said. But the league gave him something. He got to get away on his one day off, and you never knew who might be watching. 'My dream is still to find a team,' he said. 'In France, England, Spain, Russia.'

The tournament appeared to be of an unusually high quality. Several of the players claimed they had played to a professional standard in Africa, but couldn't survive in a world where wages could sometimes go a whole season without being paid. One player said he'd played in the Kenyan Premier League, another said he'd been a coach. The crowds for the Workers' Cup regularly outnumbered those at the local Qatar Stars League matches. 'I joined the team as a player but my profession is engineer, so I couldn't continue,' said Mohamed Saadeldin, Taleb Group's 30-year-old Egyptian coach. It was getting close to kick-off now and several hundred fans of L&T, almost all of them from Ghana, had filled the temporary stand opposite the dugout. 'It is a Cup for labour so they fired me!' Saadeldin laughed. 'But at least they made me the coach.' Saadeldin was now writing his teamsheet on a scrap of paper as his co-coach, a labourer himself, read out the starting line-up from his phone. 'Together we choose the teams,' Saadeldin said. But there was a problem. Their star striker had worked for the opposition earlier in the tournament and couldn't play. He was effectively Cup-tied. 'Big controversy!' he laughed again. 'Almost all of them are from Ghana, plus four or five from Egypt. We dream now of reaching the final and we need to get the Cup, *inshallah*. I think we win 25,000 riyals and a mobile or camera for each one,' he said. 'I'm looking forward to a new phone!'

The players lined up in the tunnel and walked out onto the pitch. The crowd was heavily in favour of Larsen & Toubro, whose entire team was Ghanaian. Seconds before the match started, Larsen & Toubro lined up in front of their fans, to sing an impromptu version of Ghana's national anthem, before the dancing and the drumming of old food tins restarted. It was a tight game. Taleb Group had taken a narrow 1–0 lead in the first half. But as the match continued, a fleet of luxury SUVs drove into the car park. FIFA's new president, Gianni Infantino, wearing a white shirt, his bald head gleaming in the sunshine, had arrived with the great and good of Qatari football, including the man who was in charge of implementing Qatar's controversial 2022 World Cup bid: Hassan al Thawadi. He wanted to see a game. And the Workers' Cup was the only match in town.

7.

Despite years of digging, Qatar wasn't prepared for what followed when it struck gold. Ever since announcing that it intended to bid for the right to host the 2022 World Cup finals, Qatar was seen as an outside bet, at best. Very few people could even point to Qatar on the map, and what was known about the country didn't necessarily put people's minds at rest either: a tiny outcrop in the Persian Gulf, connected to Saudi Arabia, downstream from the chaos in Iraq that bakes in a four-month long summer with daytime temperatures rarely dipping below 50 degrees. When FIFA's own technical committee evaluated all the 2022 bids – from the US, Australia, Japan and Korea – Qatar's was the only one designated as high risk, due to the extreme summer heat. And there was no football pedigree to lean on either. Qatar's league had only been professionalised relatively recently and the national team had never come close to qualifying for a World Cup finals. 'The Maroon', as they are known, constantly hover around 100th place in FIFA's rankings. When the then FIFA president Sepp Blatter pulled a piece of card out of an envelope with the word 'QATAR' written on it, even he sounded surprised. Yet the victory, if you look a little closer, was not a surprise at all – and not just because of the persistent allegations of corruption that have surrounded that day in Zurich in December 2010 ever since. Over the past decade Qatar's monarchy, through its web of investment vehicles and government departments, had invested its huge wealth in sport and was buying up football clubs, using the game as a soft-power launchpad towards global recognition.

Today, Qatar is a long way from the tiny, insignificant and crushingly poor outpost of the British empire of old. In 1940 – a period that Qataris refer to as 'the years of hunger' – the population of Qatar stood at 16,000. As described in Allen J. Fromherz's *Qatar: A Modern History*, one British civil servant posted in Doha at that time described it as 'little more than a miserable fishing village straggling along the coast for several miles and more than half in ruins. The *suq* [market] consisted of mean, fly-infested hovels, the roads were dusty tracks, there was no electricity and the people had to fetch their water in skins and cans from wells two or three miles outside the town.' The peninsula's pearling and fishing industries, its two biggest, had collapsed and Qatar would not be revived until the discovery of oil in 1949. In 1971, a few months before the UAE's seven emirates came together, Qatar announced its independence. A year later, Sheikh Khalifa bin Hamad al Thani snatched power from his disinterested brother, Ali, while he was on a hunting trip in Iran. Twenty-four years later, Sheikh Hamad bin Khalifa al Thani seized power from his disinterested father, Sheikh Khalifa, while he was on one of his many holidays in Switzerland. There was a counter-coup in 1996, but the Bedouin tribes paid to cross the border through the desert from Saudi Arabia got lost. So too did the boat full of French mercenaries, led by Sheikh Khalifa's former bodyguard, who'd been training a force of 50 men in the central African country of Chad, only to be scuppered by landing on the wrong beach.

The new Emir began with a reformist zeal that, according to an *Economist* article in 1996, had the royal families of surrounding Gulf states worried. The ministry of information was abolished, paving the way for the establishment of the Al Jazeera news network, and it was announced that democratic reforms would take place, with an elected advisory chamber. Women would have the vote; Hamad talked of a British-style constitutional monarchy where the Emir was head of state but the power resided in an elected parliament. The exploitation of the world's third-largest gas field off Qatar's coast changed everything. It suddenly made Qatar, per capita, the richest country on earth. It was under Emir Hamad – now protected by the US military's central command, CENTCOM, stationed outside Doha – and following the lead of the UAE that Qatar began to invest heavily in sport in general, and football in particular. The Emirates airline had been, at one time or another, the main shirt sponsors of Chelsea, Arsenal, Paris Saint-Germain, Real Madrid, Benfica and AC Milan. It was a major sponsor of FIFA and the World Cup, as well as the world's oldest competition, the English FA Cup. Emirates have paid over £250 million to secure the naming rights of Arsenal's new stadium until 2028.

Qatar shamelessly copied the UAE's blueprint, with one exception. Where the UAE's local football league had been largely left alone as the plaything of the UAE's many princes, Qatar invested heavily in its Q League, attracting some of the biggest names in the game as they reached the end of their careers. When I first travelled to Qatar in 2004, Marcel Desailly, both de Boer brothers and Gabriel Batistuta were playing out their final seasons for huge contracts. 'At my age, it is finished for me,' Desailly had told me when I asked why he had agreed to play in Qatar when other European leagues had come calling. 'I realised that I still wanted to play football and that is why I came here. I would go back to Europe, for what? I know everything from Europe. The crowd. The pressure. I did it for 20 years and it's enough.'

The country successfully bid for the 2006 Asian Games and floated the idea of bidding for something bigger – a World Cup finals, perhaps, or even the Olympic Games – but the thorny issue of the desert heat seemed to make it impossible. Still, there were plans to take the Qatar national team to the World Cup finals, mainly through gaming the system by naturalising foreign-born players. When Qatar was caught offering a huge seven-figure payment to Aílton, a Brazilian striker who was then top scorer in the Bundesliga, to help their bid to qualify for the 2006 World Cup finals in Germany, FIFA were forced to tighten up the rules.

Instead, Qatar invested in Aspire, a huge training complex and academy that wanted to nurture the next generation of Qatari sports men and women, while finding talent from around the rest of the world too. I stood in the main hall at the grand opening in 2005. Aspire had paid hundreds of thousands of dollars to see Maradona and Pelé both walk on stage together in Doha – a tough ask given the antipathy between the two men over the thorny issue of who is the greatest player of all time. The 2.5-kilometre-square Aspire Zone complex had world-class training facilities for most sports. Later, the 50,000-capacity Khalifa International Stadium would open and become its centrepiece.

Much of the investment appeared to fail, however. Qatar didn't qualify for the 2006, 2010 or 2014 World Cup finals. The 2006 Asian Games were a disaster after torrential rain created such hazardous conditions that several fans were killed in car accidents on their way to an event, while a South Korean equestrian rider was killed when his horse slipped in the mud. A prison ship had to be brought in to house some of the competitors due to a hotel shortage. One local paper dubbed them 'the Death Games'. The Q League had also lost its lustre, and big names were no longer coming to play their last years in the sun. After announcing its plans to host the 2016 summer Olympic Games in Doha, which would have been moved to the slightly cooler month of October, the city did not even make the shortlist when it was announced in 2008. Qatar also failed to become a candidate city for the 2020 Games.

And then it all started to make sense. In 2009 Qatar launched its long-shot bid to host the 2022 World Cup finals. Although some claim that the idea was suggested by Blatter during a 2008 meeting with Sheikh Hamad, there had been talk of a Qatari World Cup bid for at least five years before that. 'We are serious about winning the right to host the FIFA World Cup in the Arab world for the first time,' said Hassan al Thawadi, the young chief executive chosen to head the bid. 'We are offering FIFA an incredible event, with a tremendous football legacy, but also a legacy for humanity. Qatar 2022 can be a watershed moment.' Aspire, which had appeared to be little more than a well-funded sports hall, had become front and centre of the campaign. The Qataris had opened numerous academies around the globe, looking to identify and recruit talent in previously overlooked or underdeveloped footballing nations. It had set up a programme called 'Football Dreams' designed to mine for talent in Africa, opening a facility in Senegal. 'Football Dreams stands out not just because it throws money around to pluck prospects from the developing world,' wrote ESPN's Brent Latham. 'Six of the 15 programs are in countries represented on FIFA's all-powerful 24-man executive committee.' Aspire had built a presence in Guatemala, Thailand and Paraguay. All three had a member on the FIFA Exco, world football's 24-man governing body that would decide who would host the 2022 finals.

By 2011, Aspire players honed in Doha were breaking into national teams in Asia and Africa. '2010 was a watershed year for Aspire because some of the boys that came through the academy are now starting to find their way into the Qatar Olympic squad,' said Wayde Clews when I revisited Aspire in 2011. Clews was in charge of overseeing Aspire's performance and had just seen eight Aspire students make the Qatar football team headed to the 2010 Asian Games in China. 'We are also now seeing three or four players making their way into the [full] national squad,' he said. The problem, especially in Africa, was that it appeared as if Aspire was hoovering up talented African kids with one eye on naturalising them in time for the 2022 finals. Clews denied that. 'There is absolutely no obstacle of those boys playing for their home countries,' he said. Aspire's director general, Dr Andreas Bleicher, was equally as certain. 'When making agreements, we are not requiring them to play for Qatar, we leave it up to them,' he said when I asked whether Qatar would naturalise any of the Aspire graduates. 'A player might be here for five years,' he said. 'If he wants to play for Qatar, it is upon the player concerned.'

Qatar's 2022 bid was a seductive one. It talked of unity in the Middle East, of using zero-carbon cooling technology to combat the heat, of flat-packed stadiums that would be taken down and rebuilt in Africa. The bid has been tainted somewhat by the persistent allegations of corruption that bedevilled the bidding process, which the Qatar team has strenuously denied. Of the 24 Exco members that were due to vote, two were suspended beforehand after being caught in a *Sunday Times* sting discussing cash for votes. Of the other 22, nine have been banned from football over corruption allegations and another five have retired. Behind the scenes, though, hard politics were at work. A large number of trade deals appeared to have been made between Qatar and countries with which they did not traditionally have strong ties. There was the strange case of Marios Lefkaritis, FIFA's Exco member from Cyprus, who sold a strip of land back home for £27 million. The buyer was the Qatar Investment Authority. He denied that the deal, and the vote for 2022, were connected.

According to Heidi Blake and Jonathan Calvert in *The Ugly Game: The Qatari Plot to Buy the World Cup*, the Emir himself travelled to South America – the scene of several deals and alleged payments that just happened to take place in countries that also had a FIFA Exco voter – in the August before the vote. Sheikh Hamad had flown to

Paraguay to meet the country's president to discuss the building of a new gas pipeline between Uruguay, Paraguay and Bolivia that would cost hundreds of millions of dollars. Mohamed bin Hammam, the Qatari head of the Asian Football Confederation, had been due to travel for a separate trip to meet Paraguay's Exco member Nicolás Leoz but cancelled abruptly. Sheikh Hamad, it was later reported, met Leoz secretly. A $2 billion gas deal was agreed on the trip. The book also suggests that a huge gas exploration deal was cut between Qatar and Russia before the 2022 and 2018 votes. When Bin Hammam visited Russia shortly after Sheikh Hamad had met Vladimir Putin, Hammam was due to meet Russia's 2018 bid team. Strangely, though, a briefing note said that 'most of the bid committee are Gazprom officials. Gazprom is the largest extractor of natural gas in the world.'

But the most important deals were allegedly reserved for Michel Platini, the UEFA president, whose European votes would swing the decision. With two months to go before the vote, Platini held two private dinners with Sheikh Tamim bin Hamad al Thani, the crown prince of Qatar. While his younger brother Mohammed had been the face of the bid, Tamim was the future power. Platini and Sheikh Tamim met at a Chinese restaurant in Geneva, which caused little fanfare. The second meal would prove more controversial.

Ten days before the vote, French president Nicolas Sarkozy invited Sheikh Tamim to the Élysée Palace. Also there was Sébastien Bazin from Colony Capital, the American firm of investors that owned 98 per cent of Paris Saint-Germain alongside a host of other unusual investments, including photographer Annie Leibovitz's back catalogue and Michael Jackson's old house. PSG might well have been a relatively young club in European terms – having been founded in 1970 – but they were the only major club in the city. In fact, there wasn't any major capital city that only had one club. Perhaps only ADO Den Haag. Still, PSG were haemorrhaging cash, something that President Sarkozy – as a long-term fan – wanted to stop.

What went on during that meal is still fiercely debated. An investigation by *France Football* called 'Qatargate' alleged that Sheikh Tamim offered to buy Paris Saint-Germain and clear its debt if Platini voted for Qatar for 2022. On top of that a new TV channel beIN Sports – spun off from Al Jazeera Sports and rebranded – would be created and buy French TV football rights. Platini responded to the allegations forcefully. 'To say that my choice . . . was part of a deal between the French state and Qatar is pure speculation . . . and lies,' he said. 'I do not rule out legal action against anyone who casts doubt on the honesty of my vote.' Later, the French media reported that Platini admitted that Sarkozy didn't tell him he had to vote for Qatar but that it would be 'a good thing if [he] did'.

That meeting signalled the beginning of the end for Platini. After a long series of denials about what went on at the meal, Platini eventually admitted that he had indeed voted for Qatar 2022. He maintained his decision had nothing to do with the dinner, however, and still enthusiastically backed the bid, if only Qatar would host the finals in Europe's winter months. Up until then Platini had been heir presumptive to Sepp Blatter as FIFA's next president. But the admission that he voted for Qatar left him seriously exposed among his European associations. When the time came for him to challenge Blatter for the top job in 2015, he was instead undone by a new scandal. Blatter had used FIFA cash to pay Platini £1.3 million. The men claimed this was for consultancy work a decade earlier. But the payment came around the same time as Blatter's 2011 re-election campaign, and two months after the Qatar vote. Platini had decided against standing for the top job, keeping his powder dry for the 2015 election, which – many people believed – Blatter would not contest. Both men were banned from football by FIFA's ethics committee, although both deny any wrongdoing. Platini would be forced to watch his home country host Euro 2016, which should have been his swansong as UEFA president, literally at home.

Two more important developments took place in the months after the dinner at the Élysée Palace. As allegedly promised, Paris Saint-Germain found a new owner and its debts were cleared, Colony Capital announcing that it had sold 70 per cent of the club to Qatar Sports Investment – founded at the same time as the Qatar Investment Authority (the country's sovereign wealth fund, which holds a rumoured £130 billion in assets) – for a reported £50 million. QSI was formed in 2005 by Sheikh Tamim. PSG had, effectively, been bought by the Qatari state, even if the suave face of the deal was Nasser al Khelaifi, a 40-year-old Qatari former professional tennis player who once reached 995th place on the ATP tour rankings. Al Khelaifi would now be PSG's president, charged with bringing the club European glory. 'We have a very clear vision, to be honest,' he told the *Financial Times*. 'In five years, we want to be one of the best clubs in Europe and to win the Champions League. And our brand to be worth €1 billion. And we will be there.' Al Khelaifi was involved in another deal that allegedly found its genesis at the Élysée Palace, one that potentially could prove to be even bigger. BeIN Sports, the rebranded Al Jazeera Sports channel, would pay £70 million to show French Ligue 1 matches. They would go on to secure the rights for the Champions League and the 2016 European Championships. In 2014 French football rights were sold for a record price, rising by 23 per cent. The chairman of beIN Sports is Nasser al Khelaifi. In 2013, Sheikh Tamim – the crown prince of Qatar, who had been at both meetings and who had founded QSI – became Emir. Unlike his father, he did not have to instigate a coup. Sheikh Hamad abdicated and peacefully stepped aside. Sheikh Tamim was 33 years old.

QSI followed Abu Dhabi's blueprint. They had bought a historic club that was undervalued and then spent hundreds of millions making it competitive. Their first signing was Argentine midfield Javier Pastore for £35 million. Zlatan Ibrahimović would follow. Paris Saint-Germain have now won four consecutive French league titles, the French Cup two years running and the league cup three times in a row. They regularly reach the latter stages of the Champions League, and have signed a £150 million, four-year sponsorship deal with the Qatar Tourism Authority. From making a £20 million loss every year, PSG now had revenue in excess of £350 million a year.

Qatar's economy has diversified. PSG is an asset just like any other on QIA's books: Sainsbury's, Harrods, Barclays Bank, Volkswagen, Porsche or Miramax. More importantly, the country has successfully rebranded itself via football, and not just through PSG. Although the 2022 World Cup has brought nothing but trouble for Qatar, PSG and its other high-profile sponsorship deals have been an unalloyed success. Likewise, its shirt sponsorship deal with Barcelona. For decades, Barcelona's fans – or *socios* – who own and run the club had resisted any sponsorship on the front of their shirts. UNICEF briefly adorned the strip, but in 2010 it was agreed that the Qatar Foundation – a huge Qatari government-funded educational charity – would appear too. That gave way to Qatar Airways, the state airline. There was uproar among Barca fans, not just over the break with history but also the nature of the company. Qatar's treatment of migrant workers and strict use of the *kafala* system made many believe that the sponsorship deal was at odds with the club's historically left-wing identity. Worse, the CEO of Qatar Airways seemed to suggest that he was proud that unionisation was banned at his company. Meanwhile, contracts for cabin crew stipulated that women would be fired if they got pregnant. Eventually, in 2015, the company changed its pregnancy policy. 'We call on Qatar Airways to reform the rest of their labour policies to ensure freedom of association and collective bargaining,' said Sharan Burrow, General Secretary of the International Trade Union Confederation. 'Notwithstanding this victory, the workplace for courageous employees remains oppressive under a system of slavery – the *kafala* system – which must be eliminated.'

There have been other Qatari investments. A minor member of the ruling royal family – Sheikh Abdullah bin Nasser al Thani – bought Spanish La Liga side Malaga in 2010, saving the club from financial ruin and even funding the team's quarter-final run in the Champions League. But soon the money was scaled back – just at the same time as PSG's Qatari spending was ramping up – as were the club's Champions League ambitions. More unusual was Qatar's next football club purchase in Europe, found in the least expected of places.

**

Eupen, Belgium

KAS Eupen seemed a strange team for Qatar's Aspire Zone Foundation to buy. Middle Eastern money usually signalled marquee signings, but not here. KAS Eupen were in the Belgian second division and in serious financial trouble. They were also relatively cheap to buy, and the visa regime in Belgium made it easier for players to come from outside the EU and play in the league. Immediately after the purchase KAS Eupen signed a string of players from Ghana, France and Mali, all of whom had been nurtured by the Aspire Academy.

The town of Eupen itself is a little piece of Germany in Belgium, which has a small German-speaking population (it's an official language) and looks more like an Alpine town, with quiet, narrow streets and buildings made of stone and wood. Luxury cars move slowly through the town, past equally luxurious watch and fashion shops.

It is KAS Eupen's first game of the 2014–15 season, against Mons, and a familiar face is sitting in a café near the club's Kehrwegstadion, a tidy 8,000 capacity ground with four small but equally proportioned stands with seats coloured the same black and white of the club's shirt.

I'd met Dr Andreas Bleicher in Doha in 2011. He still ran the 'Football Dreams' project for Aspire, but was now also a designated board member at KAS Eupen. 'It didn't matter we didn't get promoted, we have a long-term plan,' says Dr Bleicher of KAS Eupen's first season in Belgium's second division. They finished second, but lost the promotion playoff. 'Our aim is not to win the Champions League.'

Aspire's motivations, for many, are still opaque. 'We are running a humanitarian football project!' says Dr Bleicher, pointedly, who is far more combative off home soil. The motives of the Qatari government, not just in buying Eupen but starting Aspire too, had obviously been a question he'd faced many times before. 'We screen hundreds of thousands of footballers a year. We give them education in a private school. The question is what do we do when they are 18? Do we leave them on their own? This is not the right way. The biggest step is youth to professional football. And we want to give these kids a chance to make it in professional football. So,' he adds, 'maybe we should run a football club in Europe.'

So Qatar went on the hunt for a suitable club, which was harder than it sounded. They didn't want a high-profile club in the Premier League, and didn't want one from a league that wouldn't expand their players' horizons. 'We analysed everything: language, regulations, and we came up with Belgium,' says Dr Bleicher. The biggest benefit of owning a Belgian club is the fact that there is no limit on the number of foreign players you can sign from outside the EU. And unlike in Germany, with its '50+1 rule', you can actually own a club in its entirety too. Language is also a factor. 'A lot of our players speak French,' Bleicher observes, reflecting the fact that a large proportion of the squad are players discovered in francophone West Africa. 'Eupen is perfect. It is a small town. Safe environment. It is in the heart of European football.'

KAS Eupen was ripe for a takeover. The club was formed after the Second World War when the town's two local teams were merged out of practical necessity. Eupen was close to the site of the Battle of the

Bulge. The town suffered in its aftermath, however, in part due to Eupen's German identity. 'Back then anything German was despised,' says Jeff Gerkens, KAS Eupen's former chief executive, who now works as a kind of club historian, taking Arab dignitaries, including members of the Qatar royal family, around the town and showing them the sights. '2,200 young men from Eupen went to war with the German army,' he explains. 'One third didn't come back, one third came back with a handicap, the other third with psychological problems. They could not live apart. So we made one club.'

The club spent most of its life in the second and third divisions, but with a new German investor they managed to secure promotion for their one previous season in Belgium's top flight, in 2010. Within six months the investor was in a Cologne jail over previous financial dealings and later sentenced to seven years. 'They had already spent next year's money,' says Gerkens, who'd retired from the club by that point. They slipped into the relegation playoff, and back into the second division. 'We were one centimetre from official bankruptcy,' says Gerkens, recalling the day in March 2012 when a delegation from the Qatari royal family arrived looking for a suitable club to buy. 'Christmas, Easter and everything else came in one day from Qatar.'

With Qatari money now invested in the club, the fans expected a flurry of superstars to follow. 'It is the best thing to happen here,' explains Thomas Evers, a sports reporter for the *Grenz-Echo*, Belgium's only German language daily newspaper. His office is down a quiet little alleyway, just off the main square. 'All the people in Eupen asked the same question: "Why Eupen?" I was quite surprised. We couldn't believe this big academy would buy Eupen. The club in 2012 was already bankrupt. There was a problem getting their league licence. The Qataris arrived, paid all the salaries and debts. It was a positive effect on the whole region.' The money also brought some unrealistic expectations. 'When I think of Qatar I think of PSG,' admits Evers.

'Some supporters dreamed of PSG, that Qatar would buy a lot of stars. Instead they saw fifteen 18-year-old Africans arrive.'

The players themselves appeared to thrive at Eupen, even if they narrowly missed out on promotion. The club is run in Eupen, Dr Bleicher says, but with a framework laid out in Qatar, with many of the squad trained and educated in Qatar since they were eight years old. This is what prompted the questions about naturalisation. 'We can say we are running this project for almost eight years and [have] screened 3.5 million footballers. Not one is playing for Qatar,' Dr Bleicher emphasises, angrier now. 'Also, study FIFA regulations. If you acquire new citizenship, you would have to live continuously in one place for five years after you are 18. What are we doing? The exact opposite.' He points out that over 30 Football Dreams students have represented ten different national teams, mostly in Africa, from under-17 to A-team level. 'And they are still very young, the oldest are 20. When the first players play at the Africa Cup of Nations for Cameroon or Nigeria, or the 2018 World Cup in Russia for Mali or the Ivory Coast, then people will see.'

A few hours later, Dr Bleicher saw KAS Eupen beat Mons 3–0. In the end the club narrowly missed out on promotion again, before reaching Belgium's top division in 2016 – although their promotion was highly controversial. The league went into the final game of the season with three teams capable of winning the only automatic promotion spot. One was a tiny club with just a few hundred fans, no ground, and huge debts – but White Star Brussels somehow managed to win the league, only to be refused a playing licence on the grounds that they didn't have the finances to survive in the top flight. KAS Eupen and Royal Antwerp – Belgium's oldest club – then played each other in their last game of the season, in Antwerp, with both having a shot at the title. The game ended 0–0, meaning Eupen finished ahead of Antwerp on goal difference; only for White Star to leapfrog both after winning their last game.

After the Eupen game, Antwerp's fans rioted through the city, setting fire to cars and vans in the streets outside the ground. 'Several groups of supporters hurled objects towards the police, such as signposts, fences and even a trailer,' said Antwerp police spokesperson Wouter Bruyns. 'They also threw cobblestones, or used them to smash the windows of police vans. One van was set alight.' In the end, after an appeal was rejected, White Star were refused promotion because of the licensing issue and Eupen were promoted. The experiment had so far been a success. One Qatari defender played most of Eupen's matches in their promotion season, and will stay with the squad for their second season in the top flight. One Aspire graduate was even signed for Barcelona B. Halfway through their first season in Belgium's top tier, Eupen are holding their own, in mid-table.

The experiment was so successful that Aspire bought a second club, in Spain: Cultural y Deportiva Leonesa, from the city of León, who reached the second tier of Spanish football. Several Qatari players have been in and out of their squad since. 'We hope in ten years' time some of the very best players in world football will have played in Eupen and been developed by Football Dreams,' says Dr Bleicher. 'We can say, "Look, we found these players in the middle of nowhere. We helped them to be champions in life."'

8.

Gianni Infantino stood on the touchline, watching as Larsen & Toubro pushed for a late equaliser in the semi-final of the 2016 Workers' Cup. But it never came. Taleb Group held on for a 1–0 victory. Their players celebrated wildly on the pitch while their opponents lay on the turf, shattered. Many were in tears, devastated that they would not be playing in the final. The fans, who had played Ghana's national anthem with soup ladles and cooking-oil drums, fell silent, briefly. 'We had one of our players down, we lost concentration, we thought their players would kick the ball out but they refused,' said Mohamed Yahaya, a land surveyor who played for L&T and could barely talk through the tears. 'I felt really bad. I was looking forward to getting to the finals.' In the dressing room, the Taleb Group were rapturous, singing 'Ole, Ole, Ole, Ole!' while spraying cans of Coke around the room. 'I feel happy . . . *hamdullah* [thank God],' said their Egyptian coach, Mohamed Saadeldin, gasping for air between each sentence. 'We win today . . . *hamdullah* . . . L&T were a good team . . . but we are very strong . . . *hamdullah* . . . we are in the final . . . *hamdullah!*' Infantino comforted the losing players as a scrum of photographers took photos of him embracing them.

It had been another bad week for FIFA and for Qatar. Infantino had only just been elected as FIFA president, on a reformist platform. The former general secretary of UEFA had been thrust into the battle at the last minute. When it was clear that his boss, Michel Platini, would be engulfed in corruption allegations that would prevent him from standing, Infantino was put forward to ensure European football would have at least one candidate in the vote for president. Behind the scenes, his nomination was viewed disparagingly. He was described by one FIFA figure as 'a placeholder' who would be replaced once Platini had beaten his corruption accusations. But Platini couldn't, and Infantino ended up in the final run-off, against Sheikh Salman bin Ibrahim al Khalifa. Sheikh Salman was the new president of the Asian Football Confederation, having replaced the now-disgraced Mohammed bin Hammam of Qatar, who had been banned from football for life. Sheikh Salman was a member of Bahrain's ruling royal family, and was arguably an even more divisive figure than Bin Hammam. He had been accused by several human rights organisations, and former Bahrain national team players, of (at best) turning a blind eye to the arrest and alleged torture of sportsmen and women who participated in peaceful protest against the Bahrain regime when the Arab Spring arrived in the capital, Manama, in February 2011. The issue had followed Salman's campaign and, in the final vote, Infantino prevailed, promising transparency and an end to the conveyor belt of FIFA scandal.

Shortly after his victory, Amnesty International released their savage report on Qatar's progress on migrant labour rights, *The Ugly Side of the Beautiful Game: Exploitation on a Qatar 2022 World Cup Site*. It detailed the experiences of workers building the Khalifa International Stadium and the surrounding Aspire Zone, and included the familiar litany of complaints: appalling conditions of accommodation, crippling recruitment costs, late payment of wages, lower wages than promised, the confiscation of workers' passports and evidence that firms would leverage the exit visas needed to leave the country to pay less money or get out of tight legal areas. Both Paris Saint-Germain and Bayern Munich had spent the winter training at Aspire's facilities. 'The abuse of migrant workers is a stain on the conscience of world football. For players and fans, a World Cup stadium is a place of dreams. For some of the workers who spoke to us, it can feel like a living nightmare,' said Amnesty International Secretary General Salil Shetty. 'Despite five years of promises, FIFA has failed almost completely to stop the World Cup being built on human rights abuses.'

The issue had been dogging Qatar since it won the bid in 2010, and a devastating investigation by the *Guardian* into the treatment of Nepali workers – over 40 of whom had died during one month – made sure that the issue would always be connected to the World Cup. And it wasn't just construction workers who were affected. Even footballers in the UAE and Qatar are subject to *kafala*. In 2013, French footballer Zahir Belounis was trapped in Qatar. The midfielder had signed for El Jaish, the army team who play in the newly renamed Qatar Stars League. He had played in the lower reaches of French football, so a move to Qatar was a huge opportunity. He was even, briefly, given a Qatari passport, to represent Qatar at the 2011 World Military Games (where Qatar finished fourth) but it was taken off him when he returned.

Still, he had his lucrative league contract, although soon he fell out of favour and was forced to play for another team and had his wages withheld. When he complained he was handed a contract and offered an ultimatum. 'They [El Jaish] said, "We will pay you, but you have to sign this paper that says we don't owe you anything." I said, "Give me first the cheque." They said, "Contract first." They said they would not give me an exit visa unless I stop the claim [against the club].' He was eventually given an exit visa, but only after months of negative press against Qatar.

Another footballer to experience a similar fate was former Morocco international Abdeslam Ouaddou. He had played at the highest level, in France for Nancy and in England for Fulham, then moved to Qatar on the promise of a lucrative contract playing for Lekhwiya, which is owned by the same member of the Qatari royal family that owns Malaga. After captaining Lekhwiya to the title in his first season, Ouaddou was moved to another club. He was told that he had no choice as no one could go against the decision of 'the prince'. He too was owed money and threatened with the withholding of his exit visa, but he got out and has become a vocal campaigner for workers' rights in Qatar. 'When you work in Qatar you belong to someone,' he told me. 'You are not free. You are a slave. Of course [football] is not the same situation as the [construction] workers in Qatar, but there is a parallel. It is the same methodology. They can throw you away like old socks.'

The organisation set up to make the World Cup happen – the Supreme Committee for Delivery and Legacy, headed by Hassan al Thawadi – had tried to deal with the avalanche of negative publicity surrounding the treatment of migrant workers. In 2014 they released the Workers' Welfare Standards, which required a minimum standard of treatment for workers on World Cup projects, higher than that currently in Qatari law. However, the 'standard' turned out to be not legally enforceable (although contractors believed to have contravened rules could lose contracts), and created a moral division between workers on World Cup sites and those on non-World Cup sites, often living in labour camps next door to each other. Theoretically, World Cup stadium workers could get air conditioning and the others not. In a country as small as Qatar, what constituted a World Cup project anyway? Roads, malls, apartments; they were all being built around the World Cup project, and literally around the World Cup stadiums – it was very hard to know where one World Cup project began, and another non-World Cup project ended. 'The Supreme Committee has shown commitment to workers' rights and its welfare standards have the potential to help,' said Salil Shetty of Amnesty International. 'But it is struggling to enforce those standards. In a context where the Qatari government is apathetic and FIFA is indifferent, it will be almost impossible for the World Cup to be staged without abuse.'

Gianni Infantino's first job was to put out the fire, hence his visit to various Qatari construction sites, and the brand-new 'Labor City' with improved accommodation, before being driven to the first Workers' Cup semi-final, where, after the game, sitting next to Hassan al Thawadi, he responded in a press conference to the allegations made by Amnesty International. 'Over the past two days I have been able to personally witness what has been done, and I am confident we are on the right track,' Infantino said to a packed room of journalists. 'An encouraging example of this is the Supreme Committee's responses to the issues raised by Amnesty International in their recent report, with many of those issues already being tackled before the report was published . . . We will take the Qatari authorities by their word, the concrete actions will be the real testament of their will.' The biggest issue, though, was *kafala*. 'I discussed the changes to the *kafala* legislation this morning with the prime minister. This is also something which has to be acknowledged, respected and enforced,' he said. 'We are speaking about thousands and thousands of people, but without the World Cup none of this would even have been discussed.'

In that respect he was at least partially right. The reform process for labour rights in Saudi Arabia or the UAE was virtually non-existent. Some changes were made to the UAE's labour law, in theory granting workers the right to change jobs, but practically it remained impossible. 'FIFA is not a world welfare agency,' Infantino continued, before announcing the creation of an independent body to oversee Qatar's promised reforms. 'But we can help with changes that go beyond football.' After the press conference, Infantino's motorcade swept out, towards the airport, past the ranks of Porsches and Maseratis parked up by the local dignitaries who had hosted them. Dozens of Ghanaian and Kenyan supporters had taken the chance to take selfies in front of them as security guards tried, and failed, to shoo them away.

With Infantino gone, it was time for the second semi-final. It was approaching 12 and, even in April, the sun burned in the cloudless sky. Thousands were now in the crowd to see Gulf Contracting Co., who had recently been in the British press over their alleged poor treatment of migrant workers, take on Mowasalat, a government-owned transport company. The coach of Gulf Contracting Co. was British, and it was the third year he had coached the team. 'This year we've got players from Nepal, Kenya and Ghana,' said Andy Clayton. Clayton had played in English non-league football but trained as a carpenter, moved to the Gulf and started coaching the team. He'd set up a trial three months ago, whittling down his team from a pool of 100. 'Qatar is a transient country,' he explained. 'So from my team from last year we only had four players.' I didn't ask about the *Guardian* report that claimed many of their workers were living in substandard accommodation, but he talked about it anyway. 'It is not as bad as people say at all,' he said confidently. 'I would say that we'll see 500 to 600 of our workers today from the camps and 99 per cent will be happy.'

Like the first game, the second semi-final was tight. No one wanted to miss out on the final, or the potential of a new mobile phone, especially as they were so close. On both sides, Indian, Ghanaian, Eritrean, Kenyan and Egyptian players battled it out. The crowd was equally multinational. The game finished 0–0, and went to penalties. Both teams missed as the thousands stopped banging their soup ladles and silence fell for each kick, exploding when a goal went in, getting even louder when it didn't. Finally Gulf Contracting Co.'s Jasper Abbey, a 24-year-old mason from Ghana with long dreadlocks down his back, stepped up with a chance to score the crucial kick. 'Do you see our crowd?' shouted Clayton, pointing to the huge support itching to run onto the pitch. 'I can't watch.'

The crowd sunk in silence as Abbey stood by the penalty spot before stepping back and blasting the ball into the back of the net. Hundreds invaded the pitch, past the half-hearted attempts by the security guards to prevent them from getting onto the grass. By the dugout, the fans hoisted Abbey and Clayton onto their shoulders and did a lap of honour amid a riot of music and dancing. 'In all my life in football,' Clayton shouted down, 'this is the greatest thing to have happened to me.' Others laid down their flags, hard hats and blue overalls on the turf. It was as genuine an outpouring of joy as I'd ever witnessed at a football match, a fleeting moment of anarchy and true freedom that began to ebb almost as soon as it had begun. 'I am much too happy, look at the fans, 2,000 of them! I could not let them down,' said Abbey, now out of breath from trying to escape another lap of honour. He was chased by groups of men desperate to hoist him onto their shoulders too. 'It was a big tough game. Every game we raise our game. We give thanks to the Almighty.'

The final would be played in a few weeks' time, against Taleb Group, but now it was time to return home, back to the camps. Once the celebrations had died down, the ubiquitous grey buses with bars on their windows arrived to take the players and supporters home. I climbed onto the bus too, which drove half an hour north on empty roads to Umm Salal. The bus passed the guards, there to keep track of workers getting out, or unauthorised people from getting in. The camp grounds are tidy, but isolated and far from any settlements. It is a kilometre walk to the nearest shop outside. Any journey by foot in the summer would be all but impossible. The Gulf Contracting Co. players were rewarded with buckets of KFC, which the players devoured, grateful to have a break from their usual spicy south Indian menu. 'We love KFC, because we're from Africa,' one player said, deadpan. The huge bowl of cooked biryani went untouched as the players devoured their chicken.

Outside, the fans who had travelled to the game were now quiet and listless. The camp was baking hot, the sun reflecting blindingly up from the floor. A few sheltered under a tree in the shade.

What is life like here? I asked, now that the workers were away from their bosses and back on home turf.

They began shouting out, one by one.

'It is not good. We are not good!' said one.

'It is like we are in the ghetto!' said another.

Soon each man was calling out his complaint.

'We live in a slum!'

'No, even a slum is better than this one!'

'Even the slums of *Nairobi* are better than this one,' added a third man, as if comparing their accommodation to the absolute worst place on earth.

'This is like a rabbit's house.'

'We live eight people in the room!'

And you? I asked another worker.

'12.'

And you?

'14.'

Only two things seemed to be as the workers had expected. They were paid on time (part of Qatar's reform to make sure wages were transferred into an account) and they had air conditioning, even if some of them lived 14 to a room. 'We get paid on time but we get peanuts,' said Maxwell, a Kenyan labourer. 'This is not a salary, this is peanuts.' Maxwell was like most of the workers there, who said they were getting less than 700 riyals a month (£144). Some said it was as low as 625 riyals a month (£130). 'That is what we are getting,' said Maxwell, with a shrug. He used to be in the Kenyan army and was earning five times as much. But he was the only son in the family and his mother wanted him to do something less dangerous, and feared he'd be sent to Somalia to fight the militant group Al Shabab. 'We have to work so hard for that money,' he said.

A large crowd of workers had now gathered under the tree, with more grievances being aired. 'There are better jobs, but they don't pick us for them,' said one worker, who claimed that the best jobs and paid overtime were distributed on racial lines, not on who worked the hardest. Indian bosses would prefer Indian workers. Pakistani bosses, Pakistani workers.

'They are against Africans!' shouted one worker.

Everyone agreed. But now two of the camp's security guards had noticed the growing crowd, and had tried to blend in, even though they were Indian and at least a foot smaller than everyone else. As one worker explained the low pay for back-breaking work, the guard walked behind him and put his hand over the worker's mouth when he thought I wasn't looking.

9.

The Khalifa International Stadium appears unrecognisable from what I had seen in 2011. Back then Qatar was hosting the Asian Cup finals, the equivalent of the European Championships. That was six weeks after the vote to award Qatar the right to host the 2022 World Cup finals. It was winter. It rained constantly and was so cold Qataris could be seen at the matches wearing ski jackets over their white robes. Back then I had seen 50,000 people, mainly Qataris, cheer on the Maroon as they beat China 2–0 in the Asian Cup group stage – a huge proportion of the local population. But today, the grass has gone and every surface is covered in scaffolding. The stadium has been transformed into a busy building site filled with 2,800 migrant workers.

It was here in the Aspire Zone that Amnesty International gathered the interviews for their damning report on Qatar's treatment of migrant workers building the World Cup venues. This will not be where the final is held – that stadium is being built in Lusail, a new city being constructed 20 kilometres along the coast, north of Doha – but the Khalifa International Stadium is still to be a central venue, and will be hosting at least one of the semi-finals. 'It will be finished next year,' shouts the Eastern European site foreman as he shows me around. He is keen to point out that the workers all have different skills and come from a wide range of countries, like Lebanon or Europe. But most are from Bangladesh, India and Pakistan, and are earning 800 riyals a month (£165).

That's very low, isn't it? I ask.

'It is approved from the Qatari Ministry of Labour. They decide the level of wages. They control it,' the foreman replies, defensively. 'I can show you now a photo: one labourer from India, building a duplex. It is not much for us. But it makes a lot for them.'

So how many of your workers are labourers on the lowest wages? I ask.

'Just over 50 per cent,' he replies.

Workers in blue overalls and hard hats buzz past, not wanting to make eye contact. None want to speak, until the foreman insists. 'Don't be afraid,' he says to a nervous group of Bangladeshi labourers. 'COME!'

One man shuffles forward, the only one, they say, who can speak English.

How is life in Qatar? I ask.

'Nice,' he says.

And the conditions here?

He looks at the foreman and his team all standing and watching him in silence. 'Nice,' he repeats.

Is the work good?

'Yes,' he replies. 'Good work.' His eyes dart between mine, his friends and the delegation of bosses. 'Very nice, Qatar! Very nice, Doha! Very nice, my company! There are no problems!' he says finally, before running back to work.

'See!' the foreman says, before shouting after the men and pointing at me. 'If you have any problems he will sort them out.' He laughs to himself.

The intense spotlight that the World Cup has brought has at least given fresh impetus to those who oppose the *kafala* system. But to many within Qatar, *kafala* is a positive thing. It controls mass migration and protects the citizens in a country where Qataris are a tiny minority. Many feel their culture is under threat. 'The majority of Qatari people don't want the World Cup in Qatar,' says Khalid al Hail, Qatar's most outspoken opposition figure. 'Qatar is the only country in the GCC [Gulf Cooperation Council] area that has a majority of religious people,' he says, pointing out that Qatar follows the strict, ultra-conservative Wahhabi form of Islam favoured by Saudi Arabia. This more than anything, believes Al Hail, explains why Qataris are at best ambivalent, but at worst may even directly oppose the finals: 'Our people oppose the World Cup from a religious point of view. They don't like the fact when the World Cup comes to Qatar they have to let [in] alcohol and other things against Islamic values. Do you think they will be peaceful, like now, when they see alcohol in the streets, with their Islamic principles? I know many people, especially the Islamic extremists, and they are angry. You can call it "Project Anger".'

Al Hail lives in London now, in exile. He set up the Qatari National Democratic Movement because, he says, he was against 'Islamic politics' and the fact that Qatar supported the Muslim Brotherhood, with its links to Hamas, propped up, financially, by the Qatari government who, as recently as August 2016, sent £31 million to Gaza to pay the wages of non-security civil servants there. Khaled Mashal, the political leader of Hamas, also lives in exile in Doha.

Al Hail, a wealthy construction magnate, fled Qatar in 2014. His outspoken opinions on the government and the arrest of several high-profile figures – including a poet sentenced to life in prison for writing a poem that allegedly defamed the Emir – eventually brought about his own arrest. He was tortured, he claims, and had his passport seized. When he was released, he managed to escape the country illegally: 'When I remember home, I remember the detention centre. They killed everything beautiful in me towards my country. And now, it is fear. What is going to happen to you? Life in jail? Executed? That's what happens if you oppose the head of state in a country in an absolute monarchy.' Al Hail claimed political asylum in the UK, but still has a unique perspective on the network of influence and patronage in Qatar, not least because he owned several construction companies. 'The government of Qatar try to assert control as they don't separate politics from business,' he says. 'If there is ever a political issue it comes back to business.'

**

The sun is setting in Doha as another day of work is coming to an end. As night encroaches, the grey buses filled with shattered workers, their blue overalls and skin covered in sand and dirt, leave the building sites and head back to the camps. A lucky few will have a bed in the nearby Labor City, the brand new camp that will ultimately house a few thousand workers in much better conditions than those found elsewhere in Doha. In Labor City they will have a cinema and a cricket pitch, a barber's shop and a gym. Four men will live in each room, with air conditioning.

The roads are empty as you travel for an hour northwest of Doha, until a traffic jam suddenly halts you in what appears to be the middle of nowhere. Dozens of grey buses full of workers are backed up, surrounded by a swirl of dust. Up ahead, just visible on the horizon, is the single dirt track down which every bus wants to head, towards the labour camps of Al Shahaniya. It takes another 30 minutes of queuing just to get to the turning. Our car, following a bus, bumps along the unlit track lined with a handful of garages dealing in scrap metal and reconditioned engine parts. A few enterprising men have set up grocery shops. The buses disappear, one by one, down separate unlit tracks, towards their assigned camps.

Far away from Doha, far away from Labor City and far away from where the World Cup is being built, tens of thousands of men live in these camps that have spread into a township on the edge of Al Shahaniya, a tiny town in the centre of Qatar famous for its camel-racing track. You can buy, or sell, a labour camp in Al Shahaniya easily. Real estate companies and online ads offer dozens of deals. One offers a camp that can hold 250 people, with five bathrooms and five kitchens, sleeping six men to a room. Yours for only 1,800 Qatari riyals a month – about £370.

Security guards prowl the entrance to each camp. We stop by the road that has the fewest security guards and wait in the shadows of an abandoned truck until a bus full of men turns down the track. We run next to it, hidden from the security guards on the other side of the vehicle. It's a further ten minutes down the track, past a few more shops set up to sell groceries and mobile phone credit to the workers, until we reach a track that turns right towards a camp. The smell of human sewage hits you first. Ahead, there are dozens of one-storey, breeze-block huts where the men live. Next to them is one toilet and a shower block, where the smell is coming from. One of the squat toilets is blocked, spilling its contents on the cracked, dirty white-tiled floor. On the other side of the yard is the kitchen, a block with two long sideboards carrying black heavy metal gas rings to cook on.

The walls and floors are covered in grease and dirt. 'Come, let me show you,' says Mohammed, a 36-year-old Indian who has been here for four years, working as a storekeeper. 'Everything is bad here, look . . .' He opens the door to his room. A filthy air-conditioning unit is struggling against the heat. There are ten men watching an Indian Premier League cricket match on an old TV that they have ingeniously hooked up to Indian TV. 'Look, I've had this mattress for four years,' he says, lifting a thin, threadbare, brown-stained mattress. 'The air conditioning is not in good condition. There's no maintenance. The food we are cooking ourselves. The toilets and the kitchen are very bad.' Down every narrow, bare-brick corridor live dozens of men who have similar stories. The corridors go on, seemingly indefinitely; hundreds upon hundreds of people working for a complex network of contractors and subcontractors covering every kind of work and project in Qatar.

In one room, six Ghanaian men are sitting on the floor, a large Ghana flag hanging above them. The walls are covered in plastic sheeting. A tiny, filthy air-conditioning unit rattles in the corner. 'We are building a tower. I can't remember the company, but the agent deceived us,' says Simon, a 24-year-old stonemason. 'Things in Qatar are not what we thought. We come over and we have no one over here so we just have to accept it like that and do the work. So we don't have any option.' The six men are paid half the salary they were promised. 'They said we are not qualified masons so they pay us less,' he explains. Now he is only earning 1,000 riyals a month (just over £200). But he feels lucky in one respect: 'The same agent is bringing people for 800 riyals now.' It is a buyers' market. The biggest surprise for the men is the hostility they have encountered. 'There are people who talk to you like you are not a human being,' Simon says. 'In my country I don't get treated like this. I'm working for you, we live six to a room, we don't have anything to entertain ourselves. You come back after working you eat and you sleep. Early morning to work. Then work.'

The men had each paid 7,000 Ghanaian cedi to an agent to get here (over £1,000). Once the money they spend on food and other expenses is taken out, they can only send 500 riyals back home every month at most. 'You have kids' school fees,' says Simon. 'Mum and Dad, brothers to look after. How can you sustain that? It is not an option to leave. We are here already with a three-year contract.' The lure of working in Qatar is strong. 'We're here because we were told they have money – all those buildings because of the World Cup,' says Ismail, a 25-year-old labourer wearing a white, knitted Islamic *kufi* headdress. 'We are putting all our efforts into Qatar hosting the World Cup. But the salary is so low.' Each of the six men regrets coming but feel trapped. Even if they could break their contract, what would their families do back home? And how would they repay the agent? 'I would rather stay in my own country and earn 600 cedi [around £115] a month. You cannot travel abroad to work and take this little money,' says Ismail.

It was getting late and the men had to sleep, in preparation for their 4 a.m. alarm call. Ismail walked us out of the labyrinth of identical corridors and back to the yard with the filthy kitchen and broken toilets. 'Look at the way things are,' he says. 'Tell people. We are like animals in here.'

We wait for another vehicle to pass. This time it is a lorry pulling a water tanker. As soon as it passes the security block, we run, hidden from the security guards, and dive into the shadow of the same abandoned lorry outside, back into our car, and back onto the road to Doha.

10.

The five-star La Cigale Hotel, Doha is a one-hour drive away from the workers in Al Shahaniya. Three boulder-sized cut-glass chandeliers hang in its opulent lobby. Upstairs, on its popular terrace affording views of the entire city, one meal costs the same as one month's wages for a migrant labourer from Bangladesh or Nepal or Ghana. Business is good. The cafés and bars downstairs are full with a multicultural clientele. Real Madrid are playing Manchester City in the semi-finals of the Champions League tonight and every table is booked.

Hassan al Thawadi can usually get a table, whenever he likes, anywhere he likes. The general secretary of the Supreme Committee for Delivery and Legacy has one of the most high-profile and important jobs in Qatar: not only delivering the World Cup, but also having to deal with the political fallout that has followed the decision to award it to Qatar, even though he freely admits he is no politician. 'I think he was overwhelmed by the players. He jumped on the pitch!' says Al Thawadi as he sits down in the café near the lobby, wearing his white robes, and discussing this week's visit of FIFA president Gianni Infantino. 'You saw a lot of the players take selfies with him. What he [Infantino] liked about the Workers' Cup was the atmosphere. Every year it gets better.'

It has been an intense few days for Al Thawadi. Shortly after the release of the scathing Amnesty International report, a UN conference – the 2016 Asia Regional Forum on Business and Human Rights – was coincidently held in Doha. It also heard criticism from several speakers about Qatar's workers' rights record. One speaker, Professor John Ruggie, a former UN human rights advisor and now at Harvard, had drafted an equally damaging report on FIFA's recent approach to human rights. In it, he recommended that Qatar should be stripped of the World Cup if there wasn't adequate movement on reforms. 'Reputations hang in the balance as the whole world watches not just the games and participants but what it took to get there,' he told the conference, although the Qatari delegation had left before he spoke.

The avalanche of criticism that hit Qatar had finally led the government to announce that the *kafala* system was to be abolished by

THE MIDDLE EAST: PRINCES AND SHEIKHS

the end of the year. But that also prompted other questions. Did Qatar regret investing in football in this way, inviting scrutiny it perhaps wasn't prepared for? And was the reform genuine? Guidelines had been set as to how best to treat migrant workers, yet most were still living in miserable conditions, living miserable lives, permanently in debt. The economics of migrant labour had clearly been proven to be false. Once every middle man has taken their cut, a worker is left with barely enough money to send home. It certainly didn't feel like the reforms implemented so far were having any effect. One hour earlier I had been talking to angry Ghanaian labourers living in abject conditions. Now, I was drinking an espresso from expensive china with the man who as much as anyone could influence which direction the country headed in next.

Is it ethical in such a rich country for someone to be paid $200 a month? I ask.

'I can't . . . I'm not fully aware. I'm not the right person,' Al Thawadi responds. 'In the areas we are responsible . . . I look at worker welfare, where we can influence and have a say on that. Ethical recruitment. Getting rid of worker fees so any new worker doesn't have to pay. Accommodation, making sure it is healthy. How many to a room. We can address those. Safety in the workplace, transportation. Repatriation. These are the areas we are responsible for.'

Recruitment is another issue that seems unsolvable. I point out that Bangladesh, a nation of 160 million, appears solely dependent on the recruitment industry. Even if, as Al Thawadi says, awareness campaigns are being set up in Nepal and other countries warning workers not to use an agent, the message will still be lost on half of the residents of the village near Comilla, where the Hoque brothers had returned after being deported from the UAE. Half the village, after all, is illiterate. '[The changes] are making a positive impact on workers' lives,' states Al Thawadi. 'The Worker Welfare Forum. It allow for workers to vote for a representative who raises issues. Those minutes are being shared with us.' But these changes will make no difference to the lives of men and women coming from Bangladesh. The recruitment industry is too entrenched, too powerful. And banning all Bangladeshi workers would plunge their economy into free fall.

So far 24 World Cup contractors have been blacklisted for labour violations. Two hundred thousand good-quality rooms are being built for workers too, he claims. But why herd workers into faraway camps in the first place? They live separate lives, isolated from the rest of the country, as if they were Qatar's dirty secret. And where will the new 'quality rooms' be built? I ask. 'That is for the market to dictate,' he replies.

Within Qatar, Al Thawadi had to negotiate a difficult path. He was not a member of a royal family, which makes influence harder to achieve in an absolute monarchy. There were those who objected to the World Cup for religious reasons. There were those who objected to it based on the huge cost – money that could be better spent on clearing Qatari citizens' debt. There were also those who objected to it because it was a project for foreigners, building facilities Qataris would never use, which would only make them a smaller minority in their own country. 'Qataris generally understand the situation,' he explains. 'It is a question of recognition. If you take a certain number of steps. No one is saying anything is fixed. That is not the issue. Much more developed countries face significant abuse. This is a global issue. It's complicated. The only thing I see, there needs to be a recognition of the facts being discussed. An understanding of the steps Qatar's made.'

In that respect he was correct. Reform was being discussed, even if that discussion was taking place largely because of the media coverage of the awful conditions many workers faced.

Whether they admit it or not, investing in football has become an issue of the highest political importance for both the UAE and Qatar. There was a recognition that, in a part of the world that wanted to run before it could walk, football offered a route to a basic form of nation building – or at least a collective idea of the Emirates and Qatar that could be sold abroad. But the projects and the wealth haven't been built and sustained by oil and gas alone – rather by the millions of men and women who've arrived to work in their countries for little or no return while being treated, as Ismail the Ghanaian mason I had met earlier this evening pointed out, 'like animals'.

'At the forefront is workers' welfare,' insists Al Thawadi. '*Kafala*, from what I know, the law will come in November 2016 and it will end the system. It will be a contractually based relationship between employer and employee.' That, Al Thawadi hopes, will spread to other Gulf states, even if, so far, there has appeared to be zero appetite for reform in both the UAE and Saudi Arabia. If it happened, it would, accidentally, be a hugely important legacy.

December 2016 would see the new labour law introduced. Workers will no longer need an exit permit from their employers, although they will still have to apply to the authorities three days before travel. But workers will now be able to move jobs at the end of their contract period. Currently, workers are banned from Qatar for two years if they leave their job. The reforms are unlikely to appease trade unions and human rights groups, and do nothing to address chronic low pay and the third-class status of migrant workers.

As we sipped our coffee there were still years until the World Cup in Qatar would kick off. Al Thawadi points to the café full of different nationalities and languages around us. 'Sport has this overwhelming ability to focus on an event for a short space of time. The Champions League, Madrid v Man City, every table is booked,' he notes. 'There's nothing bringing them together here other than Real Madrid or Man City. That is what the World Cup is about too.' Al Thawadi believes that, in an age of extremism, football can bridge a gap, if only for a short time. The question is: will it have been worth it? Qatar could host a World Cup built with a reformed labour system that genuinely sets a precedent to improve millions of lives. Or it could lose the finals and sink into resentment. It could put a team together for the finals that will be humiliated by being knocked out in the first round. Or it could build a football team capable of competing. Several Aspire graduates will feature, perhaps several who were born in Africa too.

Maybe *kafala* will end. And maybe the unthinkable can happen and Qatar will, with the help of Aspire, win the whole thing. 'If Qatar wins the World Cup,' replies Al Thawadi, before leaving through the opulent lobby and past the expensive sports cars being valeted out front, 'then I think the whole world will go insane.'

Postscript

Portsmouth, United Kingdom

Colin Farmery doesn't notice the man with the gun and a hawk walking around the Fratton Park pitch until I point them out to him. Colin is an archivist, historian and activist at Portsmouth FC, as well as a lifelong fan. We are sitting high up in the North Stand talking about his club's recent ownership sagas when it becomes clear that there is a man, with a rifle and the untethered bird of prey, looking to shoot vermin, rats and pigeons in particular. 'He's not here to muck about,' deadpans Colin when I ask if the gun is loaded with real bullets. 'If he sees something that needs dealing with, he'll deal with it.'

Only a few years ago it seemed more likely than not that this stadium, and this club, was as imperilled as Fratton Park's rats. The club, found on the south coast of England, had won the league twice but since then had always been on the cusp of being a top side – 'A second-tier side with ambitions for the first division,' as Colin explains it. Those back-to-back league titles were in 1949 and 1950. Yet in 2008, with an expensively assembled squad bankrolled by French-Israeli tycoon Alexandre 'Sacha' Gaydamak, the club won the FA Cup and finished eighth in the Premier League. There was debt, of course. Every club in the league had debt. Portsmouth's £65 million was comparable to other clubs like Bolton Wanderers and West Ham United. More importantly, with Gaydamak providing the funding, it was manageable. 'Winning the FA Cup was a once-in-a-lifetime moment for me, for my club to take on the big boys and win,' says Colin, who was working as a deputy principal in a local school while following the club he had supported for 40 years. In his spare time he had edited the club's programme and written several books on Portsmouth's history. 'The fans were very happy. You've got a sugar-daddy owner. We were a mini Abramovich-style club. A mini Man City,' he says. 'What we didn't appreciate was how quickly it would unravel.'

As the 2008 global financial crisis hit, the money stopped as Sacha Gaydamak effectively pulled the plug on his spending. Portsmouth went into free fall, changing ownership five times in four years, passing through the hands of a rogues' gallery of men with scarcely believable backstories. One owner was a Russian banker wanted for suspected money laundering in Lithuania. Another was an Emirati fantasist with good intentions but no money. It wasn't clear whether one of the owners, a Saudi called Ali al Faraj, even existed. Gaydamak had faced a lot of questions about his wealth when he bought the club from the Serbian-American software tycoon Milan Mandarić in 2006. For one, it appeared that the Gaydamak family wealth didn't reside with him, but with his father. Arcadi Gaydamak already owned a football club, Beitar Jerusalem in Israel, which would contravene UEFA rules on owning controlling stakes of clubs that might meet in European competition.

Arcadi was a controversial figure. He was born in Russia, made his money in France and later made *aliyah* to Israel. He had been wanted on an international arrest warrant for his alleged role in gun-running during the Angolan civil war in the early 1990s, but in Israel he was largely safe. There, he bought Beitar, a club renowned for its ultra-nationalist fan base that had a host of supporters among Israel's right-wing political elite, including the current prime minister, Benjamin Netanyahu. Arcadi had hoped that Beitar could form a springboard for political office. 'I was never a football fan, I always said that,' Gaydamak admitted when he was interviewed for *Forever Pure*, a documentary about Beitar. 'But Beitar had more fans than all the other clubs in Israel combined. And this is why it is a very interesting propaganda tool. It has a huge influence on Israel society.' He founded a new political party and ran for mayor of Jerusalem, but humiliatingly he only got 3 per cent of the vote and came in third. He lost interest in the club soon after. He was dogged by allegations of financial impropriety wherever he went. When he was investigated by Israeli authorities over accusations of money laundering, he presented a list of assets, later published in an Israeli newspaper. They totalled £1.6 billion and included Portsmouth. In 2009 he was sentenced by a French court, *in absentia*, to six years in prison over the gun-running and money-laundering charges. In the end, Arcadi presented himself to French authorities in 2015. He was arrested and sentenced to three years in prison for tax evasion and money laundering. The gun-running charges were dropped. Three months later he was released, to serve the rest of his sentence under house arrest with an electronic tag.

Sacha always maintained that he paid for Portsmouth with money from real-estate deals he made in Russia. It was an explanation the Premier League accepted. It was merely a coincidence that Sacha's money troubles coincided with his father's. 'I remember in the summer of 2007, Gaydamak had meetings with supporter representatives and I asked him a question,' says Colin. 'I asked, "What's the plan to avoid us being a Leeds?"' he said, referencing the once-dominant Yorkshire team that had flown too close to the sun, reached the Champions League but had collapsed under the weight of unmanageable debt. 'There was this frisson of horror that I had had the audacity to ask that question. Peter Storrie [the club's then CEO] was asked whether I could ask the question!' Gaydamak gave an empty answer, referring to a Deloitte report on football finances, and talking about the management of future revenues.

There was, Colin says, 'not a huge amount of dissent' to Sacha Gaydamak's tenure. Portsmouth had, after all, played AC Milan in the

UEFA Cup, drawing 2–2 with them at Fratton Park. And although the 2008–09 season didn't go to plan, they survived relegation. But that was all about to change when Gaydamak finally sold the club along with its £65 million debt to a familiar face: Sulaiman al Fahim, the Emirati who had fronted Sheikh Mansour's purchase of Manchester City. Immediately it became clear he didn't have the money to keep up the spending needed to service the debt and invest in the team. His tenure lasted 42 days, and was mired in fan protests and online threats to get out of the club. It was described by the *Guardian* as 'not only the shortest but surely the most ill-fated tenure in Premier League history'. Al Fahim sold his stake to a consortium backed by chairman Peter Storrie and led by an unknown Saudi investor with alleged royal links called Ali al Faraj.

When I met Al Fahim for a second time, in October 2009, just after the Portsmouth sale, he was very different to the brash property developer dressed in a flamboyantly coloured *kandora* who had been the face of the Manchester City deal. He was now in sports jacket and jeans, slightly balding, sitting in the lobby of a fancy Kensington hotel. 'I believe Peter Storrie from day one wanted the [rival] consortium of Ali al Faraj [because] he brought them in,' Al Fahim said, fiddling with his prayer beads as he talked. 'With me there would be no overpayment, everything would be at the right time with the right investment. Mine was £5 million as equity. But . . . they wanted £10 million in two weeks. So I sold the club.' Al Fahim thought his brief ownership was a success. 'Who would have thought that by investing £5 million you would get 10 per cent of a [Premier League] club?' he said. A few days later, despite his unpopularity, he turned up at Fratton Park to watch from the directors' box as Portsmouth beat Wigan 4–0. Colin still hears from him occasionally, enquiring about recent results. 'Let's be charitable. He overreached himself,' says Colin. 'He is not a significantly wealthy man. He might have had the trappings and appearance of it. The reality was that he was a broker, he got super-rich people into the room, and they did the deal. When he ended up at Pompey he didn't have the money required to do what was necessary.' Alas, Colin is unlikely to hear from Sulaiman al Fahim for a while. In February 2018 a court in the United Arab Emirates found him guilty of stealing the £5 million he used to buy Portsmouth from his wife. He was sentenced, *in absentia*, to five years in prison.

Sulaiman al Fahim was followed by Ali al Faraj. His reign was a disaster too. No one had ever seen him. Some started to doubt his existence. All Portsmouth had seen, according to Colin, was a 'grainy fax of a passport copy' to prove who he was. 'No one from the club ever, ever saw him,' he maintains. That season Portsmouth became the first Premier League club to go into administration and were relegated. A Hong Kong-based financier called Balram Chainrai came next. He had loaned Portsmouth £17 million. The club had effectively mortgaged the stadium and when Chainrai received no repayments he took over. The club had no money, nor even its own bank account. It was around this time that the Pompey Supporters' Trust was set up. They'd had enough of the succession of owners who were using the club, in their view, as a cash cow to settle scores and debts. It was the final ownership battle that brought Portsmouth to their second spell in administration.

Vladimir Antonov looked as if he was an Abramovich-in-waiting. He owned a Lithuanian bank and was part of London's wealthy Russian elite. The problem was that it was soon discovered that he was in trouble back in Lithuania, where he was wanted for alleged money laundering. He was arrested in London and was about to be extradited, when he went on the run. He is now believed to be in Moscow, where the Russian authorities are unlikely to extradite him. 'A cursory Google search raised question marks over him,' says Colin. 'We still had this £17 million debt. When he came to his sticky end that was the point at which we went into administration again.' Every single owner had passed English football's Fit and Proper Persons Test.

It was then, as Colin puts it, that 'the battle for the mortal soul of the football club began'. The supporters' trust began to float the idea of raising some money themselves, even though it would have been a paltry amount compared to the £100 million the first administrator demanded they raise before they'd even be allowed to sit at the table. By now, the trust had raised £1.8 million, when 1,800 fans agreed to chip in £1,000 each. 'We started to uncover what happened during the bad times of financial mismanagement from the ownership and executives at the club,' recalls Ashley Brown, the chairman of Pompey Supporters' Trust. 'Some of those stories, they are horrendous.'

What are the worst examples? I ask.

'The chief executive [Peter Storrie] was on a win bonus for the team of up to £3,000 a win. That is absolutely crazy,' he replies. 'It wasn't just the owners but some of the people who tried to be owners. We were fighting against one guy who supposedly built underwater hotels and had connections to various questionable international crime gangs. We had other people . . . they would be straight out of a novel.'

There was a court battle over the outstanding £17 million charge. The case hung on who the administrator believed had the best chance of paying off its creditors, including the taxman. At first HMRC, the British government's tax authority, refused to consider Portsmouth's choice of administrator. They had a long and strained relationship with football, an industry it believed went out of its way to deceive the exchequer at every turn. There was also the 'football creditors rule', imposed by the league, that gave preferential treatment to players, staff and clubs ahead of the taxman. In the end, they appointed Trevor Birch, the former Chelsea CEO, in the role. He told me he had never seen a club in such a mess as Portsmouth. 'There was a particular problem with the charge on the ground, that created difficulties to make a sale,' Trevor said when we spoke on the phone. 'It was worth substantially less than the charge and the players were on unaffordable contracts.' Amazingly, the community-owned option won after Birch negotiated an eleventh-hour deal with Chainrai's company Portpin to accept the money on the table from the supporters' trust. 'It is very, very difficult to let your heart rule your head as you are an officer of the court,' he explained of those last-minute dealings. 'It just so happened the stars were aligned and theirs [the PST bid] was the only game in town and enabled me to say to the court that this would save the business rather than breaking it up and selling off the stadium independently.' The deal, Trevor believes, was the first of its kind he had seen in football. 'It was the marrying of the two groups that was unique in football,' he said. 'A group of hard-headed business people, willing to stand by supporters. That doesn't happen.' Birch had now travelled full circle. In 2003 he was chief executive of Chelsea and brokered the club's sale to Roman Abramovich. He had seen the super-rich who were investing in the game up close. I asked him why he thought billionaires from around the world were buying football clubs. 'If you look at each of those billionaires there are slightly different reasons,' he replied. 'Underpinning it all is the huge global popularity of the game.' The financial possibilities that booming TV rights offered were obviously a draw too, even though many have a track record of shunning the publicity that football club ownership brings. 'It gives you global notoriety and fame,' he says of how life changes after buying a club. 'If you look at the Glazers, they shun publicity. Abramovich shuns publicity. Maybe for the Glazers it is more of a financial play. Manchester City is effectively owned by a country.'

Having sat opposite him in 2003, and agreed a deal to sell Chelsea in 15 minutes, was he any closer to understanding why Roman Abramovich bought Chelsea, I asked.

'No,' he replied.

In April 2013, Birch had played a key if dispassionate role in ensuring Portsmouth FC became the largest fan-owned club in the country. 'It was a hugely emotional moment,' says Colin. But now, Portsmouth had other pressing problems. While fighting off five owners, engaging in countless court battles, laying off most of their staff and living with the genuine fear they would go out of business, Portsmouth had been relegated four times. 'Most of players were out of contract. We had to agree settlements with the others as their wages were unaffordable,' Brown remembers. 'We literally had something like two or three players left at the club.'

Portsmouth found themselves at the bottom of League Two, the old fourth division, with a ten-point deduction and no team.

**

Does it matter who owns a football club? Does it matter where the money comes from? Does it matter why someone has chosen to buy and bankroll your team? The simplest answer I heard, whether it was Colin at Portsmouth, or Jacco from ADO Den Haag, was that most fans I met didn't care; as long as their team won silverware, they would accept almost any owner.

But not everyone wins, and that is when the questions begin to be asked. About the owners and what they are in it for. It certainly isn't an issue with foreign ownership over British owners, as the supporters of countless clubs across the country can attest. Globalisation has made the idea of foreign ownership almost redundant. Clubs owned by wealthy supporters can equally be as problematic. Look no further than Mike Ashley, the billionaire owner of Newcastle United. Ashley made his money building Sports Direct, a hugely successful sportswear retailer. In Britain, he is also one of the biggest users of so-called 'zero hours' contracts, a flexible way of employing staff that gives no actual obligation to offer any work. The contracts have been blamed for deepening poverty and raising uncertainty for millions of low-paid service sector workers. Over 90 per cent of Mike Ashley's workforce is on zero-hours contracts. A recalcitrant Ashley was dragged before a Parliamentary Select Committee to answer questions about his business after an undercover investigation by the *Guardian* revealed the terrible conditions in some of Sports Direct's warehouses. Some workers were not being paid the full minimum wage either. In the end, Ashley agreed to pay back over £1 million in lost pay, while his company faced a £2 million fine for the breach.

And then there was West Ham United, who had themselves almost gone bust when an Icelandic consortium led by banking tycoon Björgólfur Guðmundsson lost his shirt in the 2008 financial crisis. Before that the club almost ended up in the hands of Boris Berezovsky and Badri Patarkatsishvili, the two oligarchs who had fallen out with Abramovich. Through a network of offshore companies they had bought the transfer rights of two players who ended up playing at West Ham in a deal that almost ruined the club. The Carlos Tevez and Javier Mascherano affair saw two of Argentina's brightest prospects sign for a decidedly mid-table West Ham United, but it soon emerged that the deal had been against rules governing the outside influence of so-called third parties. 'If the oligarchs had been passive investors in the two players, West Ham would have complied with the rules,' Alex Duff and Tariq Panja wrote in their book *Football's Secret Trade*. 'But it would become clear that they had complete control over the next transfer of the Argentines.' Tevez's goals ultimately saved West Ham from relegation. The Premier League, meanwhile, levied a record £5.5 million fine. It could have been worse. A points deduction would have led to relegation and cost them ten times that. Sheffield United, who had been relegated, took West Ham to an independent tribunal, where £18.1 million in compensation was agreed. Shortly afterwards, David Gold and David Sullivan, lifelong West Ham fans who had sold Birmingham City to the now jailed Hong Kong hairdresser Carson Yeung, bought a controlling stake in the club. The 2012 Olympics were about to take place on their doorstep and the club agreed a potentially lucrative but controversial deal to move into the vacant Olympic Stadium. It was announced by the Conservative government that West Ham would pay a peppercorn rent in a stadium bankrolled by the British taxpayer. Karren Brady, who closed the deal, was made a Conservative peer in 2014.

In every country, following the money back to how and where it was made had revealed a trail of victims: fans, migrant workers, citizens of whole cities. In Russia and Ukraine the men who invest in football made their money from the fire sale of state assets, and kept it by propping up regimes that perpetuate corruption and restrict freedoms. Football-club ownership offers them legitimacy and insurance. Roman Abramovich has provided a model for others.

Then, in March 2018, came the attempted assassination of Russian double agent Sergei Skerpal and his daughter Yulia in the British city of Salisbury. Russia denied involvement but the British government expelled Russian diplomats. There was another lever available: the Putin-connected Russian oligarchs who had invested in Britain. 'And here there are three key surnames,' Alexi Navalny wrote after the Salisbury incident. 'Abramovich, Usmanov and Shuvalov.'

Something unusual happened next. There was a delay in renewing Roman Abramovich's British visa. Abramovich flew to Tel Aviv and, as is every Jewish person's right, requested Israeli citizenship. It was quickly granted. A few days later Chelsea announced the suspension of their new £500 million stadium project 'due to the current unfavourable investment climate.' It was a clear message to Britain. *Can you live without our money?* Chelsea's future might answer that question.

Shakhtar Donetsk owner Rinat Akhmetov wasn't doing so well either. His assets in eastern Ukraine were seized by pro-Russian rebels. He lost two-thirds of his fortune. But the club did find a new place to play: the Metalist Stadium in Kharkiv. Shakhtar was now only 300 kilometres from home.

With American proprietors like Stan Kroenke profit is king. Even as the LA Rams were raking in cash, Kroenke was busy evicting low-income residents from his 520,000-acre W. T. Waggoner Estate Ranch in Texas.

One resident, Rick Ellis, killed himself. The first line of his suicide note read: 'Stan, you took my home.'

'Kroenke gives the ultra-rich a bad name,' wrote Jeff Gordon in the *St. Louis Post-Dispatch*. 'Moving a terrible NFL team to a bigger market is one thing and ruining people's lives is another. We'll be OK without the Rams. Those people in Texas will not be OK without a place to live.'

Both American and Chinese owners are eager to join forces to push for a European Super League, where their investments in football clubs will be protected from the uncertainty of promotion and relegation. The uncertainty of merit is the enemy of profit. It was the threat of such a breakaway that saw UEFA announce proposed changes to the Champions League format in 2018. Now, the top four nations would be guaranteed four places each, cutting the number of champions from smaller countries who were already struggling to compete due to the huge inequalities between leagues. There was at least a small compensation for St Louisans. A St Louis court ruled that Rams fans who had bought Personal Seat Licences were entitled to get their deposit back. Terry Crouppen, the lawyer who aired the #slamstan Super Bowl advert, will at least get some of the money back on the four PSLs he bought for his family in 1995. At the start of 2017 the city and county of St Louis launched a multi-million dollar lawsuit against the NFL for the economic damage Kroenke's LA move caused. And the saga of state subsidies for sport stadia seemed to be settled, at least for now. Jeanette Mott Oxford finally saw a vote on the proposal to use a city-wide sales tax to fund a soccer stadium seen as essential for an MLS expansion. The city voted against it, 53 per cent to 47.

Chinese businesses continue to invest in football, although not without problems. Li Yonghong's €740 million deal to buy AC Milan was held up for eight months after a suspected forged document was used to provide proof of funds. Ever since the club has been bedevilled by questions about the owner's true wealth.

Information on most Chinese buyers was difficult to verify. A new, globalised generation was pushing the rules, built for a different age, to the limit. Take Gao Jisheng, chairman of Chinese company Lander. A 2017 bid to buy 80 per cent of Southampton FC for £210 million initially floundered. The Premier League discovered that Lander had been involved in a bribery scandal a decade before. Gao testified in return for immunity from prosecution. As there was no conviction, the Southampton deal eventually went through. The Premier League changed its rules to stop a similar situation arising.

Investment in Chinese football appears to be cooling too. A 100 per cent tax on transfer fees for foreign players over £5 million was introduced. Limits on foreign investment were also put in place. According to the *Asia Times*' Liu Hsiu Wen and Richard Cook, that move was directed at 'those who are perhaps more focused on rapidly moving their billions past China's capital controls and into the murky washing machine that is international football.'

Meanwhile, China lost 1–0 to Syria in World Cup qualification. Protestors demanded Gao Hongbo's sacking. After losing to Uzbekistan, Gao stepped down. China failed to qualify for Russia 2018. Xi's football revolution would have to wait.

Jacco, the head of the ADO Den Haag supporters' group, was at least happier. His new job in Utrecht was going well and ADO were briefly at the top of the table, the first time that had happened in years. But soon enough, ADO were sliding down the table (at one point they were rock bottom) and Wang was again missing his deadlines. 'It's the same old song, I guess,' Jacco said when I emailed him. With even more payment deadlines missed, the KNVB again placed ADO Den Haag in category one, reserved for the clubs with the worst finances. By now, the club had had enough, and took Wang Hui to court in an effort to force him to pay what they say he owed. The Dutch court removed him from the board and in January 2017 ordered him to pay over €2.5 million.

Qatar's World Cup continues to be built under intense scrutiny. The Workers' Cup returned for another year, with more teams and bigger crowds. But many of the players and supporters I had spoken to had returned to Africa, unhappy at the conditions and wages. Others had more positive stories to tell. While the Qatari government's efforts to reform the *kafala* system were derided by human rights organisations as mere window dressing, Arman – the Bangladeshi worker I had met excitedly boarding a flight to Doha in Dhaka – was at least being paid on time. 'With overtime I can be paid 3,000 riyals [£675 a month],' Arman says proudly when we speak on the phone. 'We are only here for money, so I am happy.'

He was working on an infrastructure project at Lusail, the huge coastal city being built from scratch and where the World Cup final would be held in 2022. Arman was lucky. He was being paid six times more than some, and he was being paid on time. It was midweek when we spoke, but he had felt unwell and been told to stay in bed. A doctor was called to see him, for free. But then a political crisis emerged that had the power to change everything. In June 2017 Qatar was economically and diplomatically ostracised by its neighbours, led by Saudi Arabia and the UAE. The Saudis especially had accused Qatar of supporting terrorism and for its close relationship with Iran. Neither reason was particularly plausible. Eventually, after Turkey stepped in with food imports and after spending anywhere up to a third of its vast surplus, it looked like Qatar had weathered the storm.

The blockade, as Qatar calls it, had created a political crisis which put the World Cup in jeopardy. Khalid al Hail, the outspoken Qatari opposition activist I had interviewed, had organised a conference in London to denounce Qatar's leadership. Although questions were raised as to who was backing Al Hail. A PR war broke out as each side tried to paint the other as mendacious and dangerous. This led to the crisis having one rather unusual effect. Reform of Qatar's *kafala* system sped up. It was announced that exit visas issued by companies would be abolished. Contracts would have to be lodged with a central committee so that workers would get the wages they were promised. A minimum wage would also be introduced, ending the practice of different wages for workers from different countries for doing the same jobs.

Both the International Trade Union Confederation and Human Rights Watch, two organisations sharply critical of Qatar, openly praised the move. But there was a word of caution. Promises had been made and broken in the past. As human rights advocate Nicholas McGeehan tweeted after the announcement was made: 'HRW take an optimistic view of the human rights situation in #Qatar in their World Report. It's OK to be optimistic, and I hope they're right. I'm skeptical and I hope I'm wrong.'

There was little good news on worker rights in the UAE, or for those who had been forced to leave. Anamul and Razaul Hoque, the brothers who returned to Bangladesh after being imprisoned and allegedly tortured in the UAE before being deported, have still not seen any compensation. In fact, they almost certainly never will. Almost a year after visiting them in Bangladesh and listening to their story – and their scepticism that they might receive rectitude for their suffering – Leigh Day, the British law firm representing the pair and nearly 40 other workers with similar stories, was forced to drop the case. 'Based on the specific facts of the case and the complexity of UAE law, following advice from Counsel it became apparent that there were too many risks involved in pursuing the case against the UK parent company in this instance,' said a spokesperson for the law firm. It appears that the sheer complexity of the supply chain, across multiple borders and multiple companies, had made it all but impossible to pin the blame on anyone. 'We have lost money, wasted our time and after losing everything we didn't get anything we deserved,' said Anamul after he heard the news. Both brothers were still living off their tiny patch of land. For them, working abroad remained the only option, even after everything that had happened. 'I have experience,' he said. 'I hope I will not be cheated this time.'

Manchester City, meanwhile, is thriving, posting record revenue (£391.8 million) and record profit (£20.5 million) for the 2015–16 season. Due to UEFA's allocation of TV money, their journey to the semi-final of the Champions League netted them close to £84 million alone, more than the actual winners of the competition, Real Madrid.

City Football Group also expanded further, purchasing Club Atlético Torque, a team in Uruguay's second division, providing a template other wealthy businessmen have followed. Multi-club ownership was spreading across the world. The Italian Pozzo family had already found success by owning Italian club Udinese, Premier League team Watford, and Grenada, before selling the Spanish club to Chinese owners. Red Bull, owned by Austrian billionaire Dietrich Mateschitz, had also formed a network that funnelled cash to German Bundesliga club RB Leipzig, Austria's FC Red Bull Salzburg and the New York Red Bulls. Others, like Atlético Madrid and Fiorentina have spread wider, investing in the Indian Premier League. It is an evolving area that will cause UEFA and FIFA regulatory problems. There are moral questions too. Were rich clubs securing unfair advantages in player development? And were they destroying the fabric of local leagues by imposing a homogenised club brand?

City did experience one piece of pushback though. Sun Jihai, the Chinese international footballer who once played for Manchester City, no longer appears on a list of inductees displayed in the National Football Museum's Hall of Fame, housed in the Urbis building in Manchester city centre. Curiously, Sun Jihai's name does appear on the museum's website, under 'Special Awards' which 'recognise individuals or organisations for their efforts, endeavours and contributions in the wider sphere of football'.

**

In the close season Portsmouth begged and borrowed to put a team together for the first game of the 2014–15 campaign. It was, from the start, a relegation battle. But they survived and began to build. The next season they went unbeaten during their first eleven games. For a while, it looked like they would run away with the league. But instead they finished in the playoff places.

More importantly, the Pompey Supporters' Trust has brought a degree of financial stability. The club's legacy debt had been paid off three years early. Tickets remain cheap. The club averages 16,000 supporters a game, by far the largest in the division. They had proved that a huge club, with history and support, can be supporter-owned. 'The most important thing football has to recognise is the role supporters should play in the governance of their club,' says Ashley. 'And that should happen even in the Premier League. Supporters remain the lifeblood of every football club. The biggest myth is that supporters can't own football clubs. Football fans are lawyers, accountants, entrepreneurs. The terrace is a mix of talents, and they have the club's best interests at heart.'

Can a leading club really be owned by supporters? Supporters of Swansea City have a powerful voice in the boardroom – or at least they did until it was sold to American owners – but what about being in charge of the whole club? For Colin, TV money means that the third tier is probably the furthest the current model of supporter-ownership can take you. As soon as teams compete in the Championship, Colin explains, you are dealing with clubs recently relegated from the Premier League with large parachute payments ten times Pompey's budget. 'I think it is difficult to imagine it taking shape in the Premier League,' admits Ashley, 'but everything below should be possible.'

For Ashley, his proximity to and love for his club was just one reason he would, as a director, always have the club's interest at heart. 'I find it an honour to be director,' he says, 'but if we messed it up I'd never be able to come to Portsmouth. I can't go back to Russia or Israel. This is my town.'

**

It's the last day of the 2015–16 season. At 2 p.m. the sun is again shining on the south coast. The Shepherd's Crook pub, a short walk from Fratton Park, is full of Portsmouth and Northampton fans singing together. Northampton Town, coincidently, played an important role in the supporters owning their own clubs. It was one of their fans, the late Brian Lomax, who helped to grow the supporters' trust movement in the UK through his Supporters Direct group. He died in 2015. Today, Portsmouth, AFC Wimbledon and Exeter City are all supporter-owned, with dozens of supporters now in boardrooms of football clubs across the country, largely thanks to Lomax.

'It feels like our club again,' says Wayne, a supporter with Portsmouth FC tattoos covering both arms, drinking a pint of lager in the sun. 'OK, we ain't in the Premier League. We ain't the force that we were. But it feels like a community club again. All these people, they didn't have Pompey in their heart. We finished 16th last season and should have been out of business, right.' Both sets of fans walk to the ground together. Eighteen thousand seven hundred and forty-two supporters watch Northampton beat Portsmouth 2–1. It's a party atmosphere on both sides. Northampton have won the league and Portsmouth have a potential Wembley date in the playoff final. They will first have to beat south coast rivals Plymouth.

Just a few minutes after the final whistle a queue has already formed at the ticket office, next to the mock-Tudor entrance to Fratton Park. 'It is fantastic. It is our club. The club is the city. The club is the community. It is all one. Fans owning the club puts the seal on it,' says Rob Morris, a season-ticket holder wearing a Portsmouth top and wrapped in a scarf, despite the sweltering late-afternoon sun. He is queuing for tickets for the playoff semi-final first leg against Plymouth. There won't be, he believes, a bigger match in the league. He had started going to Pompey in 1980 and vividly remembered his first match. 'Crewe Alexandra. 1–1,' he says quickly. 'Bruce Grobbelaar was in goal that day before he got famous. That is the thing that sticks out.'

Portsmouth didn't, of course, get their day out in Wembley. Plymouth beat them in the 91st minute of the second leg. But that didn't matter so much in the grand scheme of things. As the Pompey

Supporters' Trust, the fans and even the coach had said, everyone at the club knew that, whatever happened, the club was theirs. And no one could ever take it away from them again. 'We all feel a part of it,' says Morris. He went back to the queue. The club belonged to him, belonged to the fans and belonged to the city they loved. The problem was, how long would it stay that way?

**

Almost exactly a year later Colin Farmery is walking around a park in Nottingham on a Saturday morning, filling time before Portsmouth's match against Notts County. Despite being April, it is chilly and grey but Colin and his wife have travelled to the Midlands on the off chance they might witness history. 'If we win, we have to hope Luton draw,' Colin explains, sounding a little nervous. It has been another remarkable season for Portsmouth. They are third in the league and, after missing out last year, they could clinch promotion in a few hours' time. 'I made a guess this might be the game where it happens but you can't take anything for granted, can you?' he says, not wanting to jinx his team's potential promotion. Still, 4,500 Pompey fans have travelled up, presumably all with the same hopes in mind.

Portsmouth had put last season's disappointment behind them and once again proved that a supporter-owned club could thrive at this level. For once, the club had settled into a rhythm and enjoyed the anonymity of stability. It was the first time in years where there had been no off-field dramas. The memories of chaos were disappearing in the distance. Only the football mattered, and this season, the football had been very good indeed. But then, midway through the season, memories of the past returned.

An American billionaire had enquired about buying Portsmouth FC. His name was Michael Eisner and, unlike the succession of mysterious owners from the past, he had a very public reputation. Eisner had been the CEO of Disney. In fact, his two decades in charge of the company had revived its fortunes. Whereas at one time Portsmouth's staff weren't even sure if their owner actually existed, there was no doubt that Eisner was the real deal. He was independently wealthy – worth more than $1 billion – and good at his job, running major organisations and rebranding entertainment products at the very highest level.

'He is clearly a credible owner,' says Colin. 'With all the others, you had to do some digging to find out who they were. But Eisner, he's made significant money in the corporate world and turned Disney around.'

There were questions, of course. Who Eisner was wasn't difficult to find out. Why he wanted the club was harder to answer. Portsmouth was also still suffering PTSD after its recent brushes with the super-rich. Eisner's mere enquiry had for many supporters revived the trauma of the past. But for others the news of his interest had also inflamed the ambitions that had blinded the club into following the likes of Gaydamak, Antonov and Al Fahim over a financial cliff.

Eisner is a prolific Twitter user and was now tweeting his support during Portsmouth games, often with the hashtag #PUP: Play Up Pompey. Underneath each message were hundreds of replies from Pompey fans begging him to buy the club and restore it to its former glory. 'The majority are cautious and have welcomed the potential investment,' Colin says diplomatically. He himself is in favour of the move, as were 64 per cent of supporters who responded to a survey conducted by the Pompey Supporters' Trust. Any deal would have to be voted for by the PST's now 2,500-strong shareholders, the fans who had each invested £1,000 to save the club in 2013 and who own 48 per cent of the club. Following that, the members would have a vote, as would the individual shareholders who own the rest of the club.

There is, Colin admits, 'a significant proportion who are more sceptical. But the supporters will be taking the decision. It would be a huge vindication of supporter ownership. It shows we can take control of a big club and make a relative success of it. It is a good-news story.'

Michael Eisner was indeed a businessman with a long track record of success. Post-Disney, his Tornante investment company had invested in media and entertainment companies, including the hugely popular series *BoJack Horseman*, an animated show following the misadventures of a misanthropic, alcoholic horse who had fallen on hard times. But it is from his Disney days that he has received the most praise, and criticism. His tenure at Disney saw a massive commercialisation of the brand, which not everyone was happy with. When Roy E. Disney, the last family link to Walt Disney, resigned from the company in 2003 he wrote a scathing letter to Eisner deriding his 'consistent micro-management of everyone around you with the resulting loss of morale throughout this Company.' Worse, he had seen Disney stray far from its original identity. 'The Company is rapacious, soul-less, and always looking for the "quick buck" rather than long-term value which is leading to a loss of public trust.'

One example was Eisner and Disney's first foray into sports-team ownership, when they paid $50 million for an NHL expansion team. It was named the Mighty Ducks of Anaheim, home to the Disneyland Resort. *The Mighty Ducks* is a classic underdog movie starring Emilio Estevez as coach of the titular ice hockey team of misfit kids. Eisner was already a huge ice hockey fan and saw the cross-promotion opportunities of having an actual hockey team to anchor the brand. The movie, he told the *LA Times* in 1992, 'was our market research'. Two sequels followed, as well as an animated TV series. At one point it was estimated that 80 per cent of the NHL's entire merchandise revenue came from Mighty Ducks branded products. The success didn't last and the franchise began soaking up money. 'What had started out as an uplifting kids' movie about underdogs had turned into a capitalistic machine of sequels and plastic toys,' Dillon Baker wrote for Contently. 'For fans, the initial excitement of the stunt had worn off.' The franchise was sold in 2005, the same year Eisner quit the company. He had revolutionised Disney and, in many ways, the Mighty Ducks move was ahead of its time, predating other brand–sports team tie-ins now seen with the likes of Red Bull. 'Michael took a moribund company and energised it to a level I'm not sure anyone could have done,' Disney's former chief financial officer Richard Nanula told the *New York Times* after Eisner had quit. But it wasn't a happy departure. 'The team's sale was both a clean break from Eisner's ambition,' wrote Baker, 'and a return to the traditional roots of the company.'

What if Eisner wanted to do something similar, I ask Colin, like change the name of the club to the Portsmouth Mighty Ducks FC?

'Those are the kind of things that supporters will have some influence over,' he replies. 'Mr Eisner sees an iconic brand that needs burnishing rather than starting again from scratch. We need a sensitive owner to our heritage. That would be my expectation.'

Ashley Brown was holding his cards closer to his chest. The chairman of the Pompey Supporters' Trust had now devoted himself full time to the supporters' trust movement. He'd recently been appointed chief executive of Supporters Direct, the organisation founded by the late Brian Lomax. He was preparing to send out Eisner's offer and all the supporting documents to PST's members, alongside the ballot papers. A meeting had also been convened of the shareholders. Eisner would be there to present his vision for Portsmouth. Trevor Birch, the man who had played such a crucial role in ensuring Portsmouth would be owned by the fans, was negotiating the final deal to be put to a vote. 'You have to hold on to the fact that he is a well-known individual with an established track record of running a corporate group,' says Trevor. 'If you look at some of the owners over the years, you wouldn't say that at all.'

'I got the first call from our CEO and lawyer and I knew the name, I'd heard of Michael Eisner,' says Ashley. 'I was fairly sure it wasn't a wind-up.' The deal was at a delicate phase, and Ashley had to walk a difficult path. Fratton Park was in desperate need of investment. But many, including himself, were deeply sceptical of another big-money owner promising great things, even one with as high a profile as Eisner. 'It has created a division in the fan base,' Ashley admits. 'Lots of people have gone starry-eyed over the cheque book being opened. Others, the activists and those heavily involved in the club, have said, "Hang on a minute, we don't have to give this away yet. There is further to go on this journey rather than ending it and starting a new chapter as something else." It will be a wrestle for a lot of fans to let it go.'

The deal had yet to be made public when Ashley and I spoke but he had been privy to some of the initial discussions with Eisner who, he explains, was interested in Portsmouth in part because 'it is a bit of fun with the family'. There were financial reasons too. Portsmouth has no debt, owns its own stadium and could be bought relatively cheaply for just under £6 million – although there was a promise of another £10 million of investment. The shareholders would not make a profit on their £1,000 investment, although they would get their money back. 'There is a far more serious business element behind the deal,' Ashley says, 'should he get Portsmouth to the Premier League.' Still, he hadn't been overly reassured by what he had seen so far. Eisner wanted the club in its entirety, meaning no fan representation in the new ownership structure. And there was more. I asked if Ashley was in favour of the deal.

'Errr . . .' There is a long pause. 'As it stands, no. Not to the level that is being suggested,' he replies finally. 'The biggest element is that he won't agree to protection of the existing club crest because he doesn't feel that will be marketable worldwide.'

The vote, Ashley believes, will be close. It is likely to be divisive too, with the PST – and, by extension, Ashley – coming under fire for a lack of ambition. Others, though, will rightfully say they have seen this all before. Even at a club like Portsmouth that had been through so much and almost gone out of existence, the allure of success that the super-rich promise was too much to ignore. Many were willing to roll the dice again.

That afternoon in Nottingham, Colin and Ashley watch Portsmouth FC beat Notts County 3–1 thanks to two late goals by Jamal Lowe. Luton draw with Mansfield. Portsmouth are promoted to League One. The 4,500 Pompey fans who had made the trip celebrate as vociferously as when they won the FA Cup in 2008. This was their club. They had saved it. And now they were going up. Thousands of miles away, across the Atlantic Ocean, Michael Eisner had gotten up early to watch a live stream of the Notts County game. Ten minutes after the final whistle, he tweeted his congratulations: 'Congrats, Portsmouth FC, on clinching promotion to EFL League One! #PUP @officialpompey' Underneath was a picture of BoJack Horseman, dressed in a grey sports jacket and blue jumper, arms aloft in celebration. Across his chest, in large black letters, was one word: 'BOOM.'

**

A few weeks later, Michael Eisner and his two sons are on stage at the Portsmouth Guildhall, presenting their vision for the club in front of over a thousand supporters. Eisner gives a polished, hard-headed performance, again and again comparing the potential task ahead of him to his turnaround of an ailing Disney brand. Pompey's academy was the key. Just look, he says, at Disney's Mouseketeers, hosts of Disney's *Mickey Mouse Club* that made stars of Britney Spears, Justin Timberlake and Christina Aguilera. Look at the success of the Disneyland theme park. Of the Mighty Ducks of Anaheim and of the baseball franchise the Anaheim Angels, another Eisner project, who won the World Series. 'The thing I wouldn't do is Americanise Pompey,' he says. 'That would be plain dumb.'

One after another, Pompey fans rise to ask questions. Why not give the fans say over any stadium relocation? Or the final say on the club's crest? Or who Eisner would sell the club to when he was finally finished with Portsmouth? Many are booed or heckled, just as Colin Farmery had been when he had questioned Sacha Gaydamak about the future of the club before Portsmouth's financial collapse. No businessman would invest without full control, Eisner replies. And the crest? No one owns the copyright for it, so it was essential for it to change just enough to be trademarked. Eisner's son at least promises that any new stadium would not have a Southampton postcode, the club's great rivals. At the end, Eisner's voice is hoarse. He's cracking jokes, about how he never thought the *Lion King* would be such a big hit and how he is still upset that his baseball team, the New York Giants, relocated to San Francisco in 1957, when he was 15 years old. Unlike the Glazers or Stan Kroenke, who preferred life in the shadows, Eisner had at least put his vision for the club up for public scrutiny. This was the future, and the future waits for no one. 'Mickey Mouse does not look like he looked in 1935, but it's still Mickey Mouse,' Eisner says as the event comes to a close. 'You can't stand still.'

The pitch worked. A few weeks later Britain's largest fan-owned club overwhelmingly voted to approve Tornante's takeover. Not that anyone who had watched the presentation – from the thousands of supporters around the world glued to the online live feed to those inside Portsmouth's Guildhall – expected any other result. At the end of the evening, the 1,200 fans all rose as one and gave a rapturous standing ovation. Michael Eisner had brought down the house.

Acknowledgements

The Billionaires Club was perhaps the hardest book I have written, and not just because the reach of football club ownership – across politics, economics and sport – was so vast. This world was changing faster than I could keep up with. No sooner had I finished writing a chapter than a different club had been sold to a mysterious billionaire buyer or an entirely new player entered the scene. For example, when I began researching *The Billionaires Club*, the boom in Chinese ownership had not yet started. Plans had to be quickly redrawn.

So I am eternally grateful to my publisher, Charlotte Atyeo at Bloomsbury, and my agent, Rebecca Winfield, for their patience as my initially well laid plans turned to dust. I'm equally as grateful to the whole team at Bloomsbury who worked on the book as well as my editor, Ian Preece, for helping me to thread it together into a (hopefully) coherent whole.

With a book that involves this amount of foreign travel, many of the stories were built on my reporting elsewhere. I'd like to thank Andrew Das and Jason Stallman at the *New York Times*, Richard Padula at the BBC World Service, Gavin Hamilton at *World Soccer*, the team at *Delayed Gratification*, John Sinnott at CNN and Will Tidey at the Bleacher Report in particular. Without your help I would never have got this project off the ground.

Many people have also been incredibly generous in offering help with contacts and advice. I'd like to thank Jere Longman and Ken

Belsen at the *New York Times*; CNN's Jonathan Stayton; Michael Peel from the *Financial Times*; Scott McIntyre for his insights on Thailand; Olya Morvan, for helping me to keep my cool as we visited Qatar's labour camps as well as Mohamed Fahmy for his insight and help; Ralph Van Der Zijden for his help in understanding the socio-geological strata of Den Haag and Nicholas McGeehan, Showvik Das and Nilanjan Kundu in Bangladesh. Huge thanks as well to my Airbnb host in St Louis, An, who managed to find my bag, recorder and microphone and send it back to Europe after I'd got into a particularly unpleasant confrontation with a group of men after Super Bowl 50. People are good, even if I have a facial scar to prove otherwise. I'd also like to thank Jonny Mills for his help in Bangladesh, while also rectifying the fact I shamefully forgot his Herculean efforts in driving from Adelaide to Melbourne in one day during a research trip for *Thirty-One Nil*. Sorry colonel.

I have quoted from numerous sources in *The Billionaires Club*, and I'd like to thank the following for granting permission for me to build on their work. The epigraph comes from *The Wire* and is used with thanks to HBO and David Simon. I have also quoted or referenced from *Money and Football: A Soccernomics Guide* by Stefan Szymanski (Nation Books); *The Game of Our Lives: The Meaning and Making of English Football* by David Goldblatt (Penguin); *Putin's Kleptocracy: Who Owns Russia?* by Dr Karen Dawisha (Simon & Schuster); *Abramovich: The Billionaire From Nowhere* by Dominic Midgley and Chris Hutchins (Collins Willow); *Field of Schemes: How the Great Stadium Swindle Turns Public Money into Private Profit* by Neil DeMause and Joanna Cagan (Bison Books); *Bad Sports: How Owners are Ruining the Games We Love* by Dave Zirin (Scribner); *The Ugly Game: The Qatari Plot to Buy the World Cup* by Heidi Blake and Jonathan Calvert (Simon & Schuster); *Qatar: A Modern History* by Allen J Fomherz (I.B.Tauris) and *Football's Secret Trade: How the*

Player Transfer Market was Infiltrated by Alex Duff and Tariq Panja (Bloomsberg Press).

I've read many articles, features and blogs for background as well as quoting from dozens of sources including the *New York Times, Forbes*, Bloomberg, the *Guardian*, BBC, Contently, *USA Today, St. Louis Post-Dispatch, Tampa Bay Times, Tampa Bay Tribune, St Petersburg Times*, Political Economy of Football, *Sports Illustrated*, ESPN, AFP, AP, *Financial Times, Moscow Times, Bangkok Post*, Sporting Intelligence, Foreign Policy, *Wall Street Journal*, Reuters, V*anity Fair, Independent*, the *Telegraph, Evening Standard*, Radio Free Europe, *New Yorker*, Interpreter, *Der Spiegel*, CBS, *River Front Times, Denver Post, Boston Globe, Washington Post, Manchester Evening News*, Sky News, Deadspin, NOS, *Birmingham Mail, Lancashire Telegraph, La Gazzetta dello Sport, Irish Times, Watford Observer, South China Morning Post, International Business Times, FourFourTwo*, Christian Science Monitor, AS, *The Economist, L'Équipe, Telegraaf*, Omroep West, KRO-NCRV, *Liverpool Echo*, Euromoney, *Dhaka Tribune*, CNN and the Swiss Ramble.

Several quotes and an interview I use in *The Billionaires Club* originally came from my first book *When Friday Comes: Football, War and Revolution in the Middle East* (deCoubertin). The English translation of China's 50 Point Reform Plan is courtesy of Wild East Football (@ wildeastfootball). I also received help with translation and additional reporting from Remi Vorano and Richard Fitzgerald while in China. Finally, the full interview with Wang Hui in Beijing was conducted by the *New York Times*' Adam Wu. Thank you!

Several people also took the time to read early drafts of chapters and suggest changes and improvements. In particular I'd like to thank Simon Kuper, James Corbett, Michael Church, Aaron Gordon, Dave LaMattina and Chad Walker. Dave and Chad (as well as Dan Kerrigan) were also very patient during a recent filming trip in Africa for Copper

Pot Pictures, and were cool with me furiously writing the first draft in between shooting sessions in Western Sahara, Rwanda and Lesotho. At least, they said they were cool with it . . .

Finally I'd like to thank Mitra Nazar. She read my work, translated my interviews and held me together while at the same time caring for our monkey during long writing and reporting trips. I couldn't have done any of this without you, and neither would I have wanted to. Life only makes sense with both of you by my side.

Belgrade, May 2017.

Index